Rainbow of Hope for Africa's Future

Foreign Direct Investment in Africa

SAIDY V. ANDRADE

Printed by CreateSpace, An Amazom.com Company.

Distribuition; Available from Amazom.com and other online retail outlets.

Book Cover Designed by Digital Marketing 238

CreateSpace ISBN information

ISBN-13: 978-1545482049

ISBN-10: 1545482047

First Edition.

CONTENTS

FOREWORD

Africa is the birthplace of humanity. In a sense, the continent's history is a macrocosm of all history, bearing the weight humankind's most unforgiveable sins, from slavery to colonialism to environmental malevolence.

But today, at the dawn of a new millennium, Africa's most important narrative is not of history. It is of the future. That story - told here with clarity and scope - is one of hope, dynamism, and a relentless march towards progress.

Factors that were once considered detriments to Africa's progress are now its greatest strength. The legacy of colonial domination that once saw strife in its wake today translates into pan-African resilience and resolve. A footprint of neglect by industrial powers that left the continent wanting for much-needed investment for so many years now means that most of Africa's resources are still in the ground, left to be harnessed in more responsible - and more indigenous - ways. A lack of infrastructure during the telephonic boom of yesteryear hamstrung African's inclusion in global commerce; today it is a deft advantage, as Africans embrace wireless and smart technology unencumbered by legacy electronics and protectionist incumbent providers.

We live in a world where the traditional global powers are stuttering under the weight of social discontent, political partisanship, declining demographics, and a creeping skepticism of economic engagements and integration. Africa as a whole stands in refreshing contrast. Its young population is more open and exposed to the world than at any point in history. Regional economic unions are in their heyday, from the East African Community (EAC) to the Southern African Development Corridor (SADC) to the Economic Community of West African States (ECOWAS). And entrepreneurs, like this book's author, stand united in promoting a vision of hope.

The challenges, it must be acknowledged, are mammoth. At least half the continent does not have electricity. Financial inclusion is lower than anywhere on the planet. And many of Africa's political structures still embody the plutocratic corruption and instability that have scared away potential investors for decades. But Africa's new generation seems to implicitly understand the Norman Vincent Peale dictum: "Every problem has in it the seeds of its own solution."

A desperate need for electrification—combined with abundant sun and water—is driving a renewable-energy breakaway, potentially positioning Africa as a vanguard of the world's most important epochal shift. Massive numbers of unbanked people spurred the development of mobile money, a technology pioneered in East Africa that is not only changing the financial landscape of the continent but also being adopted globally. And countries like Botswana and Cape Verde, (the latter being the author's mother country) are emerging as increasingly visible and influential models of peaceful, transparent democracies.

As Peale said, if you don't have problems, you don't get any seeds.

The following is a comprehensive look at Africa's many seeds, told by an African who himself is a headspring of the optimism and ambition he narrates. These pages hold a first-hand account of lessons learned, a look at the influence of the current geopolitical complexities, a roadmap for the way forward, and a source of actionable information for those considering investing or doing business on the continent.

It is a story for the future, of countries on the rise, and of the latest—and potentially last—frontier of global business. It is as important for the global economy as it is for the everyday citizens who populate this emerging continent called Africa. I hope that many read it.

Leland Rice

Editor-in-Chief

The Business Year

INTRODUCTION:

You are probably asking why I decided to write this book, when you can find so many business books with similar titles and research about foreign investments. My main reason is to share my Passion with you and how does Africa play a part on it.

Why My Passion?

One day an American Documentary filmmaker was visiting Fogo Island, in the Cape Verde Islands, where I was born, and on a casual dinner meeting with some of US Embassy members in Cape Verde accompanying his crew, which a group of musicians from New Orleans USA where also part of, he asked me a simple question that touched my soul. The question came out basically how a normal conversation starts from trying to learn from someone you have just met. So he asked me: "What's your passion?"

Normally you expect people to ask you about you and what do you do, among other stupid questions just to keep the conversation flowing. But this guy was just to the point: "What's your passion?" It really struck me deep down in my Soul.

You are probably asking why? Because I love what I do but this simple question made me question if what I do is really what I want to do, after all the setback I have experienced so far in my crazy business life experiences around the world (Cape

Verde, Dubai, Paris, Mauritius, South Africa, Morocco, Zambia, USA).

You may be asking yourself now what exactly do I do?

Well. My passion is to Create Companies in Africa (structuring the idea, building the business model, architecture a plan to make it move forward, and design crazy financial engineering to help it attract capital to make it a reality) that no one else have the balls to set up because it seems impossible at first.

Like Peter Thiel brilliantly said it on his book *Zero to One,* if you are building something that already exists and you are not creating anything new. It is easier to copy a model than to develop something new.

Following my Passion with my Vision to help develop Africa when it comes to investment, I decided back in 2006, to set up a Foreign Direct Investment consultancy company in Cape Verde Islands, named Capital Consulting to help foreign investors invest initially in Cape Verde Islands and today all across Africa.

Why focus on Africa?

Throughout this book you will get to know some amazing facts about Africa that you probably never heard off, some exciting ones and some not at all, that you will probably end up saying you would never invest in a continent with some many issues.

I consider myself a son of Africa, but an end product of the world. I was born in a small country, named Cape Verde islands, which is part of West Africa. Cape Verde Islands is one of the few countries in Africa that are an example of Democracy, and has never seen wars and instability.

I am blessed enough to have amazing parents whom gave me and my brothers a great education and sacrificed so we could go study in Universities in Europe. *Like a raw commodity from Africa such as cocoa that is exported to Europe to become a fine and exquisite chocolate in Switzerland.*

I am also blessed that my parents always supported us since kids to have access to the best of technology of their time (well, PCs running on 2MB of space, which today is unthinkable) and to fly every year to USA and Europe on vacation to experience new cultures.

Having grown up in multicultural environments, I learned quickly how differently people can see the world. So beside all of the problems Africa face today, according to my perspective of the World and of Africa, to me Africa it's still one of the most exciting places to do business and promote Foreign Direct Investment.

Like my father once told me: "Roses are beautiful but they also have spikes."

Africa is blessed with abundant land, water and energy sources and with a young and increasingly better educated population. Such abundance, when combined with capital investment, can generate prosperity.

I have great hopes for Africa because I know the generation I belong (millennials) will be the changing force Africa needs to become a Great continent.

We are now in 2017 and the ride has been tremendously inspiring, and beside all my business setbacks in Africa I am still inspired about the future for myself, my family and for Africa.

Like Uschi Schreiber, wrote on her LinkedIn page today, as I write these pages to you, we are "living in a world in transition – from a model of business and society we know to one that still needs to be defined. We live in a world with a significant *trust deficit*. The uneven distribution of the benefits of globalization and the accelerating pace of innovation have disrupted people's confidence in those in leadership roles; local, national and global institutions and the media. However, *trust* is an important ingredient for social stability, investment and growth."

She is talking about Blockchain technology that as she puts it she believes "Blockchain has the potential to help restore trust and create stronger ecosystems among investors. It offers a way to ensure transparency, limit fraud and corruption, improve efficiency and maximize economic benefits to a broader section of society by creating a record of ownership that compels the consent of all buyers and stakeholders."

Trust! A simple word that captures everything you need to understand about business and Foreign Investment. Trust makes the world moves forward. Not Money. Money is just the instrument to make things happen. Without Trust there is no Peace of mind for no one. The investment world works the same way. If investors do not trust a destination is safe for investment they won't invest their funds in that market.

So, the basic rule of foreign investment beside safe investment destination, incentives and all the "bla bla bla" that countries tend to show that they are more attractive than others is that Money will flow to where there is TRUST and *less stress* for the investor.

Since we are in a world that is sharing everything throughout this book I will share insights, views, ideas, and statements from renowned world leaders, entrepreneurs, billionaires, politicians, musicians, successful people, and brilliant minds.

Subjects such as Foreign Investment in Africa, Economy, Economic Development, Business, Human Rights, Investment Opportunities, Leadership, Innovation, Governance, Corruption, Hope, and the Future of Africa, are mentioned among the various chapters of the book.

In a nutshell, throughout this book I will share with you my experiences, various industries data, Africa facts, my views and renowned financial institutions views and reports data, so you can see for yourself that beside all the mess that the world is in now, and the perspective that the media shows you today about Africa, that there is still see a Rainbow of Hope for Africa's future.

"Education is the most powerful weapon which you can use to change the world." Nelson Mandela

CHAPTER 1: Why is the richest continent in natural resources still poor?

Three out of every four (75%) Africans still live under poor human conditions, compared to one in five globally.

In today's Africa businesses are flourishing, from telecoms, banking, agriculture, mining, tourism, among other industries attracted by the rising middle class and the continent's natural resources. Despite all the challenges, the continent has become a beacon of hope in our difficult world today.

Africa has the potential to be the world's major driver of growth for the coming decades. It will have two billion people by 2050 and, if growth remains at the current level, the total economy of the continent would be around the current size of America.

But, whenever you hear someone talking about Africa or headlines come out in the media it's mostly bad news and it's basically the following words that you hear the most:

- AIDS
- Malaria
- Ebola
- Malnutrition
- Tension
- Corruption
- Poverty
- Conflict

- Displacement
- Starvation
- Disaster
- Coups
- Instability
- Diseases
- Inequality
- Warfare
- Greed
- Intimidation
- Dictatorship
- Genocide

Beside all the bad news you hear about Africa, for those who never been in Africa, the first thing to put in perspective and to remember is that Africa is not just one big country like the USA. Africa is 54 countries with different ethnicities, cultures, languages, leaders, and economies.

Below you will see facts about Africa, extracted from multiple references, that I thought you should know before we go in depth with this chapter.

Africa is the world's second-largest and second-most-populous continent. At about 30.3 million km^2 (11.7 million square miles) including adjacent islands, it covers 6% of Earth's total surface area and 20.4% of its total land area.

DECOLONIZATION AND THE MIXING OF RACES AND CULTURES

Prior to the decolonization movements of the post-World War II era, Europeans were represented in every part of Africa. Decolonization during the 1960s and 1970s often resulted in the mass emigration of white settlers – especially from Algeria and Morocco, Kenya, Congo, Rhodesia, Mozambique and Angola.

Between 1975 and 1977, over a million colonials returned to Portugal alone. Nevertheless, white Africans remain an important minority in many African states, particularly Zimbabwe, Namibia, Reunion, and the Republic of South Africa.

The country with the largest white African population is South Africa.

Dutch and British diasporas represent the largest communities of European ancestry on the continent today.

European colonization also brought sizable groups of Asians, particularly from the Indian subcontinent, to British colonies.

Large Indian communities are found in South Africa, and smaller ones are present in Kenya, Tanzania, and some other southern and southeast African countries.

The large Indian community in Uganda was expelled by the dictator Idi Amin in 1972, though many have since returned.

The islands in the Indian Ocean are also populated primarily by people of Asian origin, often mixed with Africans and Europeans.

The Malagasy people of Madagascar are an Austronesian people, but those along the coast are generally mixed with Bantu, Arab, Indian and European origins.

Malay and Indian ancestries are also important components in the group of people known in South Africa as Cape Coloureds (people with origins in two or more races and continents).

During the 20th century, small but economically important communities of Lebanese and Chinese have also developed in the larger coastal cities of West and East Africa, respectively.

LANGUAGES

By most estimates, well over a thousand languages (UNESCO has estimated around two thousand) are spoken in Africa.

Most are of African origin, though some are of European or Asian origin.

Africa is the most multilingual continent in the world, and it is not rare for individuals to fluently speak not only multiple African languages, but one or more European ones as well.

Following the end of colonialism, nearly all African countries adopted official languages that originated outside the continent, although several countries also granted legal recognition to indigenous languages (such as Swahili, Yoruba, Igbo and Hausa).

In numerous countries, English and French are used for communication in the public sphere such as government, commerce, education and the media.

Arabic, Portuguese, English, French and Spanish are examples of languages that trace their origin to outside of Africa, and that are used by millions of Africans today, both in the public and private spheres.

Italian is spoken by some in former Italian colonies in Africa.

German is spoken in Namibia, as it was a former German protectorate.

RELIGION

Africans profess a wide variety of religious beliefs, and statistics on religious affiliation are difficult to come by since they are often a sensitive topic for governments with mixed religious populations.

According to the World Book Encyclopedia, Islam is the largest religion in Africa, followed by Christianity. According to Encyclopedia Britannica, 45% of the population are Christians, 40% are Muslims, and 10% follow traditional religions.

A small number of Africans are Hindu, Buddhist, Confucianist, Baha'i, or Jewish. There is also a minority of Africans who are irreligious.

Who cares what the mix of regilion in terms of percentage is, and which religion is bigger than the other. What is beautifull about Africa is the Mix of Cultures, Race, and Religion.

In the late 19th century European countries colonized most of Africa. The Continent also varies greatly with regard to environments, economics, historical ties and government systems. However, most present states in Africa originate from a process of decolonization in the 20th century.

Slavery had long been practiced in Africa. Between the 7th and 20th centuries, Arab slave trade (also known as slavery in the East) took 18 million slaves from Africa via trans-Saharan and Indian Ocean routes. Between the 15th and the 19th centuries (500 years), the Atlantic slave trade took an estimated 7–12 million slaves to the New World.

In West Africa, the decline of the Atlantic slave trade in the 1820s caused dramatic economic shifts in local policies. The gradual decline of slave-trading, prompted by a lack of demand for slaves in the New World, increasing anti-slavery legislation in Europe and America, and the British Royal Navy's increasing presence off the West African coast, obliged African states to adopt new economies. Between 1808 and 1860, the British West Africa Squadron seized approximately 1,600 slave ships and freed 150,000 Africans who were aboard.

Action was also taken against African leaders who refused to agree to British treaties to outlaw the trade, for example against "the usurping King of Lagos", deposed in 1851. Anti-slavery treaties were signed with over 50 African rulers. The largest powers of West Africa (the Asante Confederacy, the Kingdom of Dahomey, and the Oyo Empire) adopted different ways of adapting to the shift. Asante and Dahomey concentrated on the development of "legitimate commerce" in the form of palm oil, cocoa, timber and gold, forming the bedrock of West Africa's modern export trade. The Oyo Empire, unable to adapt, collapsed into civil wars.

In the late 19th century, the European imperial powers engaged in a major territorial scramble and occupied most of the continent, creating many colonial territories, and leaving only two fully independent states: Ethiopia (known to Europeans as "Abyssinia"), and Liberia. Egypt and Sudan were never formally incorporated into any European colonial empire; however, after the British occupation of 1882, Egypt was effectively under British administration until 1922.

The Berlin Conference held in 1884–85 was an important event in the political future of African ethnic groups. It was convened by King Leopold II of Belgium, and attended by the European powers that laid claim to African territories. It sought to end the European powers' Scramble for Africa, by agreeing on political division and spheres of influence. They set up the political divisions of the continent, by spheres of interest that exist in Africa today.

Imperial rule by Europeans would continue until after the conclusion of World War II, when almost all remaining colonial territories gradually obtained formal independence. Independence movements in Africa gained momentum following World War II, which left the major European powers weakened.

In 1951, Libya, a former Italian colony, gained independence. In 1956, Tunisia and Morocco won their independence from France. Ghana followed suit the next year (March 1957), becoming the first of the sub-Saharan colonies to be granted independence. Most of the rest of the continent became independent over the next decade.

Portugal's overseas presence in Sub-Saharan Africa (most notably in Angola, Cape Verde, Mozambique, Guinea-Bissau and Sao Tome & Principe) lasted from the 16th century to 1975, after the "Estado Novo" regime was overthrown in a military coup in Lisbon. Rhodesia unilaterally declared independence from the United Kingdom in 1965, under the white minority government of Ian Smith, but was not internationally recognized as an independent state (as Zimbabwe) until 1980, when black nationalists gained power after a bitter guerrilla war. Although South Africa was one of the first African countries to gain independence, the state remained under the control of the country's white minority through a system of racial segregation known as apartheid until 1994.

Today, Africa contains 54 sovereign countries, most of which have borders that were drawn during the era of European colonialism. Since colonialism, African states have frequently been hampered by instability, corruption, violence, and authoritarianism. The vast majority of African states are republics that operate under some form of the presidential system of rule. However, few of them have been able to sustain democratic governments on a permanent basis, and many have instead cycled through a series of coups, producing military dictatorships.

Great instability was mainly the result of marginalization of ethnic groups, and graft under these leaders. For political gain, many leaders fanned ethnic conflicts, some of which had been exacerbated, or even created, by colonial rule. In many countries, the military was perceived as being the only group that could effectively maintain order, and it ruled many nations in Africa during the 1970s and early 1980s. During the period from the early 1960s to the late 1980s, Africa had more than 70 coups and 13 presidential assassinations. Border and territorial disputes were also common, with the European-imposed borders of many nations being widely contested through armed conflicts.

Cold War conflicts between the United States and the Soviet Union, as well as the policies of the International Monetary Fund, also played a role in instability. When a country became independent for the first time, it was often expected to align with one of the two superpowers. Many countries in Northern Africa received Soviet military aid, while others in Central and Southern Africa were supported by the United States, France or both. The 1970s saw an escalation of Cold War intrigues, as newly independent Angola and Mozambique aligned themselves with the Soviet Union, and the West and South Africa sought to contain Soviet influence by supporting friendly regimes or insurgency movements.

In Rhodesia, Soviet and Chinese-backed leftist guerrillas of the Zimbabwe Patriotic Front waged a brutal guerrilla war against the country's white government. There was a major famine in Ethiopia, when hundreds of thousands of people starved. Some claimed that Marxist economic policies made the situation worse. The most devastating military conflict in modern independent Africa has been the Second Congo War; this conflict and its aftermath have killed an estimated 5.5 million people.

Since 2003 there has been an ongoing conflict in Darfur which has become a humanitarian disaster. Another notable tragic event is the 1994 Rwandan Genocide in which an estimated 800.000 people were murdered. AIDS in post-colonial Africa has also been a prevalent issue

In the 21st century, however, the number of armed conflicts in Africa has steadily declined. For instance, the civil war in Angola came to an end in 2002 after nearly 30 years. This has coincided with many countries abandoning communist-style command economies and opening up for market reforms.

The improved stability and economic reforms have led to a great increase in foreign investment into many African nations, which have spurred quick economic growth in many countries, seemingly ending decades of stagnation and decline.

Several African economies are among the world's fastest growing as of 2017. A significant part of this growth, which is sometimes referred to as Africa Rising, can also be attributed to the facilitated diffusion of information technologies and specifically the mobile telephone.

Although it has abundant natural resources, Africa remains the world's poorest and most underdeveloped continent.

Why is the richest continent in natural resources still poor?

If you research the internet today, everyone seems to have explanation for this tragic phenomenon, citing you will find many reasons from various researches suggesting that the reasons why Africa is still poor is the result of a variety of causes that include the following:

- Corrupt Governments
- Human Rights Violation
- Failed Central Planning
- Lack of Access to Foreign Capital

- Tribal and Military conflict
- Guerrilla warfare and Genocide
- Poverty
- Coups & Instability
- Diseases
- Dysfunctional democratic institutions
- Justice systems
- Greedy multinational corporations
- Shady local and international elites
- Incompetent or ineffective international aid agencies
- Resource wars waged by domestic militias as well as outside armies
- Vestiges of colonialism — or the advent of a new type of colonialism

Like the famous comedian from South Africa, *Trevor Noah, says on his shows,* Reallyyyyy? If you haven't heard of Trevor Noah until now you should take a look at his Youtube channel and his shows on Netflix and follow him on social media to check out some of his stand up shows. The guy is hilarious.

Let's focus on the book again! Going back to the issue of *why is the richest continent in natural resources still poor?*

Out of all the reasons that academics and researchers mention as the main causes for Africa still being poor none has concluded so far that it could be for the simple reason why someone born in poverty will continue to be poor for life unless it has the opportunity to study and invest on their Education.

Yes, Education. Once you have access to knowledge (meaning you have a higher education instead of just primary and secondary education) you begin to understand the world and how things work. Specially Economics, Investments, Trading, Commodities Prices, Stock Exchange, Forward Currency Markets, bilateral and multilateral trade agreements, etc., and how business must be developed and managed.

Many studies have proved that educated politicians tend to make better decisions than those who are not educated. Highly educated leaders can easily lead their nation towards prosperity. Like David Bloom, David Chaning, and Kevin Chan mentioned on their research *Higher Education and Economic Development of Africa*, presented at Harvard University in 2006, commissioned by the World Bank and the Norwegian Education Trust Fund, they show that "higher education can enhance economic development in Africa."

Not all African Leaders received higher education. Some of them don't even have a high school certificate, or speak English properly (the world business language). Please note that there are also brilliant minds in Africa (exceptions that I will share their successes and democratic achievements in a different chapter of this book).

From my research and from my business experiences the simple factor of *Why is Africa still Poor* is Education and the Understanding by its Leaders of how policies and business practices should be implemented to protect their country and their people. Does this ring any bell to you? If not continue reading and you will understand my point.

We are now in 2017 and so much is said in the Media nowadays about the newly elected United States President, Donald J. Trump, about him trying to implement protectionist measures and going back in time with building walls to protect America. Why is the world so worried about his Policies? Maybe because it's the world biggest market (Usd18.5 trillion GDP as of end of 2016) and there is where the money is, and everyone is worried about their piece of the cake. Well, USA belongs to the American people. It is their Country. They can do whatever the f*** (my apologies for cursing) they want whether you like it or not. It is their right to protect their people first. I am quite sure this is the basic right mentioned in the Constitution of any Country on Earth.

Think about it. What if we had similar Presidents and Prime Ministers in Africa? Would Africa be different today? In my view yes. Reason is, if Presidents and Prime Ministers who run Governments care at least a little bit about their people the first thing they would focus on is the Economy. Not Votes. The problem is that 99% of African Presidents and Prime Ministers historically don't even know how the economy works and how a company is managed, because most of them took power by force or went to study sociology or political science, or any other special studies that doesn't even understand how economies work and how trade deals are negotiated between countries.

Most African Countries politicians are running for Government promising nonsense to the people just to win their Votes. Since the majority of people in Africa are still uneducated (meaning there are many people with no University degree so they can understand how an economy really works) and there is still a lot of poverty all over Africa, which makes it easy for Politicians and Dictators across Africa to buy conscious and the majority of votes.

That's why there are so many abstentions nowadays in elections across Africa among millennials because our generation understand that our votes have no weight when you only account for a percentage of the population that understands how the economy works and how the world economies are interdependent.

Majority of African Leaders don't really care about building a strong Economy to create wealth and help prosper their society. So far history as showed us that the majority of African Presidents and Prime Ministers only care to win votes, steal money from the state treasury to build wealth for themselves and their families while they are in Power. Most of the story of the 54 Countries throughout Africa is the same. There are just a few success stories in Africa but we will get to it in a bit.

Hopefully my generation will see things shake up in Africa to disrupt corrupt political regimes that have quietly survived and thrived. Why? Because dictators and failed states are bad for business.

Because of these Great African Leaders, without any economic policy for the development for their countries, Africa has mostly served as the economic engine for over decades, since their independence day, to most continents (especially Europe and China) and has fueled booming industries for several decades.

African Leaders are so brilliant that the majority of the countries give special rights to foreign investors to extract raw materials (oil, coffee, cocoa, cotton, etc.) which are exported at undervalued prices and then imported back by African companies as end products for consumption by Africans (examples: chocolates, cotton for hospitals, roasted coffee, cereals, among other commodities that are exported from Africa to come back as end products to be consumed by Africans).

What's the point to become an Independent Country and your people will still remain in Poverty for decades and without any hope for the future?

Experts in Economics believe that turning Africa's steady resilience into better lives for Africans requires strong policy action to promote faster and more inclusive growth.

To achieve the development objectives set by African institutions and the international community, African countries must deepen structural and regulatory reforms, foster macroeconomic stability, and tackle power supply bottlenecks in order to address the obstacles to the transformation of their economies. Sure! But first the Leadership running the countries must change.

With all its natural resources and potential for the future Africa could develop itself without depending on the Western banking system or the International Monetary Fund support.

What If all 54 African Leaders decided to focus their efforts on thinking about the African Economy and about creating wealth for their people first? Do you think Africa would still be the poorest continent?

Here are the Facts why Africa shouldn't be the poorest Continent in the 21st Century.

Africa remains a key territory on the global map. Rich in oil and natural resources, the continent holds a strategic position.

Africa Wealth snap shot below (Facts):

- Africa's collective GDP, at Usd2.5 trillion in 2016;

- Africa is a large continent comprised of 54 countries including islands. Although many may still have the misconception that the whole of Africa is poor and struggling, the truth cannot be further from that. There is no denying that the continent is home to some poorer countries that are in desperate need of assistance to grow their economy and provide proper health care and education systems for their nations. However, there are also many countries in Africa that have passed developing stage and are now at MIC (Middle Income Country) status. The GDP rankings in Africa show all this and more;

- It is the world's fastest-growing region for foreign direct investment, and it has approximately 30 percent of the earth's remaining mineral resources;

- The continent is believed to hold 90% of the world's cobalt, 90% of platinum, 50% of gold, 98% of chromium, 70% of tantalite, 64% of manganese and one-third of uranium;

- The Democratic Republic of the Congo (DRC) has 70% of the world's coltan, a mineral used in the production of tantalum capacitors for electronic devices such as cell phones. The DRC also has more than 30% of the world's diamond reserves;

- Guinea is the world's largest exporter of bauxite;

- North Africa counts with vast oil and natural gas deposits; the Sahara holds the most strategic nuclear ore; and resources such as coltan, gold, and copper, among many others, are abundant on the continent;

- Africa is home to the second largest tropical forest; The Continent share of the world total amount of uncultivated arable land is 60% of the entire world arable land for development of agriculture;

- The economy of Africa consists of the trade, industry, agriculture, and human resources of the continent;

- As of now writing this chapter in 2017, the population of Africa is approximately 1.233.492 billion people are living in 54 different;

- Today the rate of return on foreign investment in Africa is higher than in any other developing region.

Africa could feed itself by making the transition from importer to self-sufficiency. Africa main policies are the export of raw materials which are extracted by foreign companies.

Like mentioned above Africa share of the world total amount of uncultivated arable land is 60% of the entire world arable land for development of agriculture; Seriously???? And you see an Africa that all it does is import processed food from other countries. We should be the biggest exporters of processed food in the world (Coffee, Cotton, Chocolate, Cereals, etc.).

Why do we keep supplying the raw material to international markets and buying back the end products? Well! Food for your mind to find an answer.

Where is the African Union? I thought a Union was supposed to mean UNITY for the members of an Organization. Oh, right, I forgot, in Africa the majority of Leaders just act like it is not there problem to worry about and they don´t really care if other countries and its economy collapses. So, that why you don't hear about too many Africa Union Policies developed to benefit the whole of Africa.

Maybe we should ask the brilliant African Leaders that are running the richest countries in Africa with Natural Resources for a solution. I am quite sure they will blame colonization is why Africa is still poor.

Reallyyyyy? (Remember *Trevor Noah)*. We will get to the Colonization issue in another chapter.

WHO IS THE AFRICAN UNION?

The African Union is a pan-African organization whose goal is to propel a united continent towards peace and prosperity. It supports political and economic integration among its 54 member nations. It aims to boost development, eradicate poverty and bring Africa into the global economy.

It is the largest international economic grouping on the continent. The confederation's goals include the creation of a free trade area, a customs union, a single market, a central bank, and a common currency (African Monetary Union), thereby establishing economic and monetary union.

The current plan is to establish an African Economic Community with a single currency (sometimes referred to as the *afro* or *afriq*) by 2023.

The Abuja Treaty, an international agreement signed on June 3, 1991 in Abuja, Nigeria, created the African Economic Community, and called for an African Central Bank to follow by 2028.

Well, let's see what happens by 2023 a 2028 because from my experience in Africa there are a lot of Agreements signed and Strategic plans outlined but when it comes to put them into action nothing goes forward. Here is an example regarding the Aviation sector which is a total disaster in Africa with 130 Airlines black listed to fly to Europe and USA.

There is an agreement signed by 44 African States named the Yamoussoukro Decision that was signed in 1988 to liberalize the aviation sector (known in aviation as Open Skies) across Africa. We are now in 2017, 29 years later and there is still no Open Skies across Africa.

Specifically, the Yamoussoukro Decision calls for, among others:

- Full liberalization of intra-African air transport services in terms of access, capacity, frequency, and tariffs

- Free exercise of first, second, third, fourth and fifth freedom rights for passenger and freight air services by eligible airlines (These rights, granted by most international air service agreements, enable, among others, non-national carriers to land in a state and take on traffic coming from or destined for a third state.);

- Liberalized tariffs and fair competition;

- Compliance with established ICAO safety standards and recommended practices;

We will go more in depth into the Aviation sector in another chapter.

SO, WHY THE HELL IS AFRICA STILL THE POOREST CONTINENT?

It is particularly vexing to the many international organizations, foreign governments and private groups that have been trying since the era of independence to promote regional development, food production, education, better housing, health care, improve infrastructure, jobs and economic growth. Although more than five decades have passed since the end of colonial times, African governments often still appear clueless when it comes to lifting their people from extreme poverty.

Well, like I mentioned before, the *Cocktail mix* of no Education and Corrupt Leaders not thinking of Africa as their priority, and the Oligarchs and Corporations helping them steal Africa's wealth since Independence Day, are the main cause why Africa is the poorest continent in the World. That's the truth and the real reason most of African people in some of the richest countries on the planet are living in extreme poverty. And this is sad!

That's why you see the following headlines happening every year:

- Private equity companies amassed a $4.3 billion war chest for investment opportunities in Africa in 2015 as the global commodity rout and weakening local currencies cut prices of potential target companies;

- As commodity prices collapsed around the world between 2015 and 2016 the South African rand tumbled 29% against the dollar, the Zambian kwacha loses loses

39% and the Mozambican metical lost 30%.

- Nigeria under increasing pressure to devalue the naira, with forward currency markets predicting it will weaken by 20% in just 3 months.

Let's talk about Currency now. I didn't address this one big question yet:

What guarantees the value of a currency?

Currencies can be classified into two monetary systems: fiat money and commodity money, depending on what guarantees the value (the economy at large vs. the government's physical metal reserves).

What is Commodity money?

Commodity money is money whose value comes from a commodity of which it is made. Commodity money consists of objects that have value in themselves as well as value in their use as money.

One of the long-standing myths about modern currency is that the US Dollar it is backed by the U.S. gold supply in Fort Knox. That is, you can trade your greenback dollars to the U.S. government for the equivalent amount of gold bullion at any time. At one point, this was true of most paper currencies in the world. However, the U.S. took away the government backing of the dollar with an actual gold supply (known as leaving the gold standard) in 1971, and every major international currency has followed suit. Reallyyyyy?

So what exactly is Fiat Money?

Fiat money is currency that a government has declared to be legal tender, but *it is not backed by a physical commodity*. The value of fiat money is derived from the relationship between supply and demand rather than the value of the material that the money is made of. Historically, most currencies were based on physical commodities such as gold or silver, but fiat money is based solely on the faith and credit of the economy. Reallyyyyy? FAITH? Wow!

Breaking down Fiat Money

Fiat is a Latin word meaning "it shall be."

Because fiat money is not linked to physical reserves, it risks becoming worthless due to hyperinflation. If people lose faith in a nation's paper currency, like the U.S. dollar bill, the money will no longer hold any value. This differs from gold, which, historically, has been used in jewelry and decoration and has many modern economic uses including its use in the manufacture of electronic devices, computers and aerospace vehicles.

Most modern paper currencies are fiat currencies; they have no intrinsic value and are used solely as a means of payment. Reallyyyyy? Ohhhhh! I forgot. It's valued with FAITH. So logically Usd1.000.000 is 1.000.000 Faith! Isn't it?

So what exactly is Forex Traders exchanging in the currency markets when they sell and buy currencies (USD / EUR)? Faith! WOW. Interesting!

Historically, governments would mint coins out of a physical commodity, such as gold or silver, or would print paper money that could be redeemed for a set amount of physical commodity.

Fiat money is inconvertible and cannot be redeemed. Fiat money rose to prominence in the 20th century, specifically after the collapse of the Bretton Woods system in 1971, when the United States ceased to allow the conversion of the dollar into gold.

Many throughout the economy had thought central banks had removed the threat of depressions or serious recessions, but the mortgage crisis of 2008 and subsequent financial meltdown quickly tempered this belief.

A currency tied to gold is generally more stable than fiat money due to the limited supply of gold.

So, why the richest continent with the biggest reserve of minerals isn't creating its own currency and launch an Africa commodity currency that is not valid in FAITH but valued in real commodities.

Briefly I will just speak about the digital currency named Bitcoin.

WHAT IS BITCOIN?

Bitcoin is a digital currency created in 2009. It follows the ideas set out in a white paper by the mysterious Satoshi Nakamoto, whose true identity has yet to be verified. Bitcoin offers the promise of lower transaction fees than traditional online payment mechanisms and is operated by a decentralized authority, unlike government issued currencies.

There are no physical Bitcoins, only balances associated with public and private keys. These balances are kept on a public ledger, along with all Bitcoin transactions, that is verified by a massive amount of computing power.

Bitcoin balances are kept using public and private "keys," which are long strings of numbers and letters linked through the mathematical encryption algorithm that was used to create them. The public key (comparable to a bank account number) serves as the address which is published to the world and to which others may send Bitcoin. The private key (comparable to an ATM PIN) is meant to be a guarded secret, and only used to authorize Bitcoin transmissions.

The independent individuals and companies who own the governing computing power and participate in the network, also known as "miners," are motivated by mining rewards (the release of new Bitcoin) and transaction fees paid in Bitcoin. These miners can be thought of as the decentralized authority enforcing the credibility of the Bitcoin network. New Bitcoin is being released to the miners at a fixed, but periodically declining rate, such that the total supply of Bitcoin approaches 21 million. One bitcoin is divisible to eight decimal places (100 millionth of one bitcoin), and this smallest unit is referred to as a Satoshi. If necessary, and if the participating miners accept the change, Bitcoin could eventually be made divisible to even more decimal places.

Style notes: According to the official Bitcoin Foundation, the word "Bitcoin" is capitalized in the context of referring to the entity or concept, whereas "bitcoin" is written in the lower case when referring to a quantity of the currency (e.g. "I traded 20 bitcoin"). The currency can be abbreviated to BTC or, less frequently, XBT. The plural form of the word can be either "bitcoin" or "bitcoins."

So why isn't the African Union doing anything about creating Africa own currency?

Why do we keep seeing African Countries launching Government Bonds in foreign currencies (EUR and USD) in the Stock Exchanges in Europe, USA and Asia, to finance their economies and begging to the World Development Banks (whose loans and currencies are based on FAITH)? Food for your mind to digest!

Africa doesn't need to invent anything when it comes to thinking about a strong currency for Africa.

African Leaders just needs to learn from other success stories like the Euro created by the European Union and begin strategizing about its own single currency program. A single currency with a single market for all the regional economic blocs in Africa will form free trade areas, which will help modernize infrastructure and distribute wealth across African Countries. For instance, Ghana could choose Kenya, rather than any European Country to process its food.

Let's move on with a new subject that is the only thing that really has value and has always been over centuries the only mineral commodity with real value when economies collapse and their currencies lose value. GOLD it is!

Who do you think controls the largest reserves of Gold in the World?

Below are the top 10 countries with the largest gold holdings:

1. USA: 8.134 Tones = 75% of their Foreign Reserves

   With the largest holding in the world, the U.S. lays claim to nearly as much gold as the next three countries combined. It also has one of the highest gold allocations as a percentage of its foreign reserves, second only to Tajikistan, where the metal accounts for more than 88 percent. Donald Trump made headlines recently, claiming "we do not have the gold," but from what public knowledge is, the majority of U.S. gold is held at Fort Knox in Kentucky, with the remainder held at the Philadelphia

Mint, Denver Mint, San Francisco Assay Office and West Point Bullion Depository.

2. Germany: 3.381 Tones = 69% of their Foreign Reserves

   Germany is in the process of repatriating its gold from foreign storage locations, including New York and Paris. Last year, the country's Bundesbank transferred 210 tones, and it plans to have the full 3,381 tones in-country by 2020.

3. Italy: 2.452 Tones = 68% of their Foreign Reserves

   Italy has likewise maintained the size of its reserves over the years. A former Bank of Italy governor, when asked by a reporter what role gold plays in a central banks portfolio, answered that the metal was "a reserve of safety," adding, it gives you a fairly good protection against fluctuations against the dollar.

4. France: 2.436 Tones = 63% of their Foreign Reserves

   France's central bank has sold little of its gold over the past several years, and there are calls to halt it altogether. Marine Le Pen, president of the country's far-right National Front party, has led the charge not only to put a freeze on selling the nation's gold but also to repatriate the entire amount from foreign vaults.

5. China: 1.798 Tones = 2.2% of their Foreign Reserves

In the summer of 2015, the People's Bank of China began sharing its gold purchasing activity on a monthly basis for the first time since 2009. In December, the renminbi joined the dollar, euro, yen and pound as one of the International Monetary Fund's reserve currencies, an expected move that required the Asian country to beef up its gold holdings. The precious metal represents only 2.2 percent of its foreign reserves, so it's probably safe to expect heavier buying going forward. Recently, China, the world's largest gold producer, introduced a new renminbi-denominated gold fix in its quest for greater pricing power.

6. Russia: 1.460 Tones = 15% of their Foreign Reserves

Russia has steadily been rebuilding its gold reserves in the last several years. In 2015, it was the top buyer, adding a record 206 tones in its effort to diversify away from the U.S. dollar, as its relationship with the West has grown chilly since the annexation of the Crimean Peninsula in mid-2014. To raise the cash for these purchases, Russia sold a huge percentage of its U.S. Treasuries.

7. Switzerland: 1.040 Tones = 7% of their Foreign Reserves

Switzerland actually has the world's largest reserves of gold per capita. During World War II, the neutral country became the center of the gold trade in Europe, making transactions with both the Allies and Axis powers. Today, much of its gold trading is done with Hong Kong and China. In 2015, the Swiss National Bank posted a $5.9 billion profit, in one quarter only, largely a result of its sizable gold holdings.

8. Japan: 765 Tones = 2.5% of their Foreign Reserves

Japan, the world's third largest economy, is also the eighth largest hoarder of the yellow metal. Its central bank has been one of the most aggressive practitioners of quantitative easing - it lowered interest rates below zero -which has helped fuel demand in gold around the world.

9. Netherlands: 613 Tones = 61% of their Foreign Reserves

The Dutch Central Bank is currently seeking a suitable place to store its gold while it renovates its vaults. As many others have pointed out, this seems odd, given that the bank fairly recently repatriated a large amount of its gold from the U.S.

10. India: 558 Tones = 6.3% of their Foreign Reserves

It's no surprise that the Bank of India has one of the largest stores of gold in the world. India is home to 1.25 billion people, is the number one or number two largest consumer of the precious metal, and is one of the most reliable drivers of global demand.

WOW! No African country is in the top 10. Amazing!

As you can see, most of the world's central banks are always accumulating, holding and/or repatriating Gold. It is reported that Central Banks around the world own 32,754 tons of Gold holdings, which is about 18 percent of the total amount of gold ever mined.

It's worth noting that this global gold-buying spree coincides perfectly with the rise of unconventional monetary policies following the financial crisis massive bond buying programs, rapid money printing schemes and near zero or, in some cases, negative interest rates. The jury's still out on whether these measures have been a success or not, but for now, it appears as if banks are hedging against their own policies.

No wonder the Central Bank Governor of Italy when asked by a reporter what role gold plays in a central banks portfolio, he answered that the metal was *"a reserve of safety"* adding, it gives you a fairly good protection against fluctuations against the dollar. Reallyyyyy?

So, isn't there any Gold in Africa? Why aren't Central Banks in Africa stocking their own Gold in Africa?

Bellow you will see a list of 15 countries that shipped 85% of all gold in 2015:

1. Switzerland: Usd72.4 billion (24.4% of total gold exports)
2. Hong Kong: Usd45 billion (15.1%)
3. United Kingdom: Usd38.5 billion (13%)
4. United States: Usd19.3 billion (6.5%)
5. United Arab Emirates: Usd13 billion (4.4%)
6. Canada: Usd12.4 billion (4.2%)
7. Australia: Usd10.7 billion (3.6%)
8. Turkey: Usd7.4 billion (2.5%)
9. Peru: Usd5.7 billion (1.9%)
10. India: Usd5.3 billion (1.8%)
11. South Africa: Usd5 billion (1.7%)
12. Japan: Usd4.9 billion (1.7%)
13. Germany: Usd4.6 billion (1.6%)
14. Ghana: Usd4.3 billion (1.5%)
15. Mexico: Usd4.3 billion (1.5%)

WOW! Just South Africa and Ghana, which both combined make only 3% of total gold exports worldwide.

Guess who controls the mining of gold in South Africa and Ghana? We will get to that in the second chapter.

Fact: The US Geological Survey estimated that as of 2002, South Africa held about 50% of the world's gold resources, and 38% of reserves.

So why, don't African Countries joint forces and create a Fort Knox in Africa where in a period of 20years we can store 500Tones of Gold per year. At the end of 20years we would end up with of 10.000Tones of Gold. More than the USA Gold holding.

THE FUTURE IS BRIGHT

Beside all this mess the outlook for the future still looks bright. The future economic growth will be supported by Africa's increasing ties to the global economy. Let's take a look at what the projections from renowned financial institutions like the World Bank, IMF, Mckinsey Global Institute, Africa Development Bank, among others are saying about Africa´s outlook:

- Today, 40% of Africans live in urban areas, a portion close to China's and continuing to expand. The number of households with discretionary income is projected to rise by 50% over the next 10 years, reaching 128 million. By 2030, the continent's top 18 cities will have a combined spending power of Usd1.3 trillion;

- Sub-Saharan Africa, in particular, is expected to reach a GDP of Usd29trillion by 2050; WOW! This is in just three decades from now. Usd29trillion it's a lot of Currency (FAITH) that Africa can bank on it;

- Nearly Usd2 trillion of investments in African oil and gas are expected in the next two decades;

- Africa's economic growth is creating substantial new business opportunities that are often overlooked by global companies. Consumer facing industries, resources, agriculture, and infrastructure together could generate as much as Usd2.6 trillion in revenue annually by 2020;

- The World Bank expects that most African countries will reach "middle income" status (defined as at least Usd1.000 per person a year) by 2025. Growth has been present throughout the continent, with over one-third of Sub-Saharan African countries posting 6% or higher growth rates, and another 40% growing between 4% to 6% per year. Several international business observers have also named Africa as the future economic growth engine of the world;

- Africa generates Usd400 billion a year in oil and gas revenues. The continent's oil output is equivalent to that of Saudi Arabia, the world's largest producer. Its gas output is double that of Qatar's;

- Africa Development Bank estimates that Africa's extractive resources could contribute over Usd600 Billion in government revenue for the next 20 years (Usd30 billion per annum). The Bank also estimates that revenues from recent oil, gas and mineral discoveries could contribute between 9% and 31% of additional government revenues over the first ten years of production for countries such as Ghana, Liberia, Mozambique, Sierra Leone, Tanzania and Uganda.

As you can see the outlook and hope for the future for Africa is a beautiful Rainbow of Hope for Africa´s Future (title of this book).

Bellow I will share some data from a brilliant research done by Matthew Winkler for Bloomberg, about Africa, named "Where's the Growth? Africa":

- During the past 10 years, the gross domestic product of the 11 largest sub-Saharan countries increased 51%, more than twice the world's 23% and almost four times the 13% expansion of the U.S., the world largest economy, according to data compiled by Bloomberg;

- The robust expansion been accompanied by stabilizing inflation on the African continent, with the consumer price index for all of Africa declining to 7.8% from more than 13% in 2008, and the continent's CPI remaining less than 8% since 2013, Bloomberg data show;

- That combination of torrid growth and diminished inflation is proving an irresistible lure for global investors, who have seen the opposite trends plague the biggest emerging-market countries, Brazil, Russia, India and China;

- For evidence of investor enthusiasm, look no further than Kenya and Nigeria, whose government debt has been outperforming most of the world's economies. In the past five years, bonds issued by those two countries had total returns (income plus appreciation in local currencies converted to U.S. dollars) of 56% and 40% respectively, according to Bloomberg data. By comparison, the index of government debt of developed countries provided a dollar-equivalent return of 2% during the past five years, and a similar basket of emerging-market debt returned 12%;

- When the benchmark government bonds of 32 countries in the emerging markets are compared since 2010, Kenya and Nigeria are among the top five;

- Part of Africa's expansion can be explained by its explosive population growth. Since 2000, the population of the 11 largest sub-Saharan countries, measured by GDP, grew 41%, to 634 million, or more than twice the U.S.'s 318 million, according to data compiled by Bloomberg. During the same period, India grew 23%, the world 18%, the U.S. 13% and China 7%;

- That demographic trend won't abate soon simply because Sub-Saharan Africans are so young. In Nigeria, for example, 43.7% of the population is under 15 years old. In Kenya, its 42.1%; in Ghana, 35.3%; and South Africa, 28.3%. The world average is 25.8%. The percentage of Nigerians older than 65 is 3%, compared to 14.5% for in the U.S. and 8.3% for the world, according to Bloomberg data;

- Nigeria Oil accounts for 90% of its worldwide trade and almost 35% of its GDP, and crude oil prices have famously crashed. The currency, the naira, has failed to recover from its own collapse late last year. Yet global investors, convinced there's a lot more to Nigeria than its commodities, are driving up its bond prices anyway.

Still not convinced that Africa is where the Future is for your investments? You have nothing to lose. Just have some FAITH and invest in Africa and you will see that in the next 20 Years your money will grow exponentially more than in any Equity markets or Stock Exchanges Bond operations or speculative toxic financial products offered today.

Early entry into African economies provides opportunities to create markets, establish brands, shape industry structures, influence customer preferences, and establish long-term relationships. Business can help build a Great Africa in a near future.

So, if you are an investor and you want to be part of a success story in Africa make sure you invest to bring positive impact into the countries you target to invest in. Don't be like the thief's that are looting our continent and think it is ok to keep doing it just because they are being supported by the Corrupt Gang behind the countries they invest in (countries like Angola, the Democratic Republic of the Congo, and Equatorial Guinea).

Corruption and Inequality feed off each other, creating a vicious circle between corruption, unequal distribution of power in society, and unequal distribution of wealth.

As I finished this chapter, on 25th of January 2017, the day my son Zion J. Andrade, reached his 7 month, the Universe sends me a message. A BBC headline just comes into my outlook email, saying "Which is Africa's most Corrupt Country"? Wow! How about that for a present on my Son birthday? The news on BBC was about the 2016 Transparency International Corruption Perception Index.

Bellow I share with you some of the amazing findings on Sub Saharan Africa from the Transparency International Corruption Perception Index for the year 2016. *And the Winners Are* for Top 10 most corrupted countries in Sub-Saharan Africa:

1. Somalia
2. South Sudan
3. Guine Bissau
4. Eritrea
5. Angola
6. Republic of Congo
7. Chad
8. Central African Republic
9. Burundi
10. Democratic Republic of Congo

These are the top 10 lower-ranked countries in Sub-Saharan Africa in the index that are plagued by untrustworthy and badly functioning public institutions like the police and the judiciary system. Even where anti-corruption laws are on the books, in practice they're often skirted or ignored. People frequently face situations of bribery and extortion, rely on basic services that have been undermined by the misappropriation of funds, and confront official indifference when seeking redress from authorities that are on the take.

Tom Burgis, a journalist who covered Africa for the Financial Times for six years, makes an amazing case for all these causes in his book, "The Looting Machine: Warlords, Oligarchs,

Corporations, Smugglers, and the Theft of Africa's Wealth." Burgis goes a step farther, arguing that each of us bears responsibility for this situation every time we thoughtlessly fill our cars with gas, buy gold or a diamond wedding ring, sip a fizzy drink in an aluminum can or use a cellphone.

But who should we blame? Multinationals? Nop! Multinationals are just working to make the biggest profit for their shareholders, so they really don't care about Africa if they find Corrupt Leaders in Africa to help them steal all the wealth that they can take out of Africa. This kind of systemic grand corruption violates human rights, prevents sustainable development and fuels social exclusion.

Like Mr. Jose Ugaz, Chair of Transparency International, beautifully said, here I quote "In too many countries, people are deprived of their most basic needs and go to bed hungry every night because of corruption, while the powerful and corrupt enjoy lavish lifestyles with impunity."

The elections held across Africa in 2016 provide a good reflection of corruption trends in the region. In countries like Ghana, which is the second worst decliner in the 2016 Corruption Perceptions Index in the region, the dissatisfaction of citizens with the government's corruption record was reflected in their voting at the polls.

South Africa, which continues to stagnate this year, has witnessed the same. Joseph Kabila's Democratic Republic of Congo and Yahya

Jammeh's Gambia, which both declined, demonstrate how electoral Democracy is tremendously challenged in African countries because of corruption.

After accepting defeat guess to where Yahya Jammeh's from Gambia flew to exile in? Equatorial Guinea (*one of the Corrupt Gang Members*). Guess how he flew to Equatorial Guinea? Well, the President of the Equatorial Guinea sent him one of his Jets to pick him up. Well done Mr. President for supporting your Gang.

THE GOOD BOYS

Cape Verde and Sao Tome & Principe are the most improved African countries in the 2016 index. Both countries held democratic presidential elections in 2016.

It is no surprise that the independent electoral observer teams labelled the Cape Verde elections for 2016 as "exemplary". This election that saw Jorge Carlos Fonseca re-elected, was held in a framework of a continuously improving integrity system, as observed by various African governance reviews.

THE BAD BOYS

Despite being a model for stability in the region, Ghana, together with another six African countries, has significantly declined. The rampant corruption in Ghana led citizens to voice their frustrations through the election, resulting in an incumbent president losing for the first time in Ghana's history.

Some other large African countries have failed to improve their scores on the index. These include South Africa, Nigeria, Tanzania and Kenya. South African President Jacob Zuma was in court and in the media for corruption scandals.

Kenya – despite the adoption of a few anti-corruption measures including passing a law on the right to information – has a long way to go. President Uhuru expressed frustration that all his anti-corruption efforts were not yielding much.

Right at the bottom of the list is Somalia, whose parliamentary elections were marred by malpractice and corruption, and whose presidential elections were postponed three times last year and are yet to be held.

What needs to happen?

According to the 2016 Transparency International Index, African leaders that come to office on an "anti-corruption ticket" will need to live up to their pledges to deliver corruption-free services to their citizens. They must implement their commitments to the principles of governance, Democracy and human rights. This includes strengthening the institutions that hold their governments accountable, as well as the electoral systems that allow citizens to either re-elect them or freely choose an alternative.

As per Transparency International data 9 out of 10 people say they would fight corruption. Are you one of them? If yes, you are probably asking, what can I do to help? To begin go to the Transparency International website (https://www.transparency.org/) and sign the Declaration against Corruption!

"The Rich invest in Time, the Poor invest in Money." Warren Buffett

CHAPTER 2: Africa Businesses & Wealth. Who controls what in Africa?

The economic impact of the colonization of Africa has been debated. In this matter, the opinions are biased between researchers, some of them consider that Europeans had a positive impact on Africa; others affirm that Africa's development was slowed down by colonial rule.

The principal aim of colonial rule in Africa by European colonial powers was to exploit natural wealth in the African continent at a low cost.

Some writers, such as Walter Rodney in his book How Europe Underdeveloped Africa, argue that these colonial policies are directly responsible for many of Africa's modern problems.

Critics of colonialism charge colonial rule with injuring African pride, self-worth and belief in themselves.

Other post-colonial scholars, most notably Frantz Fanon continuing along this line, have argued that the true effects of colonialism are psychological and that domination by a foreign power creates a lasting sense of inferiority and subjugation that creates a barrier to growth and innovation. Such arguments suggest that a new generation of Africans free of colonial thought and mindset is emerging and that this is driving economic transformation.

Historians L. H. Gann and Peter Duignan have argued that Africa probably benefited from colonialism on balance. Although it had its faults, colonialism was probably "one of the most efficacious engines for cultural diffusion in world history" Reallyyyyy?

Let's change perspective. Let's imagine that the colonialism history was the opposite. Imagine that African Countries were the ones that went to Europe, made slaves out of Europeans and make everyone work for free while we steal every wealth Europe could possible provide Africa. And plus today in the 21st century African Companies would be the multinationals controlling all major businesses in Europe and making billions in profit while we would not leave any benefits in Europe.

I guess we would have a Fair World like we have today, right? Hummmmmmmmmm!

What do you think Europeans would say to Africans today if this was the History of Colonialism?

Now let's talk about a sensitive subject: Slavery!

For 500 years slavery was the biggest business between continents. There were Slave Markets for trading. People were treated as goods.

Should we blame only the Colonialist for such horrible crimes? In my humble opinion from researches made by Historians is that no one should be blamed.

Slave relationships in Africa have been transformed through three large-scale processes: the Arab slave trade, the Atlantic slave trade, and the slave emancipation policies and movements in the 19th and 20th century. Each of these processes significantly changed the forms, level, and economics of slavery in Africa

So slave trade was done by the Arabs and Africans way before the Europeans arrived in the continent. How about that?

Several nations such as the Ashanti of present-day Ghana and the Yoruba of present-day Nigeria were involved in slave-trading.

Groups such as the Imbangala of Angola and the Nyamwezi of Tanzania would serve as intermediaries or roving bands, waging war on African states to capture people to export as slaves.

Historians John Thornton and Linda Heywood have provided an estimate that Africans captured and then sold to Europeans are around 90% of those who were shipped in the Atlantic slave trade.

Henry Louis Gates, the Harvard Chair of African and African American Studies, has stated that "without complex business partnerships between African elites, European traders, and commercial agents, the slave trade to the New World would have been impossible, at least on the scale it occurred."

Cape Verde has been one of the biggest trading platform to and from where slaves were traded from. Who helped the Europeans? There are proofs in Museums in USA that shows that black people were the ones responsible for allowing this to happen at such a massive scale. This is very sad indeed!

Henry Louis Gates made a brilliant point, and let me repeat it again: "without complex business partnerships between African elites, European traders, and commercial agents, the slave trade to the New World would have been impossible, at least on the scale it occurred."

Remember the Corrupt Gang I mentioned on Chapter one? Well, this is how it all started!

I am not an Historian but here is a simple question: Which Nationality or Race until today has not been Slaved?

Like most other regions in the world, slavery and forced labor existed in many kingdoms and societies. Just search the history of what the following people did in the world: the Romans, the Othman Empire, Genghis Khan, the Egyptians, the Mayans, among others.

Karl Marx in his economic history of capitalism, Das Kapital, claimed that "...the turning of Africa into a warren for the commercial hunting of black-skins [that is, the slave trade], signaled the rosy dawn of the era of capitalist production." He argued that the slave trade was part of what he termed the "primitive accumulation" of European capital, the non-capitalist accumulation of wealth that preceded and created the financial conditions for Britain's industrialization and the advent of the capitalist mode of production.

Eric Williams has written about the contribution of Africans on the basis of profits from the slave trade and slavery, arguing that the employment of those profits were used to help finance Britain's industrialization. He argues that the enslavement of Africans was an essential element to the Industrial Revolution, and that European wealth was, in part, a result of slavery, but that by the time of its abolition it had lost its profitability and it was in Britain's economic interest to ban it.

TIME TO MOVE FORWARD

We should never forget our history but I believe it's time we forget about blaming Europe or any other colonialist countries about the problems Africa face today. We must move forward and let's work on making Africa the next industrial engine of the World.

When you can please watch the Documentary 500 Years Later. It was the first film to win a *UNESCO award for documenting slavery*. The documentary breaks the silence and speaks to the social, historical, economic and psychological impact of the slave trade, and raises public awareness of slavery's historical and contemporary manifestations.

Look at Brazil as an example. It was a colony of Portugal but today who has the biggest economy?

Brazil does. Because they learn to move on and love their history and use their knowledge to make the country great with what the country has to offer in terms of natural resources and its people, by creating smart and intelligence policies to help their country grow. Sure, Brazil has a lot of corruption, but it is an Usd1.8 trillion economy and the country is a member of the G20.

G20 comprises a mix of the world's largest advanced and emerging economies, representing about two-thirds of the world's population, 80% of the Global GDP (gross domestic product), and 75% of global trade.

The members of the G20 are Argentina, Australia, Brazil, Canada, China, France, Germany, India, Indonesia, Italy, Japan, Republic of Korea, Mexico, Russia, Saudi Arabia, South Africa, Turkey, the United Kingdom, the United States and the European Union. Wait, where is Portugal that colonized Brazil? How about that for Colonization blame?

Beside Brazil example I have also brought the G20 into this subject because the G20 Priorities for the 2017 Summit happening in Hamburg - Germany in July 2017, under the Presidency of the G20 by Dr. Angela Merkel (Chancellor of the Federal Republic of Germany), has the following in a statement as G20 2017 Priorities from Dr. Angela Merkel concerning Africa, which I quote:

Intensifying the partnership with Africa

"We wish to further intensify the important partnership with African countries in order to make a greater contribution to sustainable economic growth and stability, including beyond the borders of the G20. Building on regional and G20 initiatives, the frameworks for sustainable private sector investments and investments in infrastructure and renewable energies are to be strengthened through cooperation with interested African partner countries. A further aim of the planned G20 initiative is to support African partners to improve their population's share in sustainable economic development, particularly in the form of employment opportunities. Through this initiative, the G20 would also seek to reduce risks of climate change, contribute to more efficient health systems and strengthen the role of women. It would also contribute to the fight against the root causes of flight and displacement."

Improving food security

"Factors such as global population growth, climate change, fluctuation in precipitation, extreme weather events like droughts and flooding, and increased water consumption in industry and other sectors pose fundamental challenges to agriculture. The aim is to be able to feed the world's growing population through sustainable and more productive agriculture. The G20 will focus on

the question of how this can be achieved without increasing water consumption to unsustainable levels. Food security for present and future generations, dynamic rural economic areas, and social and political stability depend on giving opportunities to a growing young population, particularly in Africa."

AFRICAN ECONOMIES

Africa is not an isolated island in the world, and ongoing uncertainty with some of its trading partners could imperil any sustainable progress. A trade shock is just around the corner, as the continent remains reliant on a mineral-based economy. And new, rosy economic statistics have not managed to stop strikes, riots, and other protests, which are the result of the continued reality of economic inequality. What's more, Africa is complex, fragmented and multicultural. What works in Nigeria is not guaranteed to work in Kenya.

But, none of this should keep businesses from expanding into African markets. The international community should not ignore a growing market of 1 billion people.

African economies are growing, and millions have moved into the middle class category within the last decade. And Africans are buying things, from iPad to Porsche. Africans are also becoming global players, with some of their banks — such as United Bank for Africa and Guaranty Trust Bank

— opening offices in the U.S.A., France and the U.K.

Historically, the world has not seen a well-developed economy without a corresponding strong government. In contrast to a Western-style political institution of checks and balances, traditionally African tribes were not organized in such a way. Many argue that in addition to easy access to education, healthcare, and natural resources, a strong government that can balance its own power by virtue of the bureaucratic structure of itself is essential.

Effects on most African nations' wealth include, among other things, (1) residual effects of colonialism, (2) current exploitation of poor nations by wealthy nations, and (3) a pervading lack of strong political institutions to manage the economy.

Pertaining to the question about natural resources, these are often extracted by wealthy nations, who take the wealth from those resources back to their already wealthy countries. This has been the case in oil-rich Nigeria and diamond-rich South Africa. Wealthy nations also often trade extraction rights for vast amounts of extorted "dirty money".

One of the forces promoting trade liberalization has been the globalization of production, driven by transnational companies' strategies to minimize production costs by relocating phases of production of commodities across borders.

Dependency theory asserts that the wealth and prosperity of the superpowers and their allies in Europe, North America and East Asia is dependent upon the poverty of the rest of the world, including Africa. Economists who subscribe to this theory believe that poorer regions must break their trading ties with the developed world in order to prosper.

Research shows an uneven partition of value added along commodity chains between transnational firms and producers in developing countries. A great book on this subject is a book written by Gernot Kohler and Arno Tausch, named Global Keynesianism: Critique of Unequal Exchange, Global Exploitation and Global Neoliberalism, Theory of World Income, Productivity, Grow.

But why are multinationals often accused of operating in isolation from local economies and not leaving any wealth in Africa? Answer is Bad Trading Policies, and Bilateral/Multilateral Trade Agreements signed by Governments. But how can Africa have great agreements in place when it comes to international commerce if the majority of Leaders are Corrupt or lack Higher Education to understand in the first place what needs to be protected for their economy?

Here are some examples:

1. Why does Nigeria grow tomatoes but import all tomato paste from China and also from a Chinese-owned company in Italy?

2. Petroleum products are the largest UK export to Nigeria. Reallyyyyy? WOW! Last time I checked UK did not have oil. Nigeria does. Oh right, British Petroleum (BP) is UK biggest oil company.

3. Cocoa are exported as raw to Europe so Africans can import back chocolate and other products such as cookies, cereals that are all manufactured with raw materials from Africa.

4. Coffee is exported as green coffee to multinationals traders that basically buy the green coffee in Africa for Eur5/kg and sell it to coffee roasters between Eur20 to Eur35/kg giving them ridiculous margins.

But all the work is done in Africa. That's why you see a cup of coffee at Starbucks selling at premium price. Meaning that about only 10% of the value of coffee sold in the USA and Europe accrued to the producing countries.

So, why isn't there a strong African trading coffee company? And why are most of African Countries importing roasted coffee when we can roast our own coffee in Africa and just add a bag with a label on it? Isn´t it just what Starbucks business is all about? Roasting & Branding! That's it. Nothing complicated.

Don´t get me wrong with these examples I have just shared with you. I am a strong believer of globalization and fair trade, but only if it's done under FAIR principles and it benefits everyone involved in the entire supply chain. If it's done just like it has been done for decades now to benefit just one side, it is no different than when in Slavery time the Colonialist took advantage of the Slave Trade to get rich by using free labor force from the slaves.

I strongly believe that if there is transparency and fair trade agreements between the developed countries and Africa, and the benefits of profits in the supply chain are shared between Africa and developed countries multinationals, than cross-border investment and growth will be seen growing across Africa during many decades.

Today out of the big businesses in Africa WHO controls WHAT in Africa?

Without trying to develop this part too much, below you will find a snap shot per industry of the biggest multinationals controlling business and commodities in Africa, and who the main shareholders behind these multinationals are:

GOLD

> AngloGold Ashanti (South Africa / UK / Pension Funds / Norway)

> Gold Fields (South Africa / Public float on Stock Exchanges)

> Harmony Gold Mining (South Africa / Public float on Stock Exchanges)

> Anglo American PLC (UK/ South Africa – Parent company of DeBeers)

Oakbay Resources & Energy (Oakbay Investments / India Gupta family)

Kibo Mining Company (UK/South Africa)

Acacia Mining (majority controlled by Canada Barrick Gold / UK)

Kinross Gold Corporation (Canada)

Gecamines SA (Democratic Republic of Congo)

Lundin Mining (Canada)

The Fleurette Group (Gibraltar)

Barrick Mining (Canada)

Aquarius Platinum Limited (Sibanye Gold subsidiary / South Africa)

SILVER

AngloGold Ashanti (South Africa / UK / Pension Funds / Norway)

Anvil Mining (Canada)

Lundin Mining (Canada)

DIAMONDS

De Beers Group of Companies (UK/ South Africa)

Petra Diamonds (UK)

Debswana (DeBeers / Government of Botswana)

Anglo American PLC (UK/ South Africa – Parent company of DeBeers)

PLATINUM

Aquarius Platinum Limited (Sibanye Gold subsidiary / South Africa)

Anglo American PLC (UK/ South Africa – Parent company of DeBeers)

BAUXITE

Trafigura Beheer BV (Singapore)

Rio Tinto (UK/Australia)

BHP Billiton (UK/Australia)

Anglo American PLC (UK/ South Africa – Parent company of DeBeers)

Alumina Company of Guinea (USA / Guinea Government / Russia)

URANIUM

Areva (public listed company, majority owned by France State)

Somair (63% controlled by AREVA, 37% Niger Government)

AngloGold Ashanti (South Africa / UK / Pension Funds / Norway)

Gold Fields (South Africa / Public float on Stock Exchanges)

Harmony Gold Mining (South Africa / Public float on Stock Exchanges)

Sibanye Gold (South Africa)

Peninsula Energy (Australia)

Rio Tinto (UK/Australia)

Oakbay Resources & Energy (Oakbay Investments / India Gupta family)

Kibo Mining Company (UK/South Africa)

Gecamines SA (Democratic Republic of Congo)

Barrick Mining (Canada)

COAL

Anglo American PLC (UK/ South Africa – Parent company of DeBeers)

Sasol Mining (South Africa / Public float on Stock Exchange)

Glencore Xstrata (UK/Switzerland)

Debswana (DeBeers / Government of Botswana)

Exxaro (subsidiary of Main Street 333 Pty ltd / South Africa)

South Africa Energy Coal (92% Australia South32 / 8% South Africa)

Rio Tinto (UK/Australia)

Oakbay Resources & Energy (Oakbay Investments / India Gupta family)

Kibo Mining Company (UK/South Africa)

Gecamines SA (Democratic Republic of Congo)

Trafigura Beheer BV (Singapore)

Barrick Mining (Canada)

IRON ORE

Kumba Iron Ore Limited (AngloAmerican subsidiary)

Rio Tinto (UK/Australia)

Trafigura Beheer BV (Singapore)

Anglo American PLC (UK/ South Africa – Parent company of DeBeers)

COPPER

Rio Tinto (UK/Australia)

Palabora Mining Company (Rio Tinto / Anglo American / Public float)

Gecamines SA (Democratic Republic of Congo)

Trafigura Beheer BV (Singapore)

Anvil Mining (Canada)

Anglo American PLC (UK/ South Africa – Parent company of DeBeers)

Lundin Mining (Canada)

The Fleurette Group (Gibraltar)

Barrick Mining (Canada)

COBALT

Gecamines SA (Democratic Republic of Congo)

Lundin Mining (Canada)

The Fleurette Group (Gibraltar)

Barrick Mining (Canada)

FOOD INDUSTRY

Nestle (Switzerland)

Cargill (USA)

Unilever (Netherlands)

Archer Daniels Midland (USA)

Bunge (Netherlands/USA)

Louis Dreyfus Commodities (Netherlands)

Nutreco Holding N.V. (Netherlands)

Monsanto (USA)

KWS AG (Germany)

Bayer (Germany)

BASF (Germany)

DOW AgroSciences (USA)

DuPont (USA)

Syngenta (Switzerland)

Yara (Norway)

Agrium (USA)

Mosaic (USA)

K + S Group (Germany)

Neumann (Germany)

Volcafe (Switzerland)

ECOM (Switzerland)

Kraft (USA)

Sara Lee (USA)

OIL & GAS

ExxonMobil (USA)

Anadarko (USA)

Chevron (USA)

Royal Dutch Shell (Netherlands)

ENI (Italy)

British Petroleum (UK)

Perenco (UK)

Savannah Petroleum (UK)

ELF (France)

Total (France)

The Fleurette Group (Gibraltar)

Rosneft (Russia)

Sinopec (China)

CNPC (China)

ZPEP (China)

CNODC (China)

Statoil (Norway)

Petronas (Malaysia)

Aiteo (Nigeria)

Trafigura Beheer BV (Singapore)

RUBIES, CORUNDUM, EMERALDS AND AMETHYSTS

Gemfields (UK)

AVIATION

Emirates Airlines (United Arab Emirates)

Qatar Airways (Qatar)

Etihad Airways (United Arab Emirates)

Turkish Airlines (Turkey)

Air France KLM (France)

Lufthansa Group (Germany)

British Airways (UK)

TUI Fly (Germany)

Iberia (Spain)

Alitalia (Italy)

Aigle Azur (France)

Ryanair (Irland)

Saudia (Saudi Arabia)

TAP Air Portugal (Portugal)

TOURISM

TUI Group (Germany)

Thomas Cook (UK)

BANKING

These are the guys controlling the oxygen that any business needs to start, develop and grow. The FAITH Boys!

JPMorgan Chase (USA)

Credit Suisse (Switzerland)

Industrial and Commercial Bank of China - ICBC (China)

Standard Bank (South Africa / 20% China ICBC / Public float)

HSBC Bank Plc (UK)

Standard Chartered (UK)

Societe Generale (France)

Citi Bank (USA)

China Construction Bank (China)

So, do you have any doubts now WHO controls WHAT in Africa now?

Let's talk now about two (2) industries in more details: Food & Aviation.

THE FOOD INDUSTRY

The current world population of 7.3 billion is expected to reach 8.5 billion by 2030, 9.7 billion in 2050 and 11.2 billion in 2100, with India expected to surpass China as the most populous around seven years from now and Nigeria overtaking the United States to become the world's third largest country around 35 years from now, according to a United Nations report.

Moreover, the report reveals that during the 2015-2050 period, half of the world's population growth is expected to be concentrated in nine countries: India, Nigeria, Pakistan, Democratic Republic of the Congo, Ethiopia, Tanzania, the United States, Indonesia and Uganda.

Wu Hongbo, the UN Under-Secretary-General for Economic and Social Affairs, whose department produced the 2015 Revision of World Population Prospects, the 24th round of official UN population estimates and projections, noted that understanding the demographic changes that are likely to unfold over the coming years "is key to the design and implementation of the new development agenda."

8.5 billion by 2030, 9.7 billion in 2050 and 11.2 billion in 2100, that's a lot of mouths to feed. Where will all the food come from?

Half of the world's population lives in rural areas. They generate well over half of their income from agriculture. 85% of the world's approximately 450 million farms are small-scale. These produce around half of all our food.

An estimated 450 million laborers work on industrial plantations and farms. The big farms are increasingly held by banks or other big companies, which provide credit to farmers for seeds, agrochemicals, young animals, and feed.

With rising agricultural prices, the interest of investors is growing rapidly. Every year, an area the size of France is sold or leased to foreign investors. This land grabbing particularly affects Africa.

Seeds, young animals, feed, fertilizer – all things that used to be produced on the farm itself, are today separate sectors of the industrialized and globalized food value chain. This also includes trade, processing and selling of foodstuffs. The most vulnerable in this chain are those who cultivate and produce these foods: the farmers.

Small-scale farmers in the Global South come under great pressure through horizontal and vertical integration (concentration) in food production. Their right to food can be violated in many ways: by patents on seeds, expulsion from land, unfair working conditions or prices, or the squeezing out of informal markets.

Bellow I share with you the findings of a research done by ECONexus, named Agropoly - A Handful of Corporations control world food production:

The world's human population and food consumption are growing – does this mean the number of companies involved in the food sector is growing as well? The opposite is true: big corporations buy smaller companies and thus increase their market share and power. Hence, companies can dictate prices, terms and conditions and, increasingly, the political framework. Much of what we consume in the

North is being produced more cheaply in the Global South. The profits are made by only a few, predominantly Northern, companies. The big losers are the plantation workers and small farmers in the South, as they are the weakest links in the "value chain"."

- Major concentration in a few years: In 1996, the ten biggest seed companies had a market share of less than 30 %. Today, the three largest controls more than 50% of the market. Often seeds become more expensive with fewer varieties available. The three market leaders in seeds are also major pesticide producers.

- The powerful control the chain: Farmers are pressurized by corporations; they are paid low prices for their products such as soya, wheat, and maize, and they pay high prices for seeds, pesticides, energy, fertilizers and animal feed. The record food prices of 2008 resulted in higher profits for corporations, and not for farmers who have to bear all the risks.

- Who gains? Vietnamese aquaculture farmers produce Pangasius fish, for which Northern consumers pay around Usd10 per kilo. The farmer gets Usd1. After deduction of production costs their income is 10 cents per kilo. And the farmers bear all the risks of aquaculture such as fish diseases and weather problems; many also have debts to the aquaculture companies.

- Controlling the chain: In addition to horizontal integration, where one company controls a large share of the market, corporate strategies aim at vertical integration by processing the product and producing inputs. This is not about distributing business risks across several sectors but about controlling the value chain and access to cheap raw materials.

- Value chains instead of nutrient and energy circulation: What used to be produced on the farm as part of a circular economy – seeds, young animals, feed, and fertilizer – is today a global industrial "value chain" for food and agro fuels, with negative consequences for soil, water, climate, animal protection, and health.

- Lobby instead of competition: The influence of food corporations on politics and the public is growing. Thousands of lobbyists promote corporate interests. Corporate lobbyists often also work in government institutions. They often successfully lobby for corporate interests on food standards, approval of pesticides, GM seeds, trade agreements, or the public research agenda.

- World trade dominates prices: 85% of all food is consumed close to where it is produced. Nevertheless, global trade has a disproportionate influence on prices. On the stock market, batches of the same soya and maize may be traded speculatively several times over, thus increasing price volatility.

Who Controls our food? Let's look at the facts:

Animal Feed:

Turnover volume: Usd350 Billion

Market Share of top 10 Corporations: 16%

Livestock Breeding:

Only 4 companies worldwide for breeding chickens

Market Share of top 4 Corporations: 99%

Seeds:

Turnover volume: Usd34.5 Billion

Market Share of top 10 Corporations: 75%

Fertilizers:

Turnover volume: Usd90.2 Billion

Market Share of top 10 Corporations: 55%

Pesticides:

Pesticides market leaders also dominate the seed market.

Turnover volume: Usd44 Billion

Market Share of top 11 Corporations: 97.8%

Grains & Soya Trading

Market Share of top 4 Corporations: 75%

Processing

Turnover volume: Usd1.3 Trillion

Market Share of top 10 Corporations: 28%

Retail

Turnover volume: Usd7.2 Trillion

Market Share of top 10 Corporations: 10.5%

6 billion consumers

Coffee

5 Traders control 55% of the world trade of green coffee.

3 Roasters control 40% of the world coffee market.

Consumers: 500 million.

But who exactly are these Corporations controlling the entire food market production and supply chain?

The Winners are a handful of Big Corporations from Europe and USA:

Nestle (Switzerland)

Cargill (USA)

Nutreco Holding N.V. (Netherlands)

Monsanto (USA)

KWS AG (Germany)

Bayer (Germany)

BASF (Germany)

DOW AgroSciences (USA)

DuPont (USA)

Syngenta (Switzerland)

Yara (Norway)

Agrium (USA)

Mosaic (USA)

K + S Group (Germany)

Neumann (Germany)

Volcafe (Switzerland)

ECOM (Switzerland)

Kraft (USA)

Sara Lee (USA)

AVIATION INDUSTRY

Remember the Yamoussoukro Decision that I have mentioned in chapter one, which was signed in 1988 to liberalize the aviation sector (known in aviation as Open Skies) across Africa. Twenty nine (29) years have passed since its signature and there is still *"NO OPEN SKIES"* across Africa.

Why did I want to bring Aviation into this chapter? Because due to lack of leadership from the African Union to implement the Yamoussoukro Decision still after three decades, the aviation sector in Africa is a total mess and with unprofitable National Airlines (with the exception of a couple of Airlines such as Ethiopian, South Africa Airways, Royal Air Morocco), draining their State treasury funds.

Here are some facts:

- According to the International Air Transport Association (IATA) statistics, 80% of the supply of air transport services in Africa is related with non-African airlines, mostly European;

- 130 African Airlines are black listed to fly to the Europe, North America, and South America markets; 17 countries are banned to fly to the Europe;

- Passenger and cargo traffic growth is set to continue at an impressive rate driven by continued market liberalization and dramatic GDP growth in emerging markets, which will lead to increasing wealth and mobility through most Africa immediate catchment area. This supports the expectation that traffic growth will continue to outstrip the industry-wide projections of organizations such as Boeing, Airbus and IATA;

- According to Airbus Global Market Forecast, air traffic will double in the next 15 years. Further, the report calculates emerging markets are set to generate the lion's share of that growth. China, India, the Middle East, Asia, Africa, CIS, Eastern Europe and Latin America are projected to see annual revenue passenger kilometer (RPK) growth of 6.1% per annum for the next 20 years. More mature markets in North America, Europe, Australasia and Japan are projected to see 3.7% average annual RPK expansion. That in turn has and will continue to precipitate aircraft orders to serve the growing demand;

- According to Lufthansa Consulting, Africa passenger and cargo forecast will grow above the world average during 20 years (between 2008 to 2028);

African carriers face stiff competition from non-African carriers. The three Middle Eastern giants – Emirates, Qatar Airways and Etihad Airways – have put Africa at the center of their growth strategy. European carriers and Turkish airlines also control significant market share in Africa. Today, non-African airlines control and transport 80% of African passenger traffic.

Like Ethiopian Airlines Group CEO, Tewolde Gebremariam, said recently in an interview "African carriers are being driven out of the market. Some ten years ago African carriers had forty percent market share on the intra-African market. This has dwindled to 20%. Unless we wake up and do something today, ten years from now there will be no homegrown African airline. It will be the end of the African airline industry."

Here is a fact that will blow up your mind, in case you never heard about it yet. Recently United Technologies Chairman and CEO Greg Hayes said on a Goldman Sachs Global Macro Conference in New York, in a conversation about economic growth with Goldman Sachs Chairman and CEO Lloyd C. Blankfein that about 85% of the world's population has never set foot on an airplane. Meanwhile, there are about 27.000 aircraft in service around the world today - of which about half will be retired in 15 years - and we'll need about 47.000 aircrafts by 2030.

So why aren't African Countries doing nothing to develop the Airline industry?

Why aren't they developing Aviation HUBs to create strong Airlines and Aviation HUBs to connect passengers and Cargo between different continents (Europe/Americas/Africa)?

Is it difficult? Is it something new that no one ever tried so far?

Here is a success case that can be blueprinted: Dubai.

Dubai, has managed to successfully develop Dubai International Airport and Emirates Airlines, into an Aviation HUB business model which has allowed the country to promote connectivity, cargo, and global tourism.

Aviation HUBs creates connections between cities and countries. These connections represent an important infrastructure asset that benefits passengers and businesses from many countries.

In 2010 leading global research firm Oxford Economics has examined Dubai's aviation model and found that Dubai's aviation sector is a consensus based, consumer-centric and commercially driven enterprise which generates significant economic benefits for Dubai and for all countries linked to it.

Together the key players – Dubai Airports, Dubai Duty Free, Emirates and Flydubai – have combined to create a global aviation phenomenon. The emergence of Dubai as a leading global aviation center is the result of a carefully constructed and well-executed model that effectively harnesses the emirate's geocentric location and entrepreneurial spirit. It is a model that features a liberal regulatory climate, a tax-free business environment, a customer-centric focus that provides value for money, and close coordination and collaboration within the sector.

Aviation has been strategically important to Dubai's evolution and it remains instrumental in driving the emirate's future growth. The airport has served as a commercial springboard for growing hospitality, tourism, shipping, trade, finance and industrial sectors, and a conduit for its numerable infrastructural projects. It therefore forms a fundamental pillar to continual GDP growth. In total, Dubai's aviation sector supports over 250.000 jobs and contributes over Usd22 billion to GDP; representing around 19% of total employment in Dubai and 28% of Dubai's GDP.

Benefits of the Aviation sector extend beyond Dubai's borders to the global economy through enhanced global tourism and trade via the provision of efficient and high quality air services. Air travelers and shippers using Dubai and Emirates Airlines make an important contribution to many national economies. For example, associated tourism benefits contribute over Usd1 billion to GDP for both Australia and India, while connectivity benefits a total Usd1.4 billion for China and Usd800 million each for the UK and the US.

Here is a quote from His Highness Sheikh Mohammed Bin Rashid Al Maktoum, Vice

President, Prime Minister of the UAE and Ruler of Dubai, mentioned on the Emirates Group 2011-2012 Annual Report, which I share with you: "The evolving global marketplace and development of new hubs for business, finance and culture demand flexibility and innovation. This dynamic growth calls for enhanced aviation and transport infrastructure to link communities and businesses, develop environmental sustainability and expand economic development."

Quite sure you will hear excuses from most of the African Presidents that don't believe they can blueprint the Dubai success stories and replicate the same model in their country and across their regions in Africa.

Others will probably say oh Dubai is oil rich and is just one country without any conflicts, so you cannot compare it to any country in Africa. Reallyyyyy? Try and take a look at the World Map and see the countries that are very close and others that make borders with the United Arab Emirates which Dubai is part of. These countries are countries that are under war and terrorism conflict for many years, such as Syria, Yemen, Iraq, Afghanistan, and Pakistan.

Even with all the major conflicts in the Middle East, Dubai under the leadership of Sheikh Mohammed Bin Rashid Al Maktoum, has managed to make Dubai one of the most desired tourism destinations in the world and the perfect HUB for the following sectors: financial, logistics, aviation and trade.

Dubai is today considered a politically stable city-state amidst an unstable geographical neighborhood; located in an oil-rich region with minimal dependence on oil revenues; a two-tiered legal system, partly based in local tradition, and partly founded in the Western liberal tradition, especially when it comes to economics and trade.

Dubai will run out of oil soon, but its leader has managed to diversify its economy by investing alongside with the private sector to make sure the success and the wealth is made in Dubai but it stays in Dubai as well.

Dubai government planned most of Dubai's mega projects such as The Palm Jumeirah (world biggest man-made island in the shape of a palm tree), Burj Khalifa (world tallest tower), Burj Al Arab Jumeirah (world most luxurious Hotel), Dubai Mall (world biggest mall), The Atlantis Palm Dubai (world most iconic hotel), among others. Foreign investors' role in the making of what the city is today was only to take advantage of lucrative opportunities.

The government owns most of the big companies such as Investment Corporation of Dubai (public register at Dubai International Financial Center) which is the investment arm of the Government of Dubai for investments in strategic companies such as the following by sectors:

TRANSPORTATION

Emirates Airlines

DNATA

Dubai Airports

Dubai Aerospace Enterprise

Fly Dubai

FINANCE & INVESTMENTS

Emirates NDB Bank

Dubai Islamic Bank

Commercial Bank of Dubai

Borse Dubai

National Bonds

Noor Bank

Union National Bank

Dubai Investments

Emirates Investment & Development

HSBC Middle East Finance Company

Galadari Brothers

ENERGY & INDUSTRIAL

ENOC Oil

Emirates Global Aluminium

Dubai Cabel Company

REAL ESTATE & CONSTRUCTION

>EMAAR Properties

>Dubai Airport Freezone

>Dubai World Trade Centre

>Dubai Silicon Oasis

>Cleveland Bridge & Engineering ME

HOSPITALITY & LEISURE

>Atlantis The Palm, Dubai

>Golf in Dubai

>Kerzner International

RETAIL & OTHER HOLDINGS

>Dubai Duty Free

>Emirates Refreshments

>Emirates Rawabi

>Aswaaq

>Emaratech

This is how you diversify the economy and this is how wealth stays in your Country benefiting your citizens. Hand of applause please to Sheikh Mohammed. African Leaders should learn from this brilliant mind.

When you think Dubai cannot make nothing else bigger, taller or the biggest in the world, the government is building now a Usd32 billion, five-runway mega hub precisely to Emirates' specifications. Its ambitions are consonant with its name: Dubai World Central. The project will have a capacity of 220 million passengers per year, four times the number that New York's John F. Kennedy International Airport serves today.

In a nutshell, Dubai's success story is the result of its government's entrepreneurial mindset and investor oriented, business friendly attitude. Even after forty years of double-digit growth, its economy is still highly dynamic and robust. The future looks strong, with major events like World Expo 2020 scheduled to attract 22 million tourists. Reports indicate Dubai already has Usd705 billion worth of projects spread over the next 10 years, with expectations of another Usd8.1 billion worth of new projects getting added to the pipeline following the World Expo 2020.

If you want to know more about Dubai Leader, his vision and leadership buy his book named My Vision: Challenges in the Race for Excellence, where Sheikh Mohammed examines aspects of the UAE's unique development experience and how Dubai should be an example for other countries to follow. The book represents a message of optimism that if all the constituents of any given society agree to excel in all fields, different cultures and religions can coexist without the slightest problem. The proof he provides is Dubai itself.

After making this point on the success of Dubai Aviation success story, let's take a look at Who Controls Aviation in Africa?

The facts are:

With typically weak national flag carriers, foreign airlines are increasingly dominating Africa's intercontinental market, particularly Emirates, Qatar Airways and Turkish Airlines. With the exception of Ethiopian Airlines and South African Airways, African carriers will continue to struggle and lose market share.

Fragmented and usually highly inefficient African airlines have a relatively small presence in the international market and struggle to compete against larger players from outside their region. Traffic to and from Africa will grow significantly in percentage terms over the next 10 years off the existing low base, particularly between Africa and Asia. However, African airlines appear destined to continue to lose market share to competitors.

Europe is the largest intercontinental market from Africa with approximately 1.5 million weekly nonstop return seats (80million passengers per year).

Air France-KLM is the largest airline group in the Africa-Europe market while Turkish Airlines is the second largest and the fastest growing. Turkish has expanded its share of capacity in the Africa-Europe market from less than 5% to approximately 7% over the last three years as it has rapidly grown its African network.

Turkish Airlines now serves 43 destinations in Africa and plans to expand further in Africa with new destinations and, more significantly, additional capacity to existing destinations through extra frequencies, decoupling destinations and up-gauging. Turkish's share of nonstop capacity in the Africa-Europe market could reach 15% in 2025, enabling it to overtake Air France-KLM as the market leader.

Europe's three main airline groups – Air France-KLM, International Airlines Group (parent company of British Airways, Iberia, Alitalia) and Lufthansa – all have a strong presence in Africa which they are keen to grow, although the rate of growth will be much slower than Turkish. They particularly have an advantage over African competitors in the long haul markets connecting Europe with central, eastern, southern and western Africa.

In the larger north Africa-Europe market, the African airlines are relatively stronger. North African airlines allocate nearly all of their capacity to nearby Europe. However they have the disadvantage of having to compete against European Low Cost Carriers (LCCs) in addition to Europe's main full service airline groups.

European LCCs now account for 22% of capacity in the north Africa-Europe market, led by a 7% share from Ryanair. North Africa-Europe accounts for approximately two thirds of total Africa-Europe capacity. Europe's LCCs will continue to expand in North Africa over the next decade and use new generation narrow body aircraft to push further into Africa.

Given the challenges they face, African airlines will likely experience over the next decade a steady decline in their share of capacity in the Africa-Europe market. Africa's airlines generally lack the scale to compete effectively and have not been able to follow the European airline sector in pursuing acquisitions or mergers.

Ethiopian Airlines has made some moves towards consolidation, although its acquisitions have been relatively minor in terms of the airlines acquired and the size of the stakes. The political – essentially protectionist – environment in Africa makes it very difficult to pursue meaningful consolidation. As a result most of Africa's airlines will likely continue to struggle from both a profitability and growth perspective. In the Africa-Europe market this means ceding market share to stronger competitors from Europe and the Middle East.

Gulf airlines have become significant players in the eastern Africa-Europe and southern Africa-Europe markets. Emirates and Qatar Airways are particularly strong in Africa.

There are approximately 800.000 weekly nonstop seats between Africa and the Middle East. The Middle East is a large local market from Africa, particularly for northern and eastern Africa. However a large portion of Africa-Middle East traffic travels beyond the Middle East as the Gulf is geographically well placed for Africa intercontinental traffic.

Emirates is the largest airline in the Africa-Middle East market and is also the largest foreign airline in Africa overall. Middle Eastern airlines combined account for approximately a 60% share of seat capacity between Africa and the Middle East, led by an 18% share for Emirates – or 20% when including its sister airline Flydubai.

There are currently only approximately 50.000 weekly nonstop return seats in the Africa-North American market and approximately 12.000 seats between Africa and Latin America. European airlines have traditionally dominated these markets, making it difficult for African airlines to pursue growth in the Americas. European carriers currently account for approximately a 38% share of passenger traffic in the Africa-North America market.

Asia is the fastest growing international market from Africa but has a relatively limited amount of nonstop capacity. There are currently approximately 90.000 weekly return seats between Africa and Asia Pacific, making it a larger market than Africa-Americas but significantly smaller than Africa-Europe or Africa-Middle East.

Unlike the Europe or Middle East markets, African airlines have a larger share of nonstop capacity to and from Asia than their overseas competitors. Currently African airlines have an 81% share of Africa-North America nonstop seat capacity, led by a 33% share for Ethiopian. African airlines have an advantage over Asian competitors as they can offer connections throughout Africa – and in some cases even to South America.

Ethiopian has rapidly expanded in Asia, growing its network from only six destinations in 2011 to 11 currently. Africa-Asia traffic has been the main driver of Ethiopian's rapid ascent over the past five years as it has more than doubled its total passenger traffic and emerged as Africa's largest (and most profitable) airline group. Ethiopian also has pursued rapid growth regionally in Africa which has complemented the expansion of its Asia operation, which requires significant feed as the local Ethiopia-Asia market is very small.

Ethiopian is planning more expansion in Asia in the coming years and will likely at least double its Asia seat capacity by 2025. However the total Asia-Africa markets will also double or even triple in size, with other African airlines targeting a piece of the fast expanding pie.

East African airlines are particularly well placed for Africa-Asia given their geographic location. Air Mauritius is in the process of establishing a new Africa-Asia hub and Rwandair is pursuing the same pool of sixth freedom traffic as it prepares to launch services to China and India using a newly acquired wide body fleet.

EgyptAir and Kenya Airways, which have been restructuring following instability in their home markets, are also keen to resume Asia expansion over the next several years. Kenya Airways has suffered some setbacks after a fruitful partnership with KLM was established and is currently undergoing a management overhaul, but looks unlikely to become a major force in the next decade.

Asia represents a ray of hope for African airlines as they try to improve their overall position in a very challenging market. However competition in the Africa-Asia market is intensifying. Gulf airlines are very well positioned to capture a large share of the anticipated Africa-Asia growth as they continue to expand their networks in both regions.

Middle Eastern airlines already fly more passengers between Africa and Asia Pacific than African airlines. While there are opportunities for more nonstop services from African (and Asian) airlines, the majority of passengers in this market will travel via the Middle East.

Middle Eastern airlines currently account for 45% of total Africa-Asia Pacific bookings compared to a 40% share for African Airlines, a 9% share for Asia Pacific airlines and a 6% share for European airlines.

Emirates is already the leader in the Africa-Asia market with a 22% share of bookings and should be able to expand its share to 30% by 2025 as it continues to pursue expansion in Africa and Asia. Given the expected rapid growth in the Africa-Asia market, total traffic for Emirates in this market could triple or even quadruple.

Qatar Airways is currently the third largest player in the Africa-Asia market, behind only Emirates and Ethiopian. Qatar's 11% share could reach 20% by 2025.

Competing against Emirates and Qatar is not an easy proposition for any airline from any region. For African airlines the challenge is even more intense as they are generally small, inefficient and unprofitable.

Ethiopian has been the only exception in recent years and should be able to continue growing its market share. Ethiopian has the largest order book in Africa and plans to again double in size by 2025.

Ethiopian should be able to grow its share of Africa-Asia traffic from 16% currently to over 20% by 2025 and its Africa-North America share from 6% to at least 10%. Ethiopian is not as well positioned geographically for the more mature Africa-Europe market, but should be able to modestly grow its current 2% share.

Most other African airline groups do not have the scale, profitability and backing to increase their market share over the next decade. Several are likely to contract – or even exit – unless they quickly are able to reform. They do not have the cost structures to compete internationally and the current protectionist policies and interventionist ways of several African governments are detrimental to their long term health.

As you seen before the Yamoussoukro Decision, which was adopted as long ago as 1988, and designed to improve intra-African market access, has still not been implemented. Given the current environment it seems unlikely the long overdue open skies regime, or even significant liberalization, will take place by 2025.

It is hard to be optimistic about the prospects for Africa's airline sector. The market must grow, as the continent is resource rich and currently greatly underserved by global standards. But continuing political instability, government interference and poor management make for a difficult outlook. African airlines are less profitable than their counterparts in all other regions. Without major structural changes the African airlines are unlikely to be profitable by 2025. Africa in a decade will be even more dominated by foreign airlines, particularly the big Gulf groups.

Below are the top foreign airlines in Africa's controlling the international airline traffic to and from Africa:

Emirates Airlines (United Arab Emirates)

Qatar Airways (Qatar)

Etihad Airways (United Arab Emirates)

Turkish Airlines (Turkey)

Air France KLM (France)

Lufthansa Group (Germany)

British Airways (UK)

TUI Fly (Germany)

Iberia (Spain)

Alitalia (Italy)

Aigle Azur (France)

Ryanair (Irland)

Saudia (Saudi Arabia)

TAP Air Portugal (Portugal)

CONCLUSION: African Leaders please wake up if you want to see an Africa more prosperous for the next generation. If you really believe you can make your country and Africa successful please try to learn from the best success cases, such as Dubai mentioned on this chapter, and blueprint various sectors that have been successful in other countries, so you can apply them into your country.

It is totally fine to be open to the world and accept globalization as long as you make sure business is done fair between foreign investors and your country, in order for your country and your people to benefit in the process of wealth creation and distribution.

"We shall make electric light so cheap that only the wealthy can afford to burn candles." Thomas Edison

CHAPTER 3: Africa Industrial Revolution.

The Industrial Revolution first started in Great Britain and eventually progressed to the United States in the early 19th century. It was first created to raise people's standard of living. Before the revolution, the majority of Americans lived on farmland, small towns, or villages where there was little manufacturing. A farmer usually was able to make shoes, and the women spent their days making soap and candles, spinning yarn or making clothing. The manufacturing that did take place was in homes or rural areas and it was done by hand. Some products made in the home (including clothing, furniture, tools, cloth, hardware, jewelry, leather, silverware, and weapons) were even exchanged for food. But, people lived in fear that the crops they grew might fail, as many of them already suffered from malnutrition. In addition, diseases and other epidemics were unfortunately common. In the late 1700's, the first sign of a revolution occurred when the steam engine was developed. It introduced the concept of companies and factories being able to create goods using machinery, as opposed to a family working together at home. One of the purposes of the Industrial Revolution was to have more goods produced at a lower cost. An immediate change included the production of goods; what was produced, as well as where and how it cost, and efficiency. The Industrial Revolution was beginning to turn an agricultural economy into one with machines and manufacturing.

The British enacted legislation to prohibit the export of their technology and skilled workers; however, they had little success in this regard. Industrialization spread from Britain to other European countries, including Belgium, France and Germany, and to the United States. By the mid-19th century, industrialization was well-established throughout the western part of Europe and America's northeastern region.

The Industrial Revolution was growing rapidly in the United States during the early 19th century. Private investors and financial buildings (such as banks) were needed to provide money to the people who wanted to start a business. This money would allow further industrialization to take place. The purpose of it was to lessen the risks of losing money to the individual investors. This was especially crucial because the new machinery that was needed was expensive. Capital was first introduced as companies combined together their money as "joint stock companies," and soon after corporations were formally developed. The advantage to this was the most an investor could lose is the amount that they put in; as opposed to losing more money than one initially started with. By the early 20th century, the U.S. had become the world's leading industrial nation.

Believe it or not, Africa is only seeing the industrial era now in the 21st century. Yes, three (3) centuries after (300 years to be more exact. Wow!).

The developed countries in the North have managed to industrialize themselves between the 18th and 19th centuries.

THE NEXT INDUSTRIAL ENGINE OF THE WORLD

We are in the 21st century and Africa is open for business, and tomorrow's global leaders should understand both the risks and the opportunities that are available here.

There is the potential for corporations to make billions of dollars in profits in Africa. But, much more importantly, contributing to a strong and sustainable Africa could just be the next generation of global leaders' greatest legacy.

Africa needs a redesign of its economy towards a knowledge-driven one and begin industrializing Africa to manufacturer products for export.

But you are probably thinking that is impossible for Africa to catch up with the North when there is an advantage of three centuries of development, know-how and market monopoly.

Well, we live in a different world today and industrializing Africa today is not the same industrialization process that the developed countries have experienced. Africa industrialization has to be done differently, and the developed countries will have to catch up with us and do the same, which is to adapt and change their entire industries to the new rules of the 21st Century, following the Conference of the Parties (COP21) during the United Nations Climate

Change Conference in Paris in December 2015, in which all signatory countries must invest in a future based on Green Industrialization with less CO2 emissions, leading to a worldwide low-carbon economy shifting away from fossil fuels.

So basically, the Race is on between the North and South! The North hemisphere (USA, Europe, and Russia) is where all the technology, know-how and industries are concentrated. The South is where the wealth is and the future is. The South hemisphere (Africa, Latin America, China, South East Asia and Australia) controls the majority of the natural resources in the world and is where most of the arable land for agriculture is located.

If the majority of African countries joint forces now and take advantage of Africa resources and potential for the future, we will become the next industrial engine of the world in the 21st century.

Below I will share with you some insights from a research named Economic Report on Africa 2016 - Greening Africa's Industrialization, done by the United Nation Economic Commission for Africa:

- Structural transformation in Africa's economies remains the highest priority, and industrialization is the top strategy for achieving it in practice. Achieving the African Union's Agenda 2063 and fulfilling the Sustainable Development Goals will demand a major re-design of growth strategies across the continent;

- The big opportunity for Africa, as a latecomer to industrialization, is in adopting alternative economic pathways to industrialization. This requires governments to take on-board the drivers, challenges, and trade-offs in pushing for a greening of industrialization - and to build them into the vision and route-map for action. Seizing the momentum of the Paris Climate Agreement and the Strategic Development Goals provides the ideal timing for such a shift in economic strategy;

- Dispelling the myths currently surrounding green growth will promote the re-shaping of Africa's economic growth in favor of sustainable development; Investing in environmental standards should be seen not as an obstacle to competitive manufacturing, but as underpinning competitiveness, making more efficient use of energy, and de-coupling resource use from output growth.

- While some individual countries have taken the lead, there would be far greater benefits from a regional approach to greening the essential infrastructure, industrial structures, and major trade flows that span each region;

- Africa's growth has been characterized by heavy reliance on natural resources and low productivity across most sectors. It has been accompanied by high energy and material intensities, as well as waste generation. These factors drive the resource scarcity and contribute to the high production costs that undermine the global competitiveness of Africa's industrial sector;

- Greening industrialization is an opportunity for Africa to achieve the type of structural transformation that yields sustainable and inclusive growth, creating jobs while safeguarding the productivity of natural resource assets. Growth in the region has been largely jobless and associated with the degradation of Africa's valuable natural capital;

- Structural transformation through industrialization will inevitably and justifiably increase the uptake of resources. But a strategy for greening this process, in its many dimensions, will deliver a more competitive and resource-efficient industrial sector - one that provides employment, is climate resilient and is decoupled from environmental degradation; there is now a growing commitment among African countries to pursue inclusive green development. A collective commitment from across the African Union would strengthen the speed and effectiveness of such a strategic shift;

- Greening industrialization provides the impetus for turning current supply chains linking natural resources to markets, into value chains that diversify Africa's economies and ensure greater value added;

- In an era of growing scarcity, resource rich Africa must shift away from being a marginal supplier of raw commodities, to harness the full potential of natural resources by diversification into greater value addition, through processing and marketing. The Africa Mining Vision offers a good example for making this step-change;

- Taking stock of current economic trends, global economic growth slowed in 2015, reflecting a range of problems in the euro area, China, Brazil, and the Russian Federation, combined with the collapse of oil prices. This slowdown among Africa's largest trading partners has inevitably hit economic performance on the continent, with growth moderating from 3.9% in 2014 to 3.7% in 2015. Africa's reliance on exports of raw materials to other regions of the world has led to falling revenues for government and a decline in investment;

- Growth in many African countries has been underpinned by increased private consumption over the last few years, due to rising domestic demand, stemming from increased government spending in infrastructure projects and growing incomes among the middle class. An increase in inward investment has also spurred growth, thanks to improvements in the commercial environment and lower costs of doing business. But falling commodity prices now mean that most countries are experiencing growing fiscal deficits, especially those reliant on oil and gas exports, and will have to revise government spending plans. Africa's vulnerability to these external shocks calls for a rethink of its growth and broader development strategy along four (4) critical dimensions:

- First: economic growth in Africa has not been inclusive: the number of Africans in absolute poverty has risen, and inequality remains a major concern.

- Second: growth has been associated with increased exploitation of non-renewable natural resources, incurring heavy costs to the soils, water, forests and biodiversity which make up Africa's rich and diverse natural resource base.

- Third: the structures of African economies have remained largely based on raw material extraction, with very little value addition and limited employment generation.

- Fourth: Africa trades more with other parts of the world than within the continent.

A strategic re-think across Africa's regions could build much stronger domestic and regional linkages - reducing large and growing food imports, greatly improving the use of renewable resources, particularly water and energy, and establishing competitive industrial activity.

- The time has never been better for African countries to follow this route to development. The past year has seen three landmark global agreements that align well with Africa's need to industrialize, by generating greener and more inclusive growth:

The first agreement was the 21st annual Conference of the Parties (COP21) during the United Nations Climate Change Conference in Paris in December 2015. At COP21 all nations signed an agreement that - if the terms are carried out - will lead to a worldwide low-carbon economy and a shift away from fossil fuels. The agreement puts the global economy on course for transforming its energy systems. All countries have pledged to keep a global temperature rise this century well below 2°C and to drive efforts to limit the temperature increase even further to 1.5°C, above pre-industrial levels" (UNFCCC,

2015). All countries of the world have submitted plans laying out their intended contribution to achieving the global target of less than 2°C, and those plans will be subject to five-year review to ratchet up the ambition gradually.

The second agreement - on the Sustainable Development Goals (SDGs), in September 2015 - places equality, sustainability and universal basic needs at the heart of our common global economic strategy.

The third agreement is the Addis Ababa Action Agenda, the outcome of the Financing for Development summit in Addis Ababa in July 2015, offers a comprehensive framework for financing Africa's industrialization and structural transformation, with an emphasis on domestic resource mobilization.

- Properly aligned, these global agreements set the stage for international and regional partnerships that can transform Africa's growth prospects. They confirm a shift in the direction of the global economy towards a sustainable, low-carbon future based on green and inclusive growth;

- African countries can stand back and watch others take the lead in building a green economy - or they can benefit from their current low-carbon position and leapfrog the process. Following the latter strategy means that many African economies can get it right the first time; infrastructure does not have to be retrofitted to make it climate resilient, and high dependence on volatile fossil fuels can be avoided, bringing significant co-benefits for health and energy security;

- Africa is blessed with abundant land, water and energy sources and with a young and increasingly better educated population. Such abundance, when combined with capital investment, can generate prosperity, employment and sustainability needed to achieve the promise laid out in the African Union's Vision 2063. Some African countries are making good progress, with a focus on water, energy and agriculture, systematically building low-carbon development and climate resilience into their plans and decision-making. But many countries have yet to focus on how best to harness the post-2015 momentum in climate and sustainability and use it to accelerate their own plans for growth, structural transformation and sustainable industrialization.

- How best to stimulate growth and ensure it is both inclusive and environmentally sustainable? Africa cannot continue on a business-as-usual trajectory if it truly wishes to industrialize and scale up broad-based development. Looking forward to 2050, and using a set of green agenda policy tools, many of the supply-demand gaps in energy are considerably if major investments tap into Africa's vast renewable energy resources. Even water scarcity becomes manageable, largely as a result of improved governance, regional integration and green infrastructure. Critically, urban populations generate big dividends where investment is made in green infrastructure, and enhanced skills and innovation.

Beside a green industrialization Africa will need to consider also technology and how interconnected our world is today. Technology plays an important role today on how we communicate, trade, and innovate businesses across different industries.

Below are some tech facts about Africa for your brain to digest:

- Internet penetration on the continent has increased by 6.839% in the last 15 years, with Frost & Sullivan saying mobile penetration in the region will increase to 79% by 2020;

- Accommodation booking platform Airbnb, which rents out rooms or whole properties online, is scaling up its operations in the region, having already seen sizeable growth. It has more than doubled listings and seen user numbers increase by 145% over the last year;

- Airbnb is following a path already mapped out by taxi-hailing giant Uber, which has rapidly established an African presence in eight cities – Cape Town, Durban, Johannesburg, Pretoria, Nairobi, Cairo, Casablanca and Lagos;

- The majority of urban Africans own Internet-capable devices and go online regularly. If infrastructure investment continues, the Internet will take hold on a much larger scale in the coming decade - potentially adding Usd300 billion a year to Africa's GDP;

- Technology and the Internet's greatest impact in Africa are likely to be concentrated in six sectors: financial services, education, health, retail, agriculture, and Government. Technology-related productivity gains in these sectors could reach Usd318 billion by 2025, and large populations stand to benefit as a result.

THE RACE HAS ALREADY STARTED

Like Kingsley Ighobor beautifully wrote in Africa Renewal platform in 2016 about the green path to industrialization, as the only viable option for

Africa's continued development, I share below some of his findings:

The green economy train has been running at full speed due to several factors, including innovative technologies, which are bringing down the cost of renewables considerably. In addition, a crash in commodity prices, particularly in extractives, is sending some of Africa's economies – such as Angola, Nigeria and South Africa – spiraling into chaos, forcing many countries to explore opportunities in green industrialization.

Government leadership has been playing a key role in driving the growth of renewables, particularly wind and solar, in the power sector including many in Africa. As of early 2016, 173 countries had renewable energy targets in place and 146 countries had support policies. Cities, communities and companies are leading the rapidly expanding "100% renewable" movement, playing a vital role in advancing the global energy transition.

Additional growth factors include better access to financing, concerns about energy security and the environment and the growing demand for modern energy services in developing and emerging economies.

Carlos Lopes, executive secretary of the United Nations Economic Commission for Africa (UNECA), expressed optimism by saying recently, which I quote: "We have the potential to access renewable energy at a time when the price of producing this energy is comparable to fossil fuel production."

According to Professor Mark Swilling of the Centre for Renewable and Sustainable Energy Studies at Stellenbosch University in South Africa, the added value of renewables is their positive impact on the "triple bottom-line", a term that refers to a company's profit, its social responsibility activities and its environmental responsibility.

Africa's capabilities for "leapfrogging" – another buzzword at economic forums – constitute a significant economic advantage for the region. Simply put, African countries implementing green initiatives won't have to go through every intermediary stage of technology, but instead can directly access the latest available on the market.

Africa can therefore be expected to take a giant developmental step: the leapfrog. Industrialized countries, on the other hand, will have to retrofit older infrastructure, said Lopes, a burdensome expense.

Ethiopia in 2011 adopted a Climate Resilient Green Economy strategy as part of its ambitious plan to propel the country into middle-income status by 2025. The government is partnering with the private sector to help communities engage in sustainable farming.

In the Democratic Republic of the Congo, a tree-cloning project is enhancing afforestation (establishing forests on lands that have not been forested for a long time) and reforestation (establishing forests where they have been destroyed). Climate change experts consider afforestation and reforestation effective methods of combating global warming. Despite the DRC's efforts, it is considering lifting the moratorium on logging that has been in place since 2002; this could threaten the forests, experts believe.

The World Bank assisted Ghana in launching a Climate Innovation Centre in the capital, Accra, to support a green growth strategy. The center is working with about a hundred local technology companies.

Nigeria's Renewable Energy Program is, among other things, executing a low-carbon development project to provide electricity for its capital city, Abuja, through improved insulation, energy-efficient devices for apartments and local power generation.

The project, currently underway, is the first of its kind in Africa and the second in the world, after that of Masdar City in the United Arab Emirates, according to Nigeria's environment ministry.

Also, TATA Group from India is planning to establish in Nigeria a mass transit system of compressed natural gas vehicles to reduce emissions.

Overall, a general belief among Africa's development experts is that going green -and clean - is no longer a moral question; it is now a socioeconomic imperative.

GREEN PROJECTS HAPPENING ACROSS AFRICA

But how should this green industrialization be achieved, especially given that there are no blueprints from which to learn as no other region of the world has passed through the early phase of industrialization pursuing a green pathway?

Many pathways to industrialization exist. But Africa as a latecomer can define and design its own pathway – based on its own realities and learning from history and the experiences of other regions – to leapfrog traditional, carbon-intensive methods of growth and champion a low-carbon development trajectory.

About 620 million people in Sub-Saharan Africa live without access to electricity. Most countries are unlikely to connect their entire populations to the electricity grid for years, if not decades. As a result, many households rely on expensive, dangerous, pollution-causing kerosene, and diesel fuel for their energy needs.

How can you industrialize a continent that 70% of its people do not have access to electricity?

To build entire industries and their supply chain Africa will need three key ingredients: affordable electricity 24/7 + roads + logistics (intra-Africa and export).

According to a 2015 African Progress Report to achieve universal energy access by 2030, Usd55 billion of investments are needed every year.

But from where will the next energy breakthrough come from to provide us with reliable electricity that does not pollute the planet and is able to support all the industries that we will need to support the next industrial revolution?

I will share with you below a post on Energy, posted on Gates Notes, The Blog platform of Bill Gates (yes the man himself, the Founder & Big Boss of Microsoft):

GATES NOTES STARTS HERE:

By the middle of this century, the world will use twice as much energy as we use today.

There's good news in this: more energy means better lives and stronger economies.

But it also means the world needs a new energy supply - one that doesn't contribute to climate change. Climate change is a serious threat, especially in the poorest parts of the world.

We need affordable and reliable energy that doesn't emit greenhouse gas to power the future - and to get it, we need a different model for investing in good ideas and moving them from the lab to the market.

That is why today, I, along with an incredible group of people who care a lot about energy innovation, I am announcing the launch of Breakthrough Energy Ventures (BEV), a fund that will invest more than $1 billion in scientific breakthroughs that have the potential to deliver cheap and reliable clean energy to the world.

It's the next step in an effort that began last December, when we brought together private investors from around the globe who were passionate about solving this problem. We formed the Breakthrough Energy Coalition, a group of entrepreneurs, business leaders, and institutional investors committed to help bring promising new zero-emissions energy technologies to market.

The Coalition partnered with Mission Innovation, an initiative of more than 20 countries and the European Union to double their investment in clean energy research and development in the next five years.

As I've argued before, an investment in a true energy transformation requires governments, research institutions, businesses, and private investors to work together. And it's hard to overstate how important this public commitment is. Government funding gives scientists the freedom to come up with bold new ideas and try to prove they will work. But government research is not enough. The world needs the skills and resources of investors with experience driving innovation from a lab to the marketplace. The private sector knows how to take great research, turn it into a great product, and ultimately create a great company to bring a transformative technology to market.

It's this type of public-private collaboration that's given rise to advances in defense, space, medicine, and information technology. In fact, it's what brought these words to your screen right now. During the Cold War, the Department of Defense developed a network of computers that could survive a nuclear attack, and private companies saw an opportunity to expand this technology to the public. Together, they created the Internet.

When it comes to energy, though, this transition - from idea to product to company - is often complicated by the challenges of the market. Unlike a software start up, getting a new energy technology from a lab to market takes a lot of infrastructure, a lot of upfront capital, and a lot of time.

The Breakthrough Energy Coalition created BEV to address some of those challenges in the energy market. We are willing to wait a longer time for returns than other funds. We have a higher tolerance for technical risk, because we know it's tough to determine which technologies will succeed in a complicated energy market. We are led by our investors, who are a unique group of global business leaders, entrepreneurs, energy experts, and company builders who can help new companies navigate the challenges of building a business while developing partnerships with the companies and institutional investors who will help bring those products to scale.

The fund is also driven by science. Because of the technical nature of succeeding in an energy market, we will build a team that knows as much about the science behind energy breakthroughs as the investment strategies necessary to build those businesses.

Finally, the fund is committed to discovering breakthroughs, wherever they are. The world has made remarkable progress in wind and solar over the past decade, and these technologies will continue to play an important role in our zero-carbon energy mix. I have argued before that innovative industries deploy the technology they have while developing the technology they need. But because the scale of the challenge of providing reliable and affordable power without contributing to climate change is so vast, and the future energy needs are so great, we need to explore as many viable solutions as possible. As I've learned through my work in business and philanthropy: to be successful, you have to get the most out of the technology you already have while developing the technology you still need.

After talking with some of the world's greatest scientists, energy experts, and energy investors, the Coalition has developed a list of scientific priorities that will set us on the path toward the energy future we need. We see this list as a "landscape of innovation" - essentially, a roadmap that Breakthrough Energy Ventures and others can use to focus their attention and guide their investment decisions over the next two decades.

In this landscape, we've outlined five grand challenges, corresponding to the biggest contributors to greenhouse gas emissions around the world:

- Electricity: How can we deliver reliable, affordable zero-carbon electricity to the world?

- Buildings: How can we eliminate emissions from our homes, offices, hospitals, and schools?

- Manufacturing: How can we make everything we use without emitting greenhouse gases?

- Transportation: How can we get around our communities and the world without emitting carbon?

- Food: How can we feed the planet without contributing to climate change?

Of course, no investor can answer these questions alone. That's why, in addition to funding new ventures, Breakthrough Energy investors will help build a broader clean energy ecosystem. We'll explore new partnerships with governments, businesses, and institutional investors who want to be part of the global energy transition. Through these partnerships, we will not only help organize more investments, but we will also help research new solutions. One of the Coalition's partners is the University of California, which has an amazing capacity to innovate through their labs and universities. In the coming years, we'll work with them to expand our research partnerships and identify the best ways to pull great inventions out of the lab and turn them into companies.

Even though Usd1 billion is a significant step, it is just one of many steps on the path to a sustainable energy future.

With patience, flexibility, collaboration, and a clear vision backed by meaningful investment, we, the fund's investors, are confident the world can meet its energy needs in a way that is fair, safe, and sustainable. And we're excited about the role that Breakthrough Energy Ventures will play in that effort. **GATES NOTES ENDS HERE**.

THANK YOU

So all I can say is THANK YOU to Bill Gates and to all the investors that have partnered with him on the Breakthrough Energy Coalition to make this vision a reality, and for fighting to make this world a better place for our future generations.

Thank you also to the following investors of the fund that I have managed to identify from my research:

- Silicon Valley venture capitalists John Doerr and Vinod Khosla;
- Former hedge manager John Arnold;
- Amazon CEO Jeff Bezos;

- Bloomberg founder and former New York City mayor Mike Bloomberg;
- Alibaba founder Jack Ma;
- Virgin Group founder Richard Branson;
- Indian billionaire Mukesh Ambani;
- Saudi Arabian investor Prince Alwaleed bin Talal;
- Hedge fund manager Ray Dalio;
- LinkedIn founder Reid Hoffman;
- U.K. hedge fund manager Chris Hohn;
- Facebook cofounder Dustin Moskovitz and his wife Cari Tuna;
- Chinese Real estate developers Zhang Xin and Pan Shiyi;
- French telecom tycoon Xavier Niel;
- South African mining magnate Patrice Motsepe;
- German software entrepreneur Hasso Plattner (Co-founder of SAP);
- U.S. finance titan Julian Robertson;
- Japanese entreprenuer and telecom investor Masayoshi Son;
- Nat Simons & Laura Baxter Simons, Co-Founders Prelude Ventures;

After decades of neglect, energy policy is starting to move center-stage in Africa. Governments are adopting more ambitious targets for power generation, backed in some cases by far-reaching reforms of their energy sectors. Private investors, domestic and foreign, are seizing new market opportunities. Beyond the national grid, smaller firms are responding to the demand of poor households for basic lighting, heating and cooking. International cooperation is also gathering momentum. From hydro-power in Ethiopia to geothermal in Kenya, and solar power in Ghana, recent years have seen a surge of investments in renewable power generation.

While we wait for new energy breakthrough let's take a look at some amazing projects and energy initiatives already causing great impact across Africa.

1. POWER AFRICA

Power Africa is an American presidential initiative launched by President Barack Obama. The initiative aims at supporting economic growth and development by increasing access to reliable, affordable, and sustainable power in Africa.

Two out of three people in sub-Saharan Africa lack access to electricity. That's about 620 million people without access to electricity according to the International Energy Agency Africa Energy outlook. In 2013, Power Africa was launched to bring together technical and legal experts, the private sector, and governments from around the world to work in partnership to increase the number of people with access to power.

Power Africa's goal is to add more than 30.000 megawatts (MW) of cleaner, more efficient electricity generation capacity and 60 million new home and business connections.

Supporting and scaling innovations is the goal of Power Africa's newest Grand Challenge for

Development: Scaling Off-Grid Energy, a partnership with the U.S. Agency for International Development (USAID), the U.K. Department for International Development (DFID), and the Shell Foundation.

The Grand Challenge is an Usd36 million investment to empower entrepreneurs and investors to connect 20 million households in sub-Saharan Africa to modern, clean, and affordable electricity. As part of the Grand Challenge, Power Africa's partners, including USAID and DFID, supported Global LEAP in launching an off-grid refrigeration competition that will leverage Usd600.000 to catalyze technological advancements in off-grid powered refrigerators. In addition, with support from the Grand Challenge, startups such as PEGAfrica are expanding access to household solar solutions in West Africa by taking new approaches to digital repayments from rural customers.

The Millennium Challenge Corporation (MCC) which is an Agency part of the U.S. Government has already committed about Usd1.5 billion to connect people to electricity and support the goals of the U.S. Government's Power Africa effort.

To date, Overseas Private Investment Corporation (OPIC), the U.S. Government's development finance institution, has also committed Usd2.1 billion in financing and insurance commitments towards 22 Power Africa projects.

These investments will lead to the development of more than 1.700 MW of new power generation in Africa.

2. NOOR SOLAR PLANT in Morocco

On the edge of the Sahara desert, Morocco is building one of the world's biggest solar power plants in a project largely funded by the European Union.

Morocco's plan to generate more than 40% of its electricity from renewable energy sources, so it's building the world's largest solar plant named Noor solar thermal plant. In Arabic, Noor means light. Noor's director calls the project a "green megawatt."

The project is financed by loans of Usd519 million from the World Bank and Usd690 million from German state-owned bank KFW. The African Development Bank, the European Commission and the European Investment Bank have also provided financial support.

The solar complex is operated by a consortium led by NOMAC, a subsidiary of ACWA Power – a private company owned by eight Saudi conglomerates – and the Moroccan Agency for Solar Energy (Masen).

The first phase of the project, which is already in operation, involved the construction of a 160-megawatt concentrated solar power (CSP) plant named Noor I. Phase two consists of the 200MW

Noor II and the 150MW Noor III plant that will start operating in 2017 and 2018 respectively.

The final phase will see the construction of Noor IV, which will have a smaller capacity of up to 70 MW; all together, this is known as the Noor Concentrated Solar Power Project.

Once completed, Noor will cost Usd2.45 billion and generate 580 MW, enough power for a city of almost 2 million people. Morocco aims to expand at other desert regions to 2 gigawatts of solar capacity by 2020 at a cost of Usd9 billion.

"We hope we can be an inspiration," Mustapha Bakkoury, head of the Moroccan Agency for Solar Energy (Masen), told Reuters. Many African nations are pushing to boost economic growth to end poverty, while seeking greener energies.

3. Lake Turkana Wind Power Project in Kenya

The total project cost is estimated at Usd680 million and includes the cost of the envisaged 400 km transmission line from Lake Turkana to the Susua sub-station near Nairobi, as well as the cost of upgrading 200 km of roads and various bridges.

The Lake Turkana wind power project involves the development and construction of a 300 MW wind farm. The project is located at a remote location, approximately 12 kilometers east of Lake Turkana in northwestern Kenya. The project area falls within a valley between two mountains that produce a tunnel effect in which wind streams are accelerated to high speeds. The wind farm will comprise 365 wind turbines with capacity of 850 KW each. In addition to the Wind Turbine Generators (WTGs) and their foundations, a 33 kV electrical collector network will be constructed.

The project will benefit Kenya by providing clean and affordable energy that will reduce the overall energy cost to end consumers. Furthermore, the project will allow the landlocked Great Rift Valley region to be connected to the rest of the country through the improved infrastructure linked to the wind farm, including a road, fiber-optic cable and electrification. This zero-emission project will also contribute in filling the energy gap in the country, enhancing energy diversification and saving 16 million tons of CO_2 emission compared to a fossil fuel-fired power plant.

The main objective of the project is to provide clean, reliable, low cost power by increasing Kenya's national power generation capacity to approximately 17%. At a far lower cost than the imported oil the local utility now uses. And when it begins producing juice next year, it will signal to investors and companies that big clean energy projects like this are viable in sub-Saharan Africa.

4. GRAND INGA HYDROPOWER PROJECT

The Grand Inga hydro power project in the Democratic Republic of Congo is forecast to double Africa's electricity production capacity, making it the world's largest infrastructure project.

The Grand Inga hydropower complex would span the Congo river and produce as much as 50.000 megawatts of power when complete, according to the World Bank.

Inga Falls on the Congo River is a group of rapids (or cataracts) in the latter portion of the Livingstone Falls. The Congo falls ~96 meters (315 ft) within this set of cataracts. This means annual flow rate of the Congo River at Inga Falls is ~42.000 cubic meters per second (1.500.000 cubic ft/s). Given this flow rate and the 96 meter fall it is easy to calculate that the Inga Falls alone has a potential to generate ~39.6 gigawatts of mechanical energy and nearly as much electrical energy.

Inga Falls is currently the site of two large hydro power plants and is being considered for a much larger hydro power generating station known as Grand Inga. The Grand Inga project, when completed, would be the largest hydro-electric power generating facility on Earth.

The dam has an expected generating capacity of 39.000 MW (52.000.000 hp), with 52 turbines each with a capacity of 750 MW (1.010.000 hp). This is a significantly larger capacity than the Three Gorges Dam on the Yangtze River in China, which is currently known as the largest energy-generating body ever built.

5. NZEMA SOLAR PROJECT GHANA

Blue Energy, a UK-based renewable energy investor and developer is building one of Africa's largest solar photovoltaic (PV) power plant in Ghana, in a move which could spark a renewable energy revolution in West Africa.

The Usd400 million giant 155-megawatt Nzema project will be one of the biggest in the world – only three solar PV plants in operation today are bigger, and it will include 630.000 solar modules.

It will increase Ghana's current generating capacity by 6% and will meet 20% of the government's target of generating 10% of its electricity from renewable sources by 2020.

Chris Dean, CEO of Blue Energy, said: "Ghana's forward-thinking strategy puts it in a strong position to lead the renewable energy revolution in Sub-Saharan Africa. Nzema is a case study in how governments can unlock the huge potential for solar energy in Africa. We are delighted that it will make a strong contribution to the national economy, provide much needed generating capacity and help develop the skills of the future." He added: "There's huge potential to develop renewable power in the region. We believe Nzema will show other countries what can be achieved and spur them into action."

The project will boost the economy of Western Ghana. It will create 500 jobs over the two-year construction period and 200 permanent jobs in operation. It is also expected to stimulate another 2.100 jobs in the local economy, by sub-contracting activities to local companies and increasing demand for goods, services and education.

The company has put in place a wide-ranging program to satisfy its corporate social responsibility obligations and enjoys extensive support from local communities. They will also benefit through land lease revenues, access to reliable electricity, new healthcare facilities, skills training, investment in schools, and support for community projects and small businesses.

Nzema is expected to contribute Usd100 million in taxes to Ghana's government over the lifetime of the project. Its clean energy will avoid emissions of 5.5 million tons of CO_2 (based on an oil-fired power station with equivalent output).

Ghana is one of the fastest growing economies in Sub-Saharan Africa, with 14.4% GDP growth in 2011. Demand for power is growing at 10%-15% a year.

6. ETHIOPIA – AN EMERGING ENERGY EXPORTER

As one of the world's highest-growth economies, Ethiopia has seen demand for electricity rise sharply. Increased investment has expanded net electricity generation fivefold. Even so, power shortages continue to hold back economic growth and grid coverage is limited, with just 15%-20% of rural Ethiopians having access to electricity.

Ethiopia's Growth and Transformation Program aims at fivefold increase in power generation, from

2GW to 10GW, with a doubling of grid connection from 2 million to 4 million households and 75% of villages connected to the grid.

Large-scale public investments in hydropower have underpinned the strategy, including the Gilgel Gibe 3 dam and the Grand Ethiopian Renaissance Dam, a 6GW hydropower project.

The World Bank forecasts that Ethiopian electricity sales will rise from 4GW in 2011 to 17GW in 2020. By 2030, the aim is to export at least 5.000MW, up from just 223MW now. Total investment requirements are estimated at around Usd2billion annually, which are double current levels.

The World Bank and the African Development Bank (AfDB) are financing a transmission line capable of transporting 2GW of electricity from Ethiopia to Kenya. Ethiopia is also investing heavily in non-hydro renewable development. New public-private partnerships are emerging. US-Icelandic company Reykjavik Geothermal has signed an Usd4 billion agreement to build a 1GW geothermal plant by the beginning of the next decade. One of the region's largest wind-farm projects, the 120MW Adama project, is under development through an Usd290 million French investments.

The emphasis on renewable energy will lead to the abatement of 250 $MtCO_2$ by 2030, which is a decrease in greenhouse gas emissions of up to 64% compared with a business-as-usual model.

7. THE DRAGON – CHINA ENERGY INVESTMENTS IN AFRICA

Chinese foreign direct investment (FDI) and other forms of finance in Africa have increased rapidly in recent years. Chinese state and non-state companies are involved in a wide range of export, infrastructure development and domestic market activity. China is now the single largest source of external finance for power-generation investments in Africa.

Best estimates put Chinese official finance to Sub-Saharan Africa's energy sector in excess of Usd16 billion between 2000 and 2012, which is more than double the financing for IPPs.

The majority of Chinese-supported projects have received funding from the Export-Import Bank of China (China Exim Bank), which provides soft loans and export credit on the part of the Chinese government. The 2014 contract to construct the Geba1 and Geba2 hydropower developments in Ethiopia was awarded to an Ethiopian company and two Chinese partners, Sinohydro and China Gezhouba Group, with Usd582 million in finance (80% of the total) provided by China Exim Bank.

The Industrial Commercial Bank of China (ICBC) has agreed to provide Usd1.2billion of the Usd2billion required to construct a 1.000MW coal-fired electricity plant in Kenya.

Large hydropower projects dominate China's energy-financing portfolio in Africa. Engineering and procurement contracts with Chinese contractors account for around 70% of projects. Ethiopia, Nigeria, Sudan, Guinea, Ghana and Cameroon dominate transfers, although about 16 countries receive some form of Chinese finance.

Chinese development finance for energy infrastructure in Africa has been a source of controversy for traditional aid donors. There are concerns that the finance is motivated by a need to secure access to Africa's natural resources on terms favorable to China and by commercial self-interest. Some aspects of Chinese finance require closer scrutiny. In particular, the practice of securing debts against future exports of raw materials creates commercial risks.

On the other side of the equation, many African governments welcome the speed at which Chinese finance is disbursed. By contrast with the complex arrangements surrounding IPP projects, Chinese support also has the merit of operating on a "one stop shop" model that combines different types of finance with technical support, including early-stage technical development.

8. PRIVATE EQUITY INVESTMENT IN ENERGY PROJECTS ACROSS AFRICA

Foreign capital flows into Africa have increased sharply, reaching 8% of GDP in 2016. Direct foreign investment dominates the transfers. However, the past five years has also seen a marked increase in private-equity flows, attracted by high dividends in areas including financial services, telecommunications, consumer goods, construction and energy.

Liberalization in the power sector has been a magnet for equity investors. Between 2010 and 2013, there were around 27 Private equity investments in energy and natural resources, with an aggregate value of Usd1.2 billion.

A new generation of investment funds is emerging. The Carlyle Group, which raised Usd591 million on its initial African Fund, is expanding energy infrastructure investments in East Africa. In February 2015, Helios Investment Partners announced closure of a heavily oversubscribed Usd1.1 billion Africa-focused fund, part of which will target energy infrastructure. In the same month, Actis launched an Usd1.9 billion renewable energy platform, Lekela Power, aimed at funding wind and solar power investments over the next three years.

Established groups are also expanding their market presence. Sithe Global, part of the Blackstone Group, one of the world's largest Private equity companies in infrastructure, is scaling up Africa operations. During 2014, Blackstone announced a joint project with Dangote Industries, the Nigeria-registered industrial conglomerate led by billionaire Aliko Dangote, to invest up to Usd5billion over the next five years in energy infrastructure projects across Sub-Saharan Africa, with a particular emphasis on power, transmission and pipeline projects.

Development finance institutions have added to the momentum behind Private equity investment. In 2015 the Norwegian Investment Fund for Developing Countries and the UK's Commonwealth Development Corporation injected Usd225 million into Globaleq, one of the largest foreign equity investors and power-sector operators in Africa. Wholly owned by Actis, it has eight separate projects across five countries, including two independent power-generation companies generating 300MW of natural gas-fired power in Cameroon.

Another investment fund, the Usd250 million ARM-Harith Infrastructure Fund, launched by a partnership of companies in South Africa and Nigeria, in 2013 secured an Usd20 million investment from the African Development Bank (AfDB). These examples give a sense of the dynamism in private-equity markets.

Private-equity investments in the energy sector do generate very large margins. Shareholders in Uganda's privatized (and now publicly listed) electricity grid, for example, get a reported return of 20% a year on capital investment. Moreover, Government guarantees have effectively reduced the risk of the investment in the energy sector.

Equity investors themselves identify Sub-Saharan Africa as a more profitable market than other emerging markets.

AFRICA PROGRESS ACCORDING TO KOFI ANNAN

I cannot end this chapter without sharing the views of someone who is considered to be one of the brilliant minds of this world, which happens to be from Africa: it's Kofi Annan, Chair of the Africa Progress Panel and former United Nations Secretary General, foreword from the report Africa Progress Report 2015 done by Africa Progress Panel, from which I share with you bellow:

Climate change demands that we rethink the relationship between energy and development. The carbon-intensive energy systems that drive our economies have set us on a collision course with our planetary boundaries. We can avoid that collision. As a global community, we have the technology, finance and ingenuity to make the transition to a low-carbon future, but so far we lack the political leadership and practical policies needed to break the link between energy and emissions.

Some African countries are already leading the world in low-carbon, climate-resilient development. They are boosting economic growth, expanding opportunity and reducing poverty, particularly through agriculture. African nations do not have to lock into developing high-carbon old technologies; we can expand our power generation and achieve universal access to energy by leapfrogging into new technologies that are transforming energy systems across the world. Africa stands to gain from developing low-carbon energy, and the world stands to gain from Africa avoiding the high-carbon pathway followed by today's rich world and emerging markets.

Unlocking this "win-win" will not be easy. It will require decisive action on the part of Africa's leaders, not least in reforming inefficient, inequitable and often corrupt utilities that have failed to develop flexible energy systems to provide firms with a reliable power supply and people with access to electricity. Tackling Africa's interlocking climate and energy problems will also require strengthened international cooperation.

Over 600 million people still do not have access to modern energy. It is shocking that Sub-Saharan Africa's electricity consumption is less than that of Spain and on current trends it will take until 2080 to for every African to have access to electricity.

Africa has enormous potential for cleaner energy – natural gas, hydro, solar, wind and geothermal power - and should seek ways to move past the damaging energy systems that have brought the world to the brink of catastrophe.

It is indefensible that Africa's poorest people are paying among the world's highest prices for energy: a woman living in a village in northern Nigeria spends around 60 to 80 times per unit more for her energy than a resident of New York City or London. Changing this is a huge investment opportunity.

Millions of energy-poor, disconnected Africans, who earn less than Usd2.50 a day, already constitute an Usd10 billion yearly energy market.

What would it take to expand power generation and finance energy for all? We estimate that investment of Usd55 billion per year is needed until 2030 to meet demand and achieve universal access to electricity. One of the greatest barriers to the transformation of the power sector is the low level of tax collection and the failure of governments to build credible tax systems. Domestic taxes can cover almost half the financing gap in Sub-Saharan Africa. Redirecting Usd21 billion spent on subsidies to wasteful utilities and kerosene to productive energy investment, social protection and targeted connectivity for the poor would show that governments are ready to do things differently. I urge African leaders to take that step.

Reforming energy utilities is also key. Long-term national interest must override short term political gain, vested interests, corruption and political patronage. Energy sector governance and financial transparency will help bring light in the darkness. Energy entrepreneurs can join the reformed utilities in investing revenues and energy funds in sustainable power that saves the planet and pays steady dividends. Some countries in the region are already at the front of the global trend of climate-resilient, low-carbon development, including Ethiopia, Ghana, Kenya, Nigeria and South Africa.

Better and more accessible energy can also power up Africa's agriculture. Governments should take advantage of "triple-win" adaptation opportunities that integrate social protection with climate-smart strategies to raise agricultural productivity and to develop rural infrastructure, including crop storage, agro-processing and transport, cutting poverty while strengthening international efforts to combat climate change.

Governments in the major emitting countries should place a stringent price on emissions of greenhouse gases by taxing them, instead of continuing effectively to subsidize them, for example by spending billions on subsidies for fossil-fuel exploration. The political power of multinational energy companies and other vested interest groups is still far too strong.

Future generations will surely judge this generation of leaders not by principles they set out in communiqués but by what they actually do to eradicate poverty, build shared prosperity and protect our children and their children from climate disaster. Let us act now and act together. By Kofi Annan - Chair of the Africa Progress Panel and former United Nations Secretary General.

CONCLUSION: I believe the future of African Industrialization beside all that has been mentioned prior, should be focused on the following sectors:

ENERGY: Despite the abundance of resources like solar, oil, water and gas, most Africans still have no reliable energy supply. The challenge has been the cost-intensive, long-term reward nature of these projects in unpredictable political systems, but still it remains a lucrative business for investors to venture.

MINERALS: As the world economy recovers, African minerals such as crude oil and gold will remain important to the global economy, as demand increases. Investing in extracting and processing these minerals will remain a lucrative venture.

AGRICULTURE: Africa is unfed in a continent with good, and 60% of the world arable land not cultivated. Africa imports its food, despite the fact that it produces enough to feed its citizens. The problem is that harvests are poorly managed due to a lack of preservation techniques, which means that much of the food goes to waste and Africa goes hungry even after bumper harvests. Food production, processing, and preservation will remain a profitable growth area.

TECHNOLOGY: Africa has not attracted capacity-building investments, such as R&D centers and hi-tech manufacturing. In the coming years, as global buyers become more sophisticated, companies that differentiate their products within local markets will have a strong competitive advantage. Africa is no exception. For example, telecoms can be profitable in Africa not for selling airtime, but for powering value-added services such as mobile banking and mobile business, among others, that address the needs of this unique population. Equally we must leverage the potential of new technologies such as artificial intelligence, automation, telepresence, and augmented reality. Maybe our generation (Africa millennials) will come up with a Made in Africa successful tech company such as Google, Facebook, Apple, Amazon, eBay, Instagram, LinkedIn, Twitter, WhatsApp, Snapchat, PayPal, and Netflix.

AVIATION: like mentioned before Africa aviation sector has huge potential and the future is bright with the amount of people that will be in the middle class by 2050. Hopefully we will see consolidation among African Airlines to create an airline group similar to Emirates Airlines, with successful Aviation HUBs across Africa (North, East, West and Southern Africa).

LOGISTICS: with the world population expected to reach 8.5 billion by 2030, 9.7 billion in 2050 and 11.2 billion in 2100, logistics of commodities, food and products will be a huge business. Moving food from Africa to other continents to feed the world will be a very lucrative business.

FINANCE: with more investments there will be more money flow, more trade and consequently more financial institutions will be needed. The Stock Market across Africa need to unify and build a strong international financial platform to IPO, list and promote great African companies to the world.

FASHION: Africa is home to a diversity of cultures across the continent. Fashion is different from country to country. One sector that has enormous potential is to develop Made in Africa fashion products with African fabrics and art as inspiration. It's a 1billion people market that will need cloths to wear every day.

MEDIA: There is no Big Media Group until now in Africa with the power to showcase Africa success stories across the financial Medias. A Media Platform could blueprint platforms such as CNBC, Bloomberg, Aljazeera, to launch a Africa focus Platform for businesses in Africa and from the World to Africa.

MUSIC & ENTERTAINMENT: Africa is known for its love for music and entertainment. There is huge potential for the development of a multicultural platform for promotion of African Music, Artists, Movies Made in Africa, to highlight only positive and great history about Africa and its culture.

"An Entrepreneur is someone who jumps off a cliff, and builds a plane on his way down." Reid Hoffman

CHAPTER 4: Africa Entrepreneurs biggest problems.

Africa's wars, coups and famines are constantly in the news - the image of starving children is what often comes to mind every time the continent is mentioned. Like for example the recent hunger humanitarian crisis in South Sudan.

But what about the men and women who are starting businesses, and risking their own money to build Africa's economies?

Despite all the obstacles, growth rates across much of Africa are rising and there are successful ventures to be found everywhere from Cape Town to Casablanca. From telecommunications and banking to the export of fruit and flowers, Africa is now finding and cultivating niche markets around the world.

Behind these statistics are stories of initiative and drive to overcome the familiar problems of endemic corruption and mountains of red tape from Governments.

The absence of a strong business class at independence for many countries was a major inhibition to growth, argues Teddy Brett, of the London School of Economics. For this reason fighting to control the levers of politics became a key way of winning economic advantage. And the results are plain to see.

Doing business in Africa is still hard work, as the World Bank Doing business rankings shows every year. As if that isn't bad enough, roads are bad, electricity unreliable and skilled labor in short supply. But if you succeed, the profits can be large.

Africa is increasingly taking its place on the global stage as a continent of growth and opportunity. Yet critical challenges remain, particularly the need to create a significant number of jobs for the continent's booming population, and the need to build a cadre of home-grown business leaders able to access global markets and drive growth in a sustainable and inclusive manner. For this reason, African entrepreneurship is central to Africa's future prosperity.

Across Africa, necessity is the mother of invention. Reusing and recombining is a way of life and, in many cases, the lack of infrastructure, even old infrastructure, gives us a "clean slate" for new solutions. Responding to these challenges, Africa's entrepreneurs are contributing a host of cutting-edge products and services, enabling them to leap forward in such fields as mobile and information technology, and to develop innovations in agriculture, transportation, healthcare and other vital fields.

But while entrepreneurship is growing rapidly in Africa, entrepreneurs continue to face significant domestic challenges that slow down their efforts.

Reid Hoffman, Co-founder of LinkedIn networking platform, once beautifully said what an entrepreneur is: "An Entrepreneur is someone who jumps off a cliff, and builds a plane on his way down." Amazing! In Africa this is even truer than anywhere on planet earth.

Entrepreneurship in Africa is so exciting that you need to have a tremendous mix of courage, passion, faith and will to make things work and turn out successfully.

To understand this chapter I will first have to take you into a journey so you can find out what it's like to be an entrepreneur in Africa.

African entrepreneurs face some of the world's toughest business conditions. Most African countries perform poorly in the World Bank's Ease of Doing Business Rankings.

The top constraints in Africa business environment are the practices of the informal sector, corruption, government bureaucracy, limited access to financing, globalization, weak infrastructure, weak transport sector, inconsistent government regulations, and minimal assistance from the government, and cross-border payments. These problems are common in many African countries, along with a lack of skilled labor and adequate training. The resources necessary to grow a business – such as finance, human and social capital, infrastructure and transport are less accessible in Africa. Capital, in particular, is costlier in Africa than in any other part of the world.

If you don't have access to capital how can you develop a business? Capital is like oxygen for businesses to keep moving forward.

President Barack Obama has made a start on solving some of these problems, as well as drawing further attention to Africa's widely acknowledged business potential. The most prominent offering is Usd200 million from the Overseas Private Investment Corporation (OPIC), dedicated to supporting Equity Bank Kenya's initiative to support small businesses (a Usd525 million loan scheme to assist small businesses with their long-term financing requirements). Chase Bank Kenya is also set to lend more than Usd580 million to entrepreneurs over the next three years, with a focus on young people and women.

Obama has set a good precedent, but these investments are just a drop in the ocean, when it comes to creating the supportive business environments and jobs that Africa's economies need to swell over the next 25 years.

But capital is just one of the ingredients you need to move a business forward. By taking a look at the World Bank Doing Business Ranking every year, investors will have access to data to help guide them to which country is easier to do business with.

On the World Bank Doing business rankings, economies are ranked on their ease of doing business, from 1–190. A high ease of doing business ranking means the regulatory environment is more conducive to the starting and operation of a local firm.

In 2017 the Sub-Saharan Africa best country to do business in is Mauritius, occupying the number 49 in the world ranking of 1-190.

Beside access to Capital to help you move with your business, just having capital is not enough in Africa. One of the biggest obstacles is Governments bureaucracy and corruption.

I have seen some many business opportunities die along the way due to lack of leadership from Government leaders in approving projects so they can move from paper to reality.

Globalization has presented African entrepreneurs with a unique opportunity to expand their services and offerings worldwide at a scale that has never been available before. However, though globalization provides them with countless opportunities, business owners have several challenges to overcome that are mostly exclusive to Africa.

Bellow I share some of the obstacles companies need to overcome to be successful in Africa:

1. Limited access to financing

By far, the most significant obstacle to companies is a lack of funding. Though the number of businesses is increasing, the amount of financing for these companies has remained largely stagnant. Reports show that a staggering 85% of small businesses are largely underfunded.

2. Weak infrastructure

While business abilities are growing, the infrastructure in most African countries remains lacking. Poorly built roads, frequent power surges, and underdeveloped transportation can challenge a company's ability to produce and deliver services on time, to the point of inhibiting growth and losing money.

African business owners are overcoming these hurdles by investing in their own infrastructure, such as purchasing backup generators to power their factories when power fails to ensure uninterrupted production. They are also combating uncertain supply of raw materials by striking up strong working relationships with suppliers and create large stockpiles to combat delays.

If you cannot have easy access to finance and you have a weak infrastructure doing business in Africa for local entrepreneurs as you may imagine is like trying to cross the Sahara Desert with a small bottle of 100ml of water for the entire journey. By the way, the Sahara Desert is an area of 9.200.000 square kilometers (3.600.000 square miles). That is 31% of Africa surface land, and is comparable to the area of the United States of America.

How foreign investors are overcoming the infrastructure obstacles in the case of factories if you cannot have access to electricity 24/7 in some countries?

Here is an example: Heineken the world's third-largest brewer does business in Africa, but it knows it needs to play by some different rules than in Europe or USA. Not only Heineken operates breweries in Africa but also its own power and water treatment plants. That's how the company overcomes a major African obstacle: the continent's notoriously weak and undependable infrastructure. Heineken has learned that, while Africa poses substantial operating challenges for consumer products makers, those hurdles are not insurmountable. And finding innovative ways to clear those obstacles can pay off. In 2016, the company reached Usd3.4 billion for annual sales in Africa, Middle East and Eastern Europe, with operating margins of 11.7%.

According to Heineken CEO & Chairman of the Executive Board, Jean Francois van Boxmeer, statement on the 2016 full year results report, from which I quote: "We delivered strong results in 2016, with clear outperformance of our premium brand portfolio led by Heineken, and sustained momentum from our innovation agenda. Our unique diversified footprint was again a competitive advantage, enabling us to deliver more than 50 basis points margin expansion, despite more challenging economic conditions in some developing markets and significant currency pressures. Performance in key European markets was good and results in Vietnam and Mexico were strong. In Africa, Middle

East & Eastern Europe market conditions remained tough, most notably in Nigeria, DRC and Russia. Excluding major unforeseen macro-economic and political developments as well as the impact of the proposed acquisitions in Brazil and in the UK, we expect continued margin expansion in 2017 in line with our previous guidance."

3. Inconsistent government regulations

Most African countries face a wide range of confusing political, regulatory, and trading laws that are constantly evolving. Multiple currencies, combined with increasingly strict import regulations, contribute to very high import costs, thus limiting companies' abilities to do business with overseas suppliers.

4. Globalization

A two-edged sword, globalization presents businesses with opportunities of expansion while simultaneously hindering their opportunities for growth. Foreign companies are able to export production to countries with low labor costs, thus increasing competition from foreign companies in local markets. Outsourcing production to countries such as China and India has led to a decrease in production for local manufacturers, sometimes causing them to shut down completely.

5. Cross-border payments

Cross-border payments tend to be inefficient, slow, and expensive for all parties. Each country has local laws and regulations within domestic banking systems, and the lack of one global regulatory system diminishes the ability of financial institutions to seamlessly transfer data and funds. Additionally, local governments each have domestic laws to regulate cross-border payments, causing a difference in regulations between the sending and receiving countries.

6. International Expansion

Unlike their counterparts in other parts of the world, small African firms have mostly sold their products in their home market or in adjacent countries that belong to the same regional economic block as their home country. It also appears that most small businesses in Africa follow the incremental stages of international expansion model. The reasons given for the favoring of gradual internationalization by small firms in Africa include: unsaturated domestic markets, reputation for low quality products, technological requirement for success in markets in developed economies, and difficulties in joining international supply-chain networks

Beside these obstacles mentioned above African entrepreneurs face many challenges; however, all of them have solutions. Some countries are investing in alternative infrastructures, clean energy sources, improving their ranking in doing business and improving access to capital.

Like they say, you are a product of your environment. One cannot expect a rose to grow and flourish in Antarctica. Once Businesses are able to have an easy environment to do business they will increase their local offerings while expanding their business both into neighboring countries and also into the global market. All these small improvements in the doing business environment and the countries infrastructures will, ultimately, pay off exponentially in the long run, positioning African entrepreneurs as local and global leaders in their fields.

One day I was watching CNBC and Billionaire Investor Warren buffet was being interviewed by Becky Quick and he said something so amazing about doing business, which I quote now: "If someone becomes a millionaire in USA it doesn't surprise me. What surprises me is seeing someone become a millionaire in a country where nothing seems to work and there are too many obstacles for doing business."

So many companies in the West have ease of doing business because their country work and they have access to so many sources of capital and access to a lot of know-how and technology from different companies which makes it easier to launch a startup or venture into different markets to launch a product or begin a new venture.

Here is a sad example of a close friend of mine, business partner, who is a great entrepreneur and one of the wealthiest man in Cape Verde (well, if you had to measure his wealth based on his net worth in terms of assets and companies he controls he is worth close to Usd250 million).

Prior to the financial crisis he used to have millions in his bank accounts. He once had an issue with a Commercial Bank where he asked for Usd100.000 loan and because it was in the middle of the 2008-2009 financial crises the bank didn't want to accept any of his assets as collateral because banks in Cape Verde are small and they lack faith in the local economy and entrepreneurs. Reason is 90% of the Commercial Banks are controlled by Portuguese Banks. Well, everyone knows who Portugal is in Europe and how big their economy is when you compare it to countries like Germany, France or Switzerland. Moral of the story, how can someone with a net worth of Usd250 million cannot loan Usd100.000? Remember Fiat Currency = Faith! Well, basically that's how many local banks work in Africa (lack of faith).

African entrepreneurs need the same things any business across the world needs – a predictable regulatory environment, reliable and affordable transport and power infrastructure, a healthy, educated and productive talent pool and access to affordable credit. But entrepreneurs are more vulnerable when these things are absent. Countries such as Mauritius and Botswana have shown that it is possible to improve competitiveness swiftly and successfully.

Entrepreneurs across Africa beside all the challenges and obstacles mentioned prior they still believe in a brighter future for Africa and that is why they continue to invest.

It is time for other governments across Africa to follow Mauritius and Botswana success cases and support the development of the next generation of business leaders, if given the right tools and business environment will for sure become global successful companies.

Things have changed with the way big business deals with Africa. Previously a destination for CSR-related activities such as building schools and planting trees, the continent is now very much the investment destination of choice, especially for US tech giants.

It's been quite a turnaround. When, for example, Microsoft was founded in 1975, Nigeria was spiraling back into dictatorship and Portugal still had African colonies in Mozambique and Angola. Now, Africa boasts seven of the world's 11 fastest growing economies, and the likes of Microsoft, Google and Facebook are scrambling for a piece of it.

Let's look at some facts on the tech sector. Below are some facts of what is going on in Africa tech sector beside the challenges and lack of energy and infrastructure:

- Groupe Speciale Mobile Association (GSMA) forecasts that there will be 540 million smartphones in Sub-Saharan Africa by 2020, up from 160 million in 2015. And consumers aren't the only ones investing in technology: "Silicon Savannahs" have cropped up throughout the continent, offering co-working spaces, skill sets, and access to support networks to young innovators;

- Facebook announced Voyager, a new phase of their plan to improve internet access across Africa;

- A start-up in Kenya called BRCK, produces a solar-powered device that offers charging and internet capabilities for up to 20 connections at a time;

- SunSweet Solar provides low-cost solar-powered systems in Tanzania. The company plans to install over 10.000 systems in rural areas within the next five years;

- Brian Gitta a young Ugandan entrepreneur has suffered from multiple bouts of malaria. Tired of feeling sick and being poked and prodded, he wondered why there couldn't be an easier, pain-free diagnosis. He and his colleagues developed a portable device called a matiscope that is connected to a smartphone. A user's finger is inserted into the matiscope which uses a red LED to penetrate the skin and detect red blood cells. The connected Windows smartphone application then diagnoses the patient and sends results to Microsoft's Skydrive to be shared with the patient's doctor immediately - no needles needed;

- The number of technology hubs across Africa has more than doubled in less than a year as more investors and innovators grow the local startup ecosystem beyond the most popular cities. A total of 314 tech hubs and incubation centers were recorded by the global telecoms industry body GSMA's Ecosystem Accelerator, a program that works to enable partnerships between operators and developers in the continent. The more than 300 hubs are spread across 93 cities in 42 countries across the African continent. However, more than half of the hubs are concentrated in only 5 countries, namely: South Africa, Egypt, Kenya, Nigeria and Morocco.

- Researches also showcased how nascent the tech industry is in Africa, with the average launch date of these hubs being 2012. However, the coalescing between entrepreneurs, innovation hubs, telecom operators and giant tech companies is underpinning the rise of a thriving tech industry. The merging of these different sectors is driving innovation by facilitating funding, co-working spaces, skill sets, and more importantly a vast network to support the startups;

- Tech Hubs like Kenya's iHub have been wildly successful, and hope to even become self-funded sometime in the near future. Since it opened in March 2010, iHub has spurred the launch of more than 170 startups;

- Large US tech companies like Google and Microsoft are also betting big in Africa, as the continent's positions itself as a market ripe for investment. Examples of these include Microsoft's Usd75 million in 4Afrika project, which supports small and medium enterprises, driving social development and technological innovation;

- Growth in smartphone use and the decline in bandwidth costs are also boosting the digital transformation across the continent;

- Google has launched Project Link, in a bid to bring faster, more reliable internet to Africans. The company has rolled out a metro fiber network in Kampala, Uganda, and will do the same in Ghana.

- Microsoft has also been investing in white spaces technology – which uses unused radio spectrum to provide Wi-Fi connectivity at a much cheaper cost to get more people online. It has launched commercial networks with local firms in Ghana, South Africa and Kenya;

- Facebook, which has over 120 million users across Africa, is also looking to encourage the uptake of internet services through Free Basics. The Free Basics service offers user zero-rated access to services such as the BBC, and of course, Facebook, providing basic online services at no cost in a bid to encourage people to get online for the first time;

- Jumia which is an African e-commerce platform is in nine countries and valued at Usd550 million;

- There is a terrific start-up named Andela, which finds the best raw talent in Africa, gives them 1000+ hours of training, and deploys them around the world, or helping them become the next generation of global technology leaders; Andela is Backed by Chan Zuckerberg Initiative, GV (Google Ventures) and Spark Capital.

The digital revolution may have begun in Silicon Valley, but its future will be written in cities across Africa.

If you are still not in Africa, you clearly missing out on tremendous business opportunities. Below I also share with you some success stories from a few companies founded by young entrepreneurs (under the age of 35) shared by Forbes Contributor, Mfonobong Nsehe, on an article published on FORBES named "The 30 most promising young entrepreneurs in Africa 2016":

- Afrobotanics, founded in South Africa by 32-year-old Ntombenhle Khathwane; Afrobotanics manufactures premium haircare products using African botanical oils and other natural products and formulas to care for the hair and limit damage as to the barest minimum;

- Oxygen Africa, founded in Zimbabwe by 31-year-old Simbarashe Mhuriro; Oxygen Africa is an investment advisory company to help facilitate foreign investors in Zimbabwe;

- Dressmeoutlet.com, founded in Nigeria by 28-year-old Olatorera Oniru; Nigerian e-tailer of fashion products, health & beauty products and home-goods. Dressmeoutlet stocks more than 1.000 products from premium designers globally. Dressmeoutlet ships worldwide and currently has customers in different states across Nigeria, Uganda and the United States of America;

- LeoFortis Group, founded in South Africa by 29-year-old Bonolo Ramokhele; an investment holding company with investments spanning commodity trading, energy, telecommunications, engineering, and mining with a presence in South Africa, Kenya, Zambia and South Sudan.

- Repurpose School Bags, founded in South Africa by two 23-year-old Thato Kgatlhanye & Rea Ngwane; Repurpose collects and recycles plastic waste into school bags for poor South African students. The plastic bags feature a solar panel in the flap which gets charged when the students walk to and from school. These charged solar panels help to provide lighting at night for the students to study;

- Leegra, founded in South Africa by 32-year-old Lee Grant; marketing and promotion company engaged in sales, merchandising, promotions, product development and strategy. His company services a diverse range of blue-chip clients and multinationals from banking and insurance to fast-moving consumer goods and healthcare;

- Emerald Moringa Tea, founded in Cameroon by 21-year-old Vanessa Zommi; When her mother was diagnosed with diabetes, Zommi, 21, set out to find alternative treatments to keep her mother healthy. She soon discovered the medicinal moringa oleifera tree which grew in her region, and discovered that the moringa leaves could reduce blood sugar levels to treat diabetes among other medicinal qualities. She partnered with moringa farmers who supplied her with the leaves and processed the leaves into moringa tea which she put into tea bags;

- mHub, founded in Malawi by 30-year-old Rachel Sibande; mHub, which she launched in 2013, is an incubator for technology startups with a special focus on building young technology entrepreneurs through training, skills development and mentorship;

- Voyaj, founded in Morocco, by 22-year-old Yasmine El Baggari; Voyaj is an online platform that matches hosts and travelers who want to share an authentic, local experience; Voyaj allows members to create a profile that includes a video post where they describe their interests and what they have to offer during a journey.

- Christie Brown, founded in Ghana, by 30-year-old Aisha Ayensu; Christie Brown is an internationally acclaimed luxury women's fashion label that subtly infuses modernism into carefully selected traditional African fabrics to create awe-inspiring dresses with a transcontinental finish;

- Gamsole, founded in Nigeria, by 27-year-old Abiola Olaniran; Gamsole, is a Nigerian gaming company, founded in 2012. The company's games now have more than 10 million downloads;

Beside these success stories I will also share five (5) other success stories from a list of eleven (11) entrepreneurs shared by Entrepreneur Contributor, Obianuju Helen Okoye, on an article published in January 2017 on ENTREPRENEUR named " 11 African Entrepreneurs Who Are Changing the Business Landscape ":

- Gina Din-Kariuki, Kenya - award-winning management consultant and social entrepreneur, as well as honorary UNFPA ambassador and Red Cross goodwill ambassador. As the founder and executive chair of the Gina Din Group, she has served as a strategic advisor to Safaricom, steering the expansion of Kenyan telecommunications.

- Jean Bosco Nzeyimana, Rwanda - How do you describe being seated on a Global Entrepreneurship panel between Facebook CEO Mark Zuckerburg and President Obama? "Exciting and frightening!" says Jean Nzeyimana. As founder and CEO of Habona, a clean and renewable energy company, this young entrepreneur has already achieved a milestone that many can only dream about. For him, it is bigger than a business. By transforming waste in his community to briquettes, a greener alternative to wood charcoal, Nzeyimana provides jobs and a cleaner environment.

- Maavi Norman, Liberia - The founder of IRIS International Consulting, social entrepreneur Dr. Maavi Norman bridges the gap by encouraging foreign investment in Africa, while supporting "deep local impact." Through his affiliation as a mentor with the White House Young African Leaders Initiative, Norman has helped guide a cohort of like-minded entrepreneurs in Africa. For him, it all comes down to this: "Stay laser-focused on solutions but evaluate a myriad of ideas for achieving them. Be open to readjusting, recalibrating and re-launching."

- Ashifi Gogo, Ghana - As a consumer, how do you guarantee that your purchase is not counterfeit? That thought got Dr. Ashifi Gogo started on Sproxil in 2009, which was recognized with an award by the White House. "If I am paying extra, I need to know if it's organic", he responds. Sproxil engages with the world's largest brands to protect their consumers from buying counterfeit products. They reward loyal consumers to make them continue buying. Originally intended for the pharmaceutical industry to combat the huge global problem with counterfeit drugs, Sproxil has now expanded into the automotive industry and into the oil and gas sector.

- Iyin Aboyeji, Nigeria - How do you get Mark Zuckerberg to invest Usd24 million in your company? Well, ask Iyin Aboyeji, he knows how. As co-founder of technology company Andela, he launched a tech talent platform across Africa. Exiting that, he is now at the helm of Flutterwave. "My definition of success is building up others, building up the continent," Aboyiji says. Indeed he is, as Flutterwave promises to change the way financial transactions take place in Africa, by offering easy exchange of digital currency that opens Africa up to the world.

When you think it couldn't be better than this let me finish this chapter with a success story in the Fashion industry, by someone whose product ended up in the hands of Oprah Winfrey. Yes, THE OPRAH WINFREY. You know you have achieved a homerun when you see Oprah Winfrey wearing your product. How cool is that for a young Kenyan entrepreneur? Well done to Becky Ndegwa.

She takes cloth designs to another level. Her custom designs feature Maasai tribe-inspired patterns and global trends infused to make a unique combination. The clothes are characterized with bright colors, hence the name of her store, Indigo6, one of the colors of the rainbow.

Becky Ndegwa said in an interview that she stumbled upon what would become her business, Indigo6, during a cold and rainy afternoon at her home in Athi River, on the outskirts of Kenya's capital Nairobi. While trying to shield herself from the cold, Ndegwa found that the Maasai shuka (a traditional garment worn by the Maasai tribe in Kenya) wasn't warm enough. So she complemented it with a normal fleece blanket. Other well-known personalities who have received one of Indigo6's blankets include the Pope and gospel artist Don Moen.

So, as you can see, beside all obstacles we African entrepreneurs face we believe in the future of Africa and we are going to make Africa Great even if Governments do not act and do their job.

"The ones, who are crazy enough to think that they can change the world, are the ones who do." Steve Jobs

CHAPTER 5: Why doing business in Africa is a Safari adventure?

Whenever you hear the word Africa is an evocative one that usually goes hand-in-hand with mental images of vast savanna plains dotted with exotic game. The majority of tourist visitors to Africa will indulge in a Safari and in doing so will find that there is nothing more magical than a close encounter with the continent's famous wildlife. Most of the species one sees on a safari are unique to Africa, and many of them are instantly recognizable.

This chapter is about Safari. Yes, Safari. What's the point talking about Africa if we cannot talk about Safari?

What is the exact definition of Safari? The exact dictionary definition of Safari is "a journey or expedition, for hunting, exploration, or investigation."

Africa abounds with incredible sights, from soaring sand dunes to savannas teeming with wildlife. Safari in Africa is like nothing you have ever experienced. The continent's offers many wonders on Safari trips to Tanzania, South Africa, Botswana, Rwanda, Morocco, and more. You can witness the annual wildebeest migration on safari in the Serengeti, or explore the sun-washed cities of Morocco. In Tanzania, you can spot lions, elephants, giraffes, and more on a thrilling family safari.

I will use the following pages to share with you some of the Best African Safari Tours, in case you ever decide to experience one, before we get into more in depth into this chapter. According to Go2Africa.com tourism platform, which is specialized in tourism packages to Africa, they have made a careful selection of their best African safari tours, rated most popular by both their Africa Safari Experts and their customers, and have shared their Top 10 tours in Africa in their platform blog, which I share here with you.

Iconic destinations - the Kruger National Park, Cape Town, Masai Mara and Serengeti - feature highly on these itineraries but so do off-the-beaten-path destinations in Tanzania and Botswana as well as tucked-away beaches in the Seychelles and Mozambique.

1. Luxury Migration, Lake & Crater Safari

One of their best African tours is a 9-day safari which kicks off in Kenya's Masai Mara before heading south into Tanzania for the Serengeti, Lake Manyara and the Ngorongoro Crater. Focused on wildlife, this is a great opportunity to witness the wildebeest migration.

2. Honeymoon Cape Town and Kruger

Two of South Africa's landmark destinations feature on this classic 9-day combination tour and the accommodation ranks among the best on the continent. Expect fine wine, gourmet food, huge views and all the thrills of a Big 5 safari in an exclusive Kruger reserve.

3. Private Guided Botswana, Victoria Falls & Zimbabwe

Four incredible southern Africa destinations await the adventure traveler on this 14-day experiential safari: the Okavango Delta in northern Botswana, and Victoria Falls, Hwange National Park and the unique Matobos in Zimbabwe. With a private guide on safari with you for the duration of the trip, you'll enjoy well-rounded expertise and a completely tailored experience. It's one of the best southern Africa safari tours.

4. Masai Mara, Serengeti & Selous Luxury Safari

Experience the very best of Kenya and Tanzania on this exclusive safari, as you explore the Masai Mara, Serengeti, Ngorongoro Crater and Selous Game Reserve. Stay in personalized tented camps, and enjoy quality service and superb crowd-free game viewing. This is authentic Africa at its best.

5. Luxury Kenya Safari & Uganda Gorilla Trekking

Perfect for the traveler looking for an authentic safari experience, this 14-day Kenya safari and gorilla adventure focuses on special cultural encounters, exceptional game-viewing and breathtaking scenery. Highlights include a balloon safari over the Masai Mara and gorilla trekking in Bwindi Impenetrable Forest National Park in Uganda.

6. Best of Namibia & Botswana

Dividing your time equally between the stark, otherworldly beauty of Namibia and world-class game viewing in private Botswana reserves, this 2-week fly-in safari adventure is one of the best and most luxurious ways to experience the highlights of Southern Africa.

7. Cape, Kruger & Mozambique Insights

Start a 2-week vacation in Cape Town, Africa's favorite city. Then search for the Big 5 in a private Kruger reserve before swopping the binoculars for a mask and flippers as you explore the teeming reefs of the Bazaruto Archipelago. Featuring excellent spa facilities throughout, this safari & beach itinerary is perfect as a honeymoon or spoil-me-rotten holiday.

8. Epic Rail Journey across Africa

A genuine once-in-a-lifetime experience: ride the world's most luxurious train on a 3-week journey that packs in a Big 5 safari, iconic sight-seeing and a tropical beach getaway as you sweep across the continent from Cape Town to Dar es Salaam.

9. Scenic Tanzania Safari

Explore some of the most beautiful wildlife regions in Tanzania on this sensational 10-day safari. Start your journey in the Tarangire National Park before travelling to the Ngorongoro Conservation area for some game viewing on the crater floor, then end off your trip in the Big 5 star of the show - the Serengeti National Park.

10. Highlights of Cape Town, Kruger & Seychelles

Sensational accommodation in three of Africa's most sought-after destinations is the order of the day with this diverse and highly rewarding 15-day tour. Perfect for a honeymoon or exclusive celebration, this tour blends the Big 5 with dreamy scenery and luxurious barefoot beach living.

Let's get down to business now!

Now that you have managed to imagine how the best Safaris in Africa are like, let me drop you an interesting question: Is business in Africa the same as going in a Safari Adventure?

Well, in my opinion investing and doing business across Africa is no different than going in a Safari adventure. Doing business across Africa is trying to develop business in different countries, with different people, different culture, different languages and ultimately different ways of doing business.

If you decide to invest in various countries you will have to be prepared to be challenged and experience an exciting journey that only a Safari adventure can provide you, which is to be ready to be amazed, scared, shocked and out of breath.

Let me make my point when it comes to invest in Africa by sharing some facts and Foreign Direct Investment data with you.

Africa's population is expected to more than double from 1.1 billion to 2.4 billion by 2050, the biggest increase of any continent. Its people are the youngest in the world, with a median age of just 19.4 years. And their youthful demographic profile is expected to endure. By 2050, their median age will still be a mere 24.7 years, compared with 39.8 years for Asians and 40.6 years for residents of Latin America and the Caribbean.

Africa is home to four of the world's megacities: Cairo, Johannesburg, Kinshasa and Lagos. Many others are expanding rapidly, including Abuja, Accra, Addis Ababa, Luanda, Lusaka, Maputo and Nairobi.

Growing urban populations need homes and, as they travel more, hotels and restaurants also serve an influx of business travelers and tourists.

The continent's domestic markets are among the most compelling attractions for foreign investors, compounded by rapid urbanization across Africa. Domestic demand will drive private sector growth, especially in consumer-facing industries, business and health care services, accelerating diversification of FDI in Africa.

Investors who already have operations in Africa believe it is the most attractive investment destination in the world, it has become more attractive in the past year, and its appeal will strengthen further in the future.

Foreign investors continue to highlight Africa's operating environment as an ongoing challenge to doing business on the continent. African countries generally lag other emerging markets in the World Bank's Doing Business ranking.

Whenever you think to invest in any African market, it is best to gain a deep understanding of the broad trends - demographic, socioeconomic, technological and political - shaping specific sub regions, and combine that with access to the best real-time on-the-ground data available.

When you finally decide to invest in Africa you have to be ready to go in a Safari that will challenge you with the following barriers on your FDI across many countries, such as:

- Unstable political environment;

- Corruption;

- Operating environment;

- Weak security;

- Poor basic infrastructure;

- Lack of highly skilled labor;

- Inconsistency and lack of transparency in regulatory policy;

- Unattractive tax policies and financial incentives;

From these barriers political instability is the biggest obstacle for companies doing business in Africa.

Despite barriers Africa is still rising. Even with these barriers Africa has attracted substantial capital flows in the past decade, bolstered by strong growth prospects and better economic management. A joint study by the African Development Bank (AfDB), the Organization for Economic Cooperation and Development (OECD) and the United Nations Development Program (UNDP) estimates that external financial flows to Africa have quadrupled since 2000.

External capital inflows are vital to the well-being of African economies. In 2016, they were equal 7.5% of the continent's GDP. Not only have these flows grown rapidly overall, but their sources have changed fundamentally. FDI has grown almost five-fold since 2000. It has overtaken official development assistance (ODA), which more than tripled in the same period.

Meanwhile, remittances from Africans working abroad have become the biggest source of foreign inflows to African states. After a six-fold increase, they are expected to have topped Usd70 billion in 2016.

While remittances help build homes, start businesses, and support consumption, FDI plays an equally vital role, helping to build infrastructure, supply necessities, reduce poverty, develop skills, and more. FDI is helping diversify the continent's economies, many of which are over dependent on extracting and exporting natural resources.

Where are investors coming from and where are they investing in Africa, according to an Ernest & Young's Africa attractiveness survey?

Here are some facts:

- Usd16 billion plan by French oil major TOTAL to develop the Kaombo offshore oil project in Angola (in a JV). This project is expected to produce 230.000 barrels per day from reserves estimated at 650 million barrels;

- Usd10 billion FDI approved in Egypt by Greek based Mac Optic to invest Usd4.8 billion to build a new refinery with a production capacity of 250.000 barrels per day, and Usd5.2 billion to build a petrochemical plant;

- Usd5 billion FDI approved in the energy sector in Nigeria to be build a 3.000 megawatts solar photovoltaic by a Joint Venture developed between SkyPower Global and FAS Energy;

- Opening of the Usd8.5 billion Suez Canal in Egypt which the waterway connects the Mediterranean to the Red Sea, providing the shortest sea link between Asia and Europe. The Suez Canal is one of the most important international waterways in the world;

- The West Africa region saw a rebound in FDI projects by 16.2%, and, interestingly, in 2015, the region became the leading recipient of capital investment on the continent, outpacing Southern Africa;

- Morocco is increasingly positioning itself as a gateway to the fast-growing African continent, particularly for investors from the US and Europe. These investors have the advantages of a relatively stable business environment and support services, combined with good air links to many other African countries. The national carrier, Royal Air Maroc, flies to more than 30 African cities.

- European investors continue to dominate investment in Africa; Collectively, European investors, among the traditional investors in African markets, continue to launch, by far, the largest number of direct investment projects in Africa. A decade ago North Americans were their strongest challengers - and indeed, the US continues to top the table by nation, rather than region of origin European nations, led by the UK, remain keen investors overall;

- The US Strategy toward Sub Saharan Africa, unveiled in 2012, makes encouraging growth, trade and investment one of four strategic objectives for US policymakers. It was followed by the launch of U.S. Government programs to facilitate trade and investment in Africa, most notable President Barack Obama's 2013 Trade Africa initiative, aimed at expanding US Africa trade and investment, beginning initially with the EAC. The US Doing Business in Africa campaign is backed by Usd7 billion funding. Another key initiative is Power Africa, that I have mentioned in the previous chapter, which intends to add more than 30.000 megawatts of electricity generating capacity across the continent, and double the number of people in Sub-Saharan Africa who have access to power. The African Growth and Opportunity Act (AGOA), grants qualifying African countries tariff-free access to the US market for some goods and services;

- US companies have traditionally been the largest group of foreign investors in Africa. Since 2007, they have launched 700 FDI projects across the continent, pouring in Usd52.7 billion and creating nearly 98.000 jobs;

- US companies also initiated more projects in business services, cleantech and chemicals. South Africa remained the favorite investment destination, though they also invested more in the key hubs of Kenya, Morocco and Egypt;

- In August 2014, leading American companies including Coca-Cola, Blackstone Group and Carlyle Group announced more than Usd14 billion investments in Africa at the first US-Africa Leaders' Summit;

- General Electric (GE), a US-based multinational manufacturer with products ranging from pumps to medical scanners, has been present in Africa since 1898. In 2013, it achieved sales of Usd5.2 billion in Africa. Responding to rising African demand, in August 2014, the company announced that it would invest up to Usd2 billion in Africa and double its workforce on the continent to 4.000 during the five years to 2018;

- IBM announced in February 2014 that it will open innovation centers in Morocco and Nigeria, working on big data, analytics and cloud computing. Mobile subscriptions and data traffic are rising strongly in Africa, opening up opportunities to supply education, banking and health care via the internet, adding to the sector's appeal;

- The European Union (EU) is seeking to promote growth in Africa by negotiating Economic Partnership Agreements (EPAs) with regional blocs in the continent. These EPAs are designed to deliver duty free and quota-free access for African goods to the EU market. Three EPAs have been signed, with the Economic Community of West African States (ECOWAS), the East African Community (EAC) and with the Southern African Development Community (SADC);

- French bank BNP Paribas set up corporate and investment banking activities in Casablanca, which is striving to develop as an African financial hub;

- Investors from the Middle East have been increasingly active in infrastructure projects in Africa, including ports and telecommunications, with a growing focus on power generation. According to the Economist Intelligence Unit, Gulf companies have invested at least Usd30 billion in African infrastructure over the past decade. Going forward, their investments are now expected to average Usd5 billion per year;

- South Africa is the favorite destination for Chinese projects, securing 34.4% of them. Tanzania, Ghana and Kenya are also popular, each taking a 9.4% share. Nearly a third of Chinese FDI projects are in Technology, media and telecommunications, though Chinese companies are also investing in coal, oil and natural gas, mining and metals, and aerospace and defense;

- After completing the acquisition of the South-African based Protea Hospitality Group, Marriott International became the largest hotel company in Africa. In October 2014, the company announced plans to expand its African presence further, from 120 properties across 10 countries to 150 properties in 17 national markets by 2020. It also intends to add 10.000 more African associates to its workforce. These developments will involve an outlay of about Usd1.5 billion by Marriott and its Real estate partners across the continent;

- International hotel chains are also striving to meet burgeoning demand in Africa, where supply of hotels in all categories is often inadequate. With few properties or chains to buy, global hotel groups have largely to rely upon organic growth. According to the UN World Tourism Organization, international arrivals in Africa exceeded 50 million in 2012 and are expected to top 85 million by 2020. Increasing regional and international trade in Africa has buoyed the number of business travelers, prompting leading hoteliers to develop ambitious plans;

- The World Bank predicts that African agriculture and agribusiness will generate sales of Usd1 trillion by 2030. A United Nations report predicts that FDI in African agriculture will grow more than fourfold in the decade to 2020, to reach Usd45 billion a year;

- Consumer spending in Africa reached Usd600 billion in 2010, and is expected to hit almost Usd1 trillion by 2020;

- Capital investment in Uganda rose to Usd4.6 billion following a joint investment in the coal, oil and natural gas sector by a Russian based investor;

- Egypt recorded Usd5.9 billion of announced FDI projects in solar power in 2015. Almost 60% of this can be attributed to Terra Sola's plans to invest in a Usd3.5 billion solar plant;

- France-based TOTAL, an oil and gas major, plans to invest Usd16 billion to develop the Kaombo offshore oilfield in Angola. The development will be established through a joint-venture initiative, with Total as the main operator with a 30% share;

- Italy-based EniSpA, an oil and gas major, plans to develop a newly discovered gas field in Egypt. Located offshore, the Zohr gas field is expected to require a minimum of Usd6 billion to fully develop;

Below I share with you what The Big Boys are doing to change their strategy towards the continent while they try to get a slice of the 'Africa Growth Story' cake, by adapting their operating business model according to each country culture, rules, regulations, language, and taste of local markets:

Coca-Cola

A model that has worked well for bottling company Coca-Cola Sabco in parts of East Africa is the Official Coca-Cola Distributor (OCCD) approach, whereby the local bottling factory partners with a number of "micro-distributors" - local entrepreneurs, each of which is given responsibility for a particular territory (generally a 1km radius in an urban environment, servicing at least 500 outlets). These OCCDs have become a central element in Coca-Cola Sabco's distribution strategy in several countries, and are responsible for 70% or more of sales volumes in Ethiopia, Kenya, Uganda and Tanzania. In this way, Coca-Cola Sabco has found an effective route to consumers, while simultaneously creating business opportunities for local entrepreneurs and their employees.

Nestle

Nestle, the foods group, has also tackled the route-to-consumer challenge by creating opportunities for micro-entrepreneurs in African countries. As part of its *My Own Business initiative*, Nestle provides vendors with a Nescafe coffee dispenser they can strap on their back, enabling them to sell coffee by the cup in markets, at events and at the roadside. Launched in Nigeria in 2012, this initiative is now operational in Burkina Faso, Cote d'Ivoire, Cameroon, Ghana, Senegal and Kenya, and is being extended to other countries.

Samsung

Samsung recently brought out extra-loud stereos to appeal to Nigerian consumers, and fridges that can withstand power loss and fluctuations, to cope in African markets where electricity supplies regularly suffer cuts and surges.

Oriflame

Swedish beauty company Oriflame set up in east Africa, but could only introduce 300 products from its 1.500-strong line. Some of its make-up was developed for the Indian market, but the company plans to introduce darker shades of foundation for an African range soon.

Uber

While Uber continues its push into Africa the company is making allowances to local markets and testing unique service models users wouldn't see in other parts of the globe. Anyone can now use the mobile app to hail a car in 12 cities across South Africa, Nigeria, Uganda, Kenya, Morocco and Egypt. And in all of those countries users can pay drivers in hard cash.

Passengers in Kenya, Nigeria, Egypt, and Morocco have the option to pay in physical or digital currency.

Shift to cash in Kenya led to a three-fold increase in Uber use, which is a bit surprising. Kenya has the highest mobile payments use in the world, largely due to the success Safaricom's M-Pesa service. Uber has payment partnerships with M-Pesa and Nigerian digital payment startup Paga.

In addition to payment models, Uber Africa is also testing methods to overcome addressing challenges. Streets are not as well mapped across the continent as many of Uber other markets, which poses challenges to drivers.

In Kenya, Uber is testing a pilot program with local directions startup OkHi, which uses smartphones and digital images to overcome inaccurate or non-existent postal codes, street names, or physical addresses.

Rather than the Uber driver aiming for number, say, 7 Mombasa Road - which may not be mapped - he or she can aim for the white fence or green gates of the exact location as seen on a mobile device.

Diageo

Diageo, the global beer and spirits producer, faces multiple challenges as it expands in Africa: limited consumer incomes, unreliable power and water supplies, poor transportation networks, a fragmented retail landscape and inconsistent regulatory regimes.

In its priority markets, Diageo follows a strategy of investing to create integrated supply chains: it builds production sites with their own power and water supplies. It invests in local suppliers, in developing a salesforce and in working jointly with distributors to enhance their capabilities. As a result of these models, Africa accounts for nearly 13% of Diageo's total net sales. The continent contributes 30% of Diageo's global sales growth and 40% of its global operating profit increase.

Diageo has developed a strong presence in a number of key markets on the continent with its iconic brands including Guinness. Nigeria was chosen as the first market outside of Ireland and the UK for a Guinness brewery. Due to the long heritage in the country and the strong brand equity built through localized brand communication, the brand is deeply rooted in the country and Nigeria has emerged as the largest Guinness Stout market in the world by net sales value.

Danone

French diary giant, Danone acquired 49% of West Africa's largest frozen dairy producer Fan Milk International. The acquisition of the Ghana-based company provides access to consumers in Ghana, Nigeria, Togo, Burkina Faso.

The remaining 51% of Fan Milk International was acquired by Dubai based Private equity firm

Abraaj Group. The acquisition of Fan Milk International forms part of Danone's Africa expansion and follows the purchase of an additional 37% in Centrale Laitiere du Maroc, which increased Danone's overall shareholding in the Moroccan dairy company to 67%.

JCDecaux Group

In order to gain a foothold and expertise in Africa, global outdoor advertising leader France based JCDecaux Group acquired in 2015 a 70% stake in Continental Outdoor Media, Africa's largest outdoor advertiser. Through the acquisition of Continental Outdoor Media, which owns in excess of 36.000 advertising panels in 16 countries across the continent, JCDecaux Group became the largest outdoor advertising firm on the continent.

Vodafone Safaricom

Safaricom, a subsidiary of Vodafone Group, whom controls 40% of the company, is a leading mobile network operator in Kenya.

Safaricom branched out from its core service of telecommunication, to financial services including the aleady-mentioned highly successful M-Pesa platform and payroll solutions. Through the M-Pesa platform users are able to access transactional services such as payment for airline tickets, utility bills and school fees. The success of Safaricom's diversification into financial services was supported by the insufficient development of the banking sector, a shortcoming that deterred investors from developing financial products for the Kenyan market. Backed by its dominant market position in the telecommunication sector and the strength of the brand as the leading telecommunication provider in Kenya, the firm was able to use this advantage to offer additional services piggybacking on its core service offering.

Still believe that the future of Africa is not bright?

As you can see investing and doing business in Africa is a Safari, and when you decide to invest in Africa you need to learn to navigate in a complex operating environment and develop solutions to ensure business success across different countries, as business models from advanced economies does not apply to the emerging markets of Africa.

Below is a list of the animals you see in a Safari and their correlation with the Top 10 strongest African economies (with 2016 GDP data):

1. Lion = Nigeria = Usd1.089 trillion GDP

2. Leopard = South Africa = Usd736 billion GDP

3. Cheetah = Egypt = Usd1.1 trillion GDP

4. Elephant = Algeria = Usd609 billion GDP

5. Rhino = Angola = Usd187 billion GDP

6. Hippopotamus = Morocco = Usd283 billion GDP

7. Buffalo = Ethiopia = Usd175 billion GDP

8. Nile Crocodile = Kenya = Usd153 billion GDP

9. Giraffe = Tanzania = Usd150 billion GDP

10. Zebra = Tunisia = Usd131 billion GDP

Let's talk about Risks now:

Just because a country shows exciting opportunities does not mean you can dive in without analyzing many risks prior to taking final decision to invest.

Ernest & Young (EY) has recently published a 2016 Africa Attractiveness Index, which basically is published to support investors in adapting to a more uncertain environment, and to assess variable opportunities and risks across the continent. EY have developed an interesting tool that provides a balanced set of shorter- and longer-term-focused metrics. This tool – the Africa Attractiveness Index (AII) – helps to measure both likely resilience in the face of current macroeconomic pressures, as well as progress being made in critical areas of longer-term development, namely governance, diversification, infrastructure, business enablement and human development.

I share with you now some findings of the overall results from EY Africa Attractiveness Index, as well as the country ranking for the Top 20 most attractive investment destinations in Africa:

EY's AAI country ranking:

1. South Africa

2. Morocco

3. Egypt

4. Kenya

5. Mauritius

6. Ghana

7. Botswana

8. Tunisia

9. Rwanda

10. Côte d'Ivoire (Ivory Coast)

11. Senegal

12. Tanzania

13. Uganda

14. Ethiopia

15. Nigeria

16. Algeria

17. Zambia

18. Namibia

19. Benin

20. Mozambique

Despite macroeconomic challenges (and a low-growth environment), South Africa still outperforms most other African economies due to relatively high scores across every other dimension (partly a reflection of the fact that the South African economy is more developed than any other African economy).

- Kenya and Cote d'Ivoire benefit from strong economic growth performance and prospects, with both performing moderately well in terms of infrastructure and business enablement.

- Botswana, Mauritius and Rwanda, although small markets have all got a strong track record in areas of business enablement, social development and economic management, and perform relatively well.

- The North African countries of Egypt, Morocco and Tunisia, as well as Ghana, in West Africa, remain under some pressure economically, but have the advantage of a relatively business-friendly environment, good infrastructure and, in the case of Ghana, a strong governance track record.

- Nigeria's relative underperformance on the AAI (ranked at number 15 overall) is perhaps somewhat surprising; while the Nigerian economy ranks as one of the most resilient in Africa, lower scores on the business enablement, governance and human development pillars are reflected in the overall ranking.

- Similarly, other high-growth economies like, Tanzania, Uganda and Ethiopia, are all ranked in the top 10 in terms of macroeconomic resilience (with Ethiopia at number 1), but are also relative underperformers on other longer term focused dimensions.

- South Africa, Egypt and Morocco are ranked in the top five of the AAI, and are also in the top 5 in terms of FDI project numbers and value.

- In contrast, despite a top 10 ranking on the AAI, Botswana, Rwanda and Mauritius do not feature strongly from an FDI perspective.

- At the same time, Algeria, Mozambique and Angola have a relatively low AAI ranking, but perform strongly in terms of FDI capital value.

This illustrates that strategic significance (e.g. natural resources and geographic location) and market size really do matter, particularly in the context of a region as vast, diverse and fragmented as the African continent:

- Egypt, Algeria, Angola and Nigeria are all resource rich and, because of this, they have attracted a large proportion of FDI capital into their capital-intensive extractive sectors (primarily oil and gas). In the last few years, FDI into Mozambique's gas sector has also grown substantially. With lower commodity prices, capital investment into extractive sectors is likely to come under pressure though; these countries are going to have to intensify their efforts to address longer-term factors, such as diversification and infrastructure (areas where Egypt and Nigeria, in particular, have already made some progress).

- FDI into South Africa, Kenya and Morocco has tended to be more diverse, with a growing emphasis on the less capital intensive services and manufacturing sectors. These three countries are also important hubs for investment into the wider southern, eastern and northern African sub regions respectively, and are among the highest-ranked countries on the AAI. Therefore, they have been among the top performing markets in terms of attracting FDI projects.

- Ghana stands out from most other African markets in terms of its positive FDI performance over the past five years, and provides a good example of a country that has made the most of a strong AAI ranking, a market that at least has some critical mass (with a population of approximately 25 million and the 12th highest level of consumer spending in Africa) and the fairly recent discovery of substantial oil reserves.

However as we look forward over the next decade, this picture is likely to change somewhat:

- Some of the top-performing countries from an FDI perspective are among those under the most macroeconomic pressure on the continent, including South Africa, Egypt, Morocco and Ghana. Of these, Ghana is probably most at risk of a significant decline in FDI projects. Although there may be some volatility in the numbers in the other three over the next few years, given their positive AAI ranking, relative size and strategic significance, we anticipate them remaining among the leading FDI destinations in Africa for the foreseeable future.

- The sheer size of the Nigerian market, together with some progress made on diversification, has already led to a significant shift in the nature of FDI (e.g., between 2006 and 2010, 75% of FDI capital was invested into extractive sectors; this fell to 36% between 2011 and 2015, with the far larger proportion now going into a range of service sectors, renewable energy, manufacturing and construction). Assuming progress is made on other dimensions of the AAI (notably business enablement, governance and human development), we would anticipate Nigeria becoming the largest market in Africa for FDI over the next decade.

- Kenya's strategic significance as a hub for investment into East Africa will ensure that it continues to attract a fair proportion of FDI projects (while recent oil discoveries may also transform the investment landscape over the next decade, albeit off a platform of an already diversified economy).

CONCLUSION:

It is perhaps inevitable that, as the prolonged global slowdown has exerted increasing pressure on many African economies, so too have doubts increasingly been raised about the sustainability of Africa's growth momentum of the previous 15 years. The reality is that growth has slowed substantially in the last year. However, at the same time, growth rates will remain resilient in coming years – across the region as a whole, and in many of the key regional economies.

Given the scale, complexity and fragmented nature of the African continent, making well informed choices about which markets to enter when, and via which mode, will be more critical than ever. While there is clearly no substitute for feet on the ground in key markets, an analytical approach that combines available data with frameworks that encourage strategic engagement should help enhance the quality of analysis and accelerate decision-making. More so than ever, the organizations that succeed in doing business in Africa will be those that plan systematically, and revisit their plans frequently to align and recalibrate.

"Business has only two basic functions: Marketing & Innovation" Peter Drucker

CHAPTER 6: Why Africa is not attracting more FDI than it should?

Beside all the potential that you read about in the previous chapters and all the major Foreign Direct Investment that you have had seen on the facts that I have shared with you, this chapter talks about why is Africa not attracting more FDI.

Like Peter Drucker brilliantly said once, business has two basic functions – marketing and innovation. One of Africa biggest issue in attracting Foreign Investment is called: NO Marketing.

Most countries in Africa, with the exception of South Africa, Egypt, Seychelles, Mauritius, Morocco, and Kenya, do not believe that spending money on marketing will make them attract more FDI.

When was the last time you saw Cape Verde on CNBC, or BBC with a nice marketing about its amazing beach destinations and sun the entire year? Never! Cape Verde has been growing at more than double digits in tourist arrivals and we are among the top 10 destination for European Tourists.

So, why do Politicians spend millions in Political Campaign to win elections, and when they win they forget that they have to work to attract foreign investment to help grow the country, and reduce poverty?

We had a ridiculous case in Cape Verde, at the end of 2016, with the National Airline of Cape Verde, named TACV Cabo Verde Airlines, which was at the brink of bankruptcy and the Government contacted our company via the National Airline Executive Board to request for our help the support the National Airline to attract a strategic aviation partner to help the Airline get out of the financial bankruptcy situation and structure a solution to help privatize the National Airline.

This request came in a turbulent time in my life, which was the birth of my son, and I couldn't focus on any business cases at all until he was safe. Remember Zion. Well, when he was born he didn't bread at first so they had to induce him into a coma during 3 days under a cold treatment at one (1) degree Celsius and then he had to stay at the Intensive Care Unit at the Hospital for 17 days to recover. These were scary days and nothing else matter at all. During this period the National Airline Board wanted me to fly in and out for just 3 days to speak to them about a solution because the World Bank, and the group of Countries, including the European Union, which helps Cape Verde Government Budget was pressuring the Government to come out with a solution for the troubling National Airline that was draining millions of the State Treasury.

After I could focus on business we presented a solution to the Board of National Airline and to the Minister of Transport of Cape Verde, on the condition that the Government would need to support the costs of an international investment road show to promote the solution to equity investors and to the big three airlines in the Middle East (Emirates, Qatar Airways, Etihad Airways). After a couple of weeks they decided that the costs of a road show were too expensive so they agreed to issue us mandates to market the solution internationally to investors, based on success fees.

A few weeks after we presented more guidance and solutions to be presented to equity investors but the Government in the beginning of 2017 decided that they had received a lot of other solutions and they couldn't give us the mandates. According to Chairman of the Executive Board of the National Airline they were surprised by the Government decision and they didn't know of any better solutions than the one we had presented and they were expecting that we could continue to help them. Amazing! Well, this is Africa!

What is more disgusting is seeing our Prime Minister giving interviews publically on an international TV Channel about the solution we have provided to the Government as the best solution to help with the privatization of the National Airline.

What exactly was the solution presented? Remember the Dubai Aviation success model I shared with you before? The solution was an Aviation HUB with complex financial engineering to help the national airline capitalize on Eur500million worth of assets that they couldn't see for themselves, by integrating an international airport with over 800ha of land and infrastructure under one Holding named Cabo Verde Airlines Group which would control the National Airline (TACV Cabo Verde Airlines), the operation of the International Airport in an island named Sal Island, and various other aviation business under the holding developed around an Aviation HUB business model, such as Maintenance Repair and Overall of Aircrafts, JET A1 fueling and refueling, Catering, Ground Handling, Hotels & Resorts, Tour Operation, among other.

This solution was provided fast because during the previous Government, which was being run by another political party, in 2012, our company proposed the Government to launch an Aviation HUB project named West Africa Aviation HUB & Group. We did an enormous international promotion in Dubai, Abu Dhabi and Europe, on investment road shows to attract investors into the project and we received many big international investors with interest on the project, being one of them Munich Airport, which is one of the biggest Airports company in the world with one of the biggest aviation HUB in Europe.

The then Government in 2012 decided that they didn't want to help fund the feasibility studies of the International Airline operations for the National Airline. So the project was put on hold by us because we couldn't believe what was happening.

As you can see, the same thing happen with both Governments, which is basically trying to get free work and use your ideas to benefit their own political agenda.

So, my question is, do both Leaders in both Governments believe the Country should always be controlled by the Government and their Ministers? How is this different from the rich natural resources country not letting their country grow because they believe protecting their own and still all they can still is the right way to move forward?

Well, we decided to leave the answer to the Gods to let us know one day, because all we can say is that these cases makes us feel sad and ashamed for being part of a country that unfortunately only works to those who decide to lick politicians ass. Meaning Political Patronage.

You are probably asking why we still insist in doing business in Africa. Well, we believe the future is Africa and we will keep fighting until every country is changed and the World Bank Doing Business Ranking as at list 25 African Countries of the top 50 list. Impossible? Nop! I don't believe in impossible. Like Mandela once said, "It always seems impossible until it's done."

WHAT ARE THE FOREIGN INVESTMENT AGENCIES DOING?

If you ask any of the Foreign Investment Agencies across Africa how many funds they have spent in the last 10 years in comparison to the FDI that the country has received, the shocking answer will be less than 0.0001%.

One my ask, how can you expect to attract more investors to your country if you don't believe marketing your country will attract investors to invest in your country?

From my experience Leaders of most of African Countries and the Presidents of the Investment Agencies believe their country is the most secure, beautiful and offers most opportunities than any other country, so that's why they don't think they should spend funds in marketing their country.

Let me share two examples using brands, which is no different than marketing a country to investors internationally.

Imagine if Apple had the same believe that they didn't need to make marketing of the Iphone, Ipad, MAC, itunes, because their product and solutions are the best in the world and people will come and buy it at their door step.

Imagine Ferrari saying they have the most amazing super cars and not showing you the images and telling you about the car features and capabilities before you decide if you want to buy it.

Well, this is basically how most African Foreign Direct Investment agencies market the countries they promote FDI. No marketing at all. They basically wait to see what happens after they go abroad to some B2B Events or International Fairs to compete with 200 other countries doing the same at the same place trying to convince Investors that their country is the best in Africa to invest in.

But Governments are smart what they tell the people that don´t understand what they are doing with public funds, when there is no transparency and no accountability. They will say, Oh we are using the diplomatic channels and our partners abroad to promote the country. Well the diplomatic channels cost millions to the State every year and most of the Ambassadors I have had the pleasure to meet have never run a business in their life. So, where are the results based on GDP growth and how many of the FDI that has come into the country actually came due to your marketing efforts?

COUNTRY BRANDING. WHY IS IT IMPORTANT?

In a world of global trade, communications, tourism and supra-national political organizations the meaning and value of place has never been more complex or contentious. But where we choose to work, study, travel and invest is still informed as much by associations and experiences of a country as it is by regulatory, economic and social conditions.

FutureBrand is one of the world's leading authorities in country brand strategy and management. They have done Country Branding for many countries.

FutureBrand helped to pioneer the study of countries as brands, understanding that they can be managed and measured for trade, investment and tourism growth.

The Country Brand Index (CBI) was first published in 2005 and has evolved to measure the dimension of country of origin or 'made in' that is an increasingly important driver of choice for corporate and consumer brands, as well as demonstrating that countries which qualify as brands have a measurable competitive advantage. Their practice draws on these insights, and includes country, destination, event and 'made in' branding for some of the world's most celebrated places.

So, the million dollar question is: Which African Country as used Future Brand to do Country Branding and Marketing for their destination to help boost trade, investment and tourism growth? The answer is NONE!

Who are the big names using FutureBrand?

Here are just a few big names, which is one of the reasons why their brands are so successful:

- American Airlines
- Nespresso
- Cadillac
- Chicco
- London 2012 Olympics
- Bentley
- Barilla

- Sephora
- Arena
- Nike
- ICC Cricket World Cup
- Movenpick
- Remy Martin
- NFL
- Beck's Vier
- The George Washington University
- INTEL
- MasterCard
- DOW
- Juventus Football Club
- British Airways
- Nakheel Dubai - The Palm Jumeirah

In 2016 FutureBrand launched the FutureBrand Index which shows a list of how the Top 100 companies rank on their list of where they measure global public perception of the Global Top 100 Companies by market capitalization. Making the Top 10 on this list are the following brands:

1. Apple :: Sector: Technology – Market Cap: Usd604 billion;

2. Microsoft :: Sector: Technology – Market Cap: Usd437 billion;

3. Samsung :: Sector: Consumer Goods – Market Cap: Usd167 billion;

4. Walt Disney :: Sector: Consumer Services – Market Cap: Usd162 billion;

5. AbbVie :: Sector: Healthcare – Market Cap: Usd92 billion;

6. Facebook :: Sector: Technology – Market Cap: Usd325 billion;

7. Toyota Motor :: Sector: Technology – Market Cap: Usd177 billion

8. Amazon :: Sector: Consumer Services – Market Cap: Usd280 billion

9. Celgene Corp :: Sector: Healthcare – Market Cap: Usd78 billion

10. Gilead Sciences :: Sector: Healthcare – Market Cap: Usd124 billion

You can take a look at the entire list on FutureBrand website. But out of the Top 100 there is no African company. Yep! NONE. Majority of companies are from USA, Japan, UK, China, France, Switzerland, Germany, and Canada.

MORE BARRIERS ON INVESTMENT AND DOING BUSINESS

Remember in previous chapters we spoke about many obstacles and barriers that entrepreneur in Africa need to overcome to be successful, such as:

- Limited access to financing

- Weak infrastructure
- Inconsistent government regulations
- Globalization
- Cross-border payments
- International Expansion
- Unstable political environment
- Corruption
- Operating environment
- Weak security
- Poor basic infrastructure
- Lack of highly skilled labor
- Inconsistency and lack of transparency in regulatory policy
- Unattractive tax policies and financial incentives

Well there is more. You are probably saying, Bloody Hell, MORE? Yes. One that is very important. It's called Bureaucracy from Government Agencies & Lack of Leadership from Government Leaders.

There are many countries with the right branding, spending millions in marketing, showing on the best to doing business in Africa, politically stable, top of the list when it comes to governance, low corruption, macroeconomic stability, good infrastructure, with huge potential for high return on investment, but still does not see increases in Foreign Direct Investment. What happens in these countries that FDI does not increase even with all the right ingredients to attract investors? Cape Verde is one of the examples of such a bad mess.

We have seen so many projects cancelled and investors deciding not to invest due to Government agencies Bureaucracy, Bad Policies and Bad Leadership from Prime Ministers, which I will share more in details in a different chapter, but below, are a few examples:

- Government sell beachfront lands to investors to develop resorts but takes 10 years to transfer the title and still does not refund the investor its money back;

- VAT refund is a joke; you must pay taxes on time but when it comes for the State to refund your VAT taxes back, waiting for 5 years seems to be normal to them; but if you don't pay in time they run after your business and try to freeze your accounts and your assets;

- It is totally normal to wait 1 year to 2 years for a project to be completely approved before you are able to start marketing it;

- Agreements are not respected unless you go to court; Government really doesn't care when they default on contracts and they don't comply with the conditions and obligations that they were supposed to guarantee to the investor so the investment can move forward;

In a nutshell, due to these issues, in 12th of May 2015, the Head of the European Union in Cape

Verde, Ambassador Jose Manuel Pinto Teixeira, came up publicly to the Media to say that the business environment in Cape Verde is bad. And Cape Verde is one of the success stories in Africa, being one of the few African Countries with a Special Partnership with the European Union.

According to this interview the Ambassador and Head of the European Union in Cape Verde said the following which I share with you:

- It is necessary for the business environment to improve. Cape Verde has a business environment that is not compatible with the rankings of all other indicators: Democracy, freedom of the press, good governance, corruption. Here the levels are very good, in terms of business environment the indicator is very bad. This is something that is not normal and it is necessary to make an effort.

- Obviously, the Cape Verdean government has to lead the whole process: reducing bureaucracy, improving coordination of decision-making processes, speeding up decisions, because there is still a mentality at the level of obstacle institutions rather than facilitators. This is the most important thing for Cape Verde in the near future, obviously, in order to respond to economic growth and job creation, because if there is no economic growth, no job creation will fail to respond to population growth.

- We organized a European Union business mission, which was attended by more than 50 entrepreneurs from 11 different countries, most of whom knew little or nothing about Cape Verde, so there was this positive aspect to put Cape Verde on the map, but to follow up these actions the business environment has to improve. If not, these actions, instead of being of investment encouragement, are the opposite. Because when they arrive and see the difficulties, when talking with other businessmen who are here or with the association, they lose the will to invest. We know that government has as a priority the attraction of investments, there are missions abroad, meetings, etc., so it seems nonsense to make all this effort without improving what is the first thing that the businessman wants to see. Because otherwise we are attracting attention and then it is a disappointment with what is found.

CAPE VERDE IN THE WORLD BANK 2017 DOING BUSINESS RANKING

The World Bank Doing Business Ranking sheds light on how easy or difficult it is for a local entrepreneur to open and run a small to medium-size business when complying with relevant regulations. It measures and tracks changes in regulations affecting 11 areas in the life cycle of a business: starting a business, dealing with construction permits, getting electricity, registering property, getting credit, protecting minority investors, paying taxes, trading across borders, enforcing contracts, resolving insolvency and labor market regulation.

In a series of annual reports Doing Business presents quantitative indicators on business regulations and the protection of property rights that can be compared across 190 economies, from Afghanistan to Zimbabwe, over time. The data set covers 48 economies in Sub-Saharan Africa, 32 in Latin America and the Caribbean, 25 in East Asia and the Pacific, 25 in Eastern Europe and Central Asia, 20 in the Middle East and North Africa and 8 in South Asia, as well as 32 OECD high-income economies. The indicators are used to analyze economic outcomes and identify what reforms have worked, where and why.

So where exactly is Cape Verde in the doing business ranking of 190 countries in the world?

Sadly Cape Verde is in 129. No wonder. With all the bad leadership, bureaucracy and no know how from the leaders in promoting foreign direct investment the country has plunged in the doing business ranking. So, it's not easy to do business here.

When my book is launched you will probably have some Politicians saying, Oh he is opposition that's why he mentioned those facts on his book. Reallyyyyy? What do you mean? These are facts from the World Bank, European Union

Ambassador. No argument needed and no Politics in the middle.

So, as a Politician, and a Minister, if you have bought my book please try to look at the facts and do your job to serve your people. That's the concept of being a politician and a member of the Government. To protect your people and fight so your country can develop for the greater good of every citizen, and not just the ones that belong to a specific political party.

Recently the Prime Minister of Cape Verde said publicly that we will see Cape Verde in the Top 50 countries of doing business. Hopefully. History will tell. FACTS matter, not Politics and promises.

Today my soul cries for Cape Verde because I want to see the country I was born like Mauritius and Dubai, or any other well developed economies, which are friendly to investment and want to see their citizens happy. Let me end this chapter with a subject that is important to all of us, no matter your race, religion or citizenship.

HAPPINESS

Ah, happiness, that elusive state. Philosophers, theologians, psychologists, even economists, have long sought to define it, and since the 1990s, a whole branch of psychology - positive psychology - has been dedicated to pinning it down and propagating it. More than simply positive mood, happiness is a state of well-being that encompasses living a good life - that is, with a sense of meaning and deep satisfaction.

Research shows that happiness is not the result of bouncing from one joy to the next; achieving happiness typically involves times of considerable discomfort. Money is important to happiness, but only to a certain point. Money buys freedom from worry about the basics in life - housing, food, and clothing. Genetic makeup, life circumstances, achievements, marital status, social relationships, even your neighbors - all influence how happy you are. So, if most of the people in your country are not happy what's the point?

Again a Dubai success case which I cannot end this chapter without mentioned it to you. Recently the Ruler of Dubai, Sheikh Mohammed Bin Rashid Al Maktoum announced that they have launched the World Happiness Council, headed by Columbia University Professor Jeffrey Sachs, who is joined by 12 other members. The Council will focus on 6 sectors: health, education, environment, personal happiness, happy cities and community standards for happiness. The Council aims to support international goals to standardize happiness as a measure of development, as they are doing in the UAE. How cool is this?

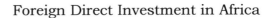

"Patience is a key element to Success."
Bill Gates

CHAPTER 7: Mastering Patience with Africa FDI Airplane mode.

Before starting this chapter more in depth I will share with you the definition of Patience according to Cambridge Dictionary: "The ability to wait, or to continue doing something despite difficulties, or to suffer without complaining or becoming annoyed."

How about the definition or understanding of what Airplane mode is?

Airplane mode, flight mode, offline mode, or standalone mode is a setting available on many smartphones, portable computers, and other electronic devices that, when activated, suspends radio-frequency signal transmission by the device, thereby disabling Bluetooth, GPS, telephony, and Wi-Fi. The name comes from the prohibition by many airlines of using equipment transmitting radio-frequency signal while in flight; using airplane mode prevents devices from transmitting.

You are probably saying fine but what does this has anything to do with Foreign Direct Investment.

Well, from my experience in Africa when it comes to investing in any country you will need to become a Master of Patience if you want to succeed in Africa.

WHY MASTER OF PATIENCE?

Because the process of Foreign Investment in many African countries is not easy, and most of the time you have to wait a long time so you can see results.

It is totally normal for example in Africa for you to experience the following:

- You meet the Foreign Investment Agencies and it's all roses at the first meeting and the country seems welcome to foreign investment and easy to do business;

- When you decide to move ahead with your project you will then need to set a local company which nowadays is easy in many African countries, and then sign a Memorandum of Understanding, a Protocol of Intention, or a Concession Agreement, or any type of agreement that you will sign with the Government to give you peace of mind so you can move ahead with your investment;

- Once your agreement is signed it all seems too good to be true that things moved that fast;

- Problems start happening along the way when it's time for you to wait for approval of you project by different Government Agencies so you can have green light to move forward with the project; this is when the Airplane mode begins; fasten your seat belt because the flight will be long and you will have to wait;

- It's totally normal for you to wait for months or even one year and a half for your project to have its full approval so you can move forward with it;

- It's totally normal for letters or phone calls to be replied back to you 3 to 6 months later; so this is Airplane mode on; you must Master Patience and always be ready to wait because no matter how well connected you are or your local partner are, Governments in Africa doesn't seem to believe time is important;

- We have experienced cases in many countries where Governments told us in writing, and in meetings with the Prime Ministers and Board of Ministers, and also in signed agreements that your project will be approved in maximum 45 days, or they would transfer a title of the land that they have received funds for it into the treasury accounts in 15 days; in one of the cases 10 years later we are still waiting for the Government to comply and the case is now going to Court for a Eur20million claim against the Government;

So, when you decide to invest in any African country make sure you have a local partner that understands the market well and knows how to help your company structure the perfect agreement that will protect you from losing money and waiting too long for things to move forward.

Warren Buffett once said, "No matter how great the talent or efforts, some things just take time. You can't produce a baby in one month by getting nine women pregnant." Brilliant!

It's important to acknowledge that Africa tests an investor's Patience. Time horizons and return models that fit other markets don't always work. Even the most experienced, sophisticated companies can be forced to recalibrate their business plans. Nestle for example, had to cut 15% of its workforce across 21 African countries after delays and lack of progress in many markets.

What's important is that investors realize there is a lot of money to be made in Africa for those bold enough that understand how to close the gaps.

But even with these challenges you won't be able to ignore the facts on Africa's potential and its markets. So fasten your seatbelt and enjoy the flight because even with the Airplane mode and the waiting you must always find a way to prevail and win in different markets.

THE AFRICAN WAY

Perhaps we should realize and accept that there is an African way of doing business and entrepreneurs must adapt to it. But Why? It doesn't make any sense!

Perhaps Africa needs new generation of leaders that really understands that money will only go where it feels comfortable and there is no stress on the investment process. Most of us know time is money, and sometimes time is more valuable than money because you cannot buy the time lost back.

Our millennial generation doesn't care if the President or Prime Minister is one party or another. What we care for is to see our country develop and attract wealth to everyone so poverty can end one day, so our generation can one day say I HAVE A DREAM like Martin Luther King had one during his time.

Sure, Martin Luther King lived in USA and he wasn't fighting inequality, poverty or fighting to see a better President running USA. He was fighting for racism and on his famous I have a dream speech he said:

"I have a dream that one day the state of Alabama, whose governor's lips are presently dripping with the words of interposition and nullification, will be transformed into a situation where little black boys and black girls will be able to join hands with little white boys and white girls and walk together as sisters and brothers."

"I have a dream today. I have a dream that one day every valley shall be exalted, every hill and mountain shall be made low, the rough places will be made plain, and the crooked places will be made straight, and the glory of the Lord shall be

revealed, and all flesh shall see it together. This is our hope. This is the faith with which I return to the South. With this faith we will be able hew out of the mountain of despair a stone of hope. With this faith we will be able to transform the jangling discords of our nation into a beautiful symphony of brotherhood. With this faith we will be able to work together, to pray together, to struggle together, to go to jail together, to stand up for freedom together, knowing that we will be free one day."

Well, my generation has a Dream for Africa:

"We have a dream that one day we will see a strong African Union that cares about Africa as a whole. A union so strong that one day we will see Africans so proud of their history and so proud of being part of Africa."

"We have a dream that one day we will see young Presidents and Prime Ministers in power with the same views as our generation and willing to fight for their country to grow so we can see African Countries reach the level of development that many countries have managed to achieve."

"We have a dream that all the crooked Presidents and Ministers will be made straight, and the glory of the Lord shall be revealed one day, and all shall restore countries leadership to leaders that truly believe they can do better and help their country prosper. This is our hope. This is the faith with which we Millennials fight for Africa and we will continue to fight until we see Africa Rise to its Greatness."

"We have a dream that one day we will make our children proud to say that the Africa Dream is similar to that of Europe, or the United States of America, or any developed nation, which is Happiness and Freedom."

While there was a time when African leaders were idolized as liberation heroes, the tide is turning. With the emergence of a well-informed and ambitious youth population, all countries on the continent will soon start seeing the full impact of this dynamic between a powerful, old elite and the next generation of aspiring leaders.

In response to this often opaque political world, where access involves compromising patterns of patronage – or is simply not conducive to safe, alternative forms of political expression – many young people are instead turning to entrepreneurialism.

As political elites have much better access to all kinds of resources, new forms of tension and opportunity will arise, creating different instruments of leverage. These might range from new political parties to novel forms of geopolitical and economic alliances forged by African youth as they create their own supra-national identity.

While other countries or regions find themselves tackling issues such as the technological revolution, climate change and religious conflict, Africa's biggest challenge over the next five years will be how it reconciles the demands of its strident youth – and their take on how to shape the post-colonial continent – in the face of established and entrenched power structures.

DIGITAL & CULTURAL REVOLUTION

While our generation fight and wait for our dream to become a reality you need to understand what cultural challenges you will face while doing business across Africa.

"We are at the beginning of a revolution that is fundamentally changing the way we live, work and relate to one another," Klaus Schwab, the founder and Executive Chairman of the World Economic Forum, writes in his book, The Fourth Industrial Revolution. This is the digital revolution which is already transforming Africa.

Africa – largely bypassed by previous industrial revolutions – stands in a unique position to reap the benefits of these changes. Its young and growing population, vast resources and largely untapped markets could provide the foundations for a continent-wide renewal, powered by technological innovations.

We have seen in previous chapters how many IT innovations are changing the Africa tech sector. But without a change in leadership and a cultural change how can we see this revolution happening for African Entrepreneurs? When do you think we will see a company with the greatness of Facebook being launched by a young and passionate African from his/her house or dorm room?

On May 14th, 1984, Mark Zuckerberg was born in New York, USA. Twenty (20) years later, he launched the initial version of "The Facebook" out of his Harvard University dorm room. A decade after opening to its first members, Facebook has one billion users in a single day, and it is worth today about Usd325 billion. Zuckerberg is undoubtedly brilliant. But what if he had been born into a working class family in Africa? Would Facebook exist today? Would the social-media revolution have unfolded in the same way? Not quite sure, it will happen with the business environment Africa has today and the business culture that doesn't believe in projects that you don't have a blueprint to compare too. It is like expecting a rose to grow in the North Pole and make someone believe it will. Without the right environment you cannot see brilliant minds achieving greatness, no matter how hard you try.

In the future, raw ability will be more important than the circumstances of one's birth, reinforcing this fundamental truth: Brilliance and talent are evenly distributed, opportunity is not. An example of the disconnect between innate ability and opportunity can be found in Africa. With more than one billion people, approximately 60% of them under age 25, and more than 25% of young people out of work in many places, Africa is home to the world's largest pool of untapped brainpower and talent. In the past, there was no scalable, cost-effective way to leverage and empower this human capital. But technology is quickly upending this paradigm, especially when it comes to identifying technical and quantitative aptitude.

This is way we see brilliant companies like Andela being launched now. Andela was found and co-funded by Facebook to find and train the top 1% of tech talent across Africa. After six months in their software-development program, young men and women work remotely for Fortune 500 companies and startups around the world while receiving continuing training and support. Clients such as Microsoft looking to tap into Africa's talent, integrating the continent's best and brightest into their workforces in new ways.

As other companies adopt similar approaches, this new, meritocratic model of workforce development will expand across the world, accelerated by massive demographic shifts already under way. Indeed, while the populations of rich countries shrink and age, Africa's overall population is expected to double by 2050. It's time to stop viewing this as simply a youth bulge - it is a talent bulge. And when the next Mark Zuckerberg is born in Africa, he (or she) will have far greater access to the opportunities that enabled Mark to reach a billion people in a single day and become one of the youngest billionaires the world has ever seen.

So, culture defines how we act and how we do things in our daily lives and it's basically one of the greatest barriers to Africa Business climate and doing business rankings.

THE ROLE OF CULTURE IN DOING BUSINESS IN AFRICA

Culture refers to the accepted norms and values and rational behavior of groups. It's "How we do things!" Countries, as well as people within the country, may operate differently according to beliefs, values, norms, morals and attitudes.

Understanding and being sensitive to the local "culture" is a critical factor for any organization to succeed, especially in international business. What works in your country might not work well in another, and could even be interpreted as an insult!

While doing business, there should be a conscious attention to behavior, ethics, etiquette visions, working style, beliefs and habits. The cultural nuances that affect organizations obviously go beyond the ability to greet or choose the correct gift. The issues related to the culture's time orientation, whether it's at an individual level or collectively as a society, not to mention conflict assumptions and non-verbal communication, all affect the understanding(s) across the table, as well as the chances of being understood. It helps make us knowledgeable about the questions to ask, not the answers.

A study from the NTU-SBF Centre for African Studies, of the Nanyang Business School, shares an African Perspective about the Role of Doing Business in Africa, which I share with you here:

The effects of colonialism past and present are visible all over Africa. It is not an overstatement when Edem Kodjo, author of 'Africa Tomorrow', describes the condition of an African as "torn away from his past, propelled into a universe fashioned from outside that suppresses his values, and dumbfounded by a cultural invasion that marginalizes him. The African,...is today the deformed image of others."

The contributions and cultural influences stemming from Africans have been greatly undermined in schools worldwide. As is the case in the distant memory of colonialization, enslaved Africans were forced to abandon traditional customs, camouflage spiritual rituals, and perish cultural artefacts. However, lifestyle from traditional folklore, practices of worship & healing, cuisine to song and dance is not only prevalent in today's society, but have a widespread, deep-rooted impact throughout the world; though largely unnoticed. It's therefore important to understand the cultural diversity of Africa.

Cultural diversity is a central part of the African collective identity. This central aspect has not always proven to be a blessing for Africa in dealing with itself and also in its encounter with the rest of the world. This is due to, among other things, the fact that the intrinsic African identity is dominantly an ethnicized cultural diversity. This implies that respective African cultures are bonded and integrated, mostly within particular groups, and hence emphasizes more on the local context at the expense of the collective Africa perspective.

According to Richard Bell in his "Understanding African Philosophy" (2002), the African "regional cultures were broken up and destroyed (or at least radically altered) primarily by the European and Islamic incursions going back some 500 years. The slave trade, introduction of new diseases, forced colonization, foreign language and religious impositions, and new administration threw most of the continent into social, religious, political, and cultural confusion. Some of these regional cultures once had great civilizations and kingdoms, but a minimum of texts survived to record their ideas and achievements. What remains of them are fragmentary pictures: icons from ritual life, histories of smaller communities passed on orally...."

According to Chibueze C. Udeani's "Cultural Diversity and Globalisation" (2007), in the age of globalization, it's a fact that "local contexts in the world are getting dissolved into a worldwide network of interaction under the influence of technology... It is therefore all the more necessary to pose the question of cultural diversity and globalization from an African perspective".

Cultural diversity in Africa has to be seen and understood from two sides: the diversity within the African cultural landscape; and the diversity of cultures with which Africans are now being more intensively confronted within the process of globalization.

Africa is 30 million square miles. It covers the same surface as 13 countries - including the United States, China and India - and the whole of Eastern Europe and in all kinds of riches, especially in raw materials such as platinum, cobalt, uranium, tantalum, gold, diamonds and oil. There is hardly an agricultural product that cannot be grown in Africa. Africa's arable land for food security is reported to be the largest in the world.

A glaring example of the riches of Africa is the Democratic Republic of Congo, the country of Patrice Lumumba. Economic experts have pronounced that, when developed, Congo alone can feed and provide electricity for the whole of Africa.

In Africa, social and business culture reflects the past colonial history to a very large extent, with the African identity playing in the background. Doing business among the same ethnic African groups is prevalent with the propensity to 'network,' much before the word came to be used as a verb. The psychological orientation here is 'n-affiliation', which is characterized by a need to belong to a group and readiness to help each other within that group.

There are many factors that must be considered in order to successfully conduct business in a marketplace foreign from your own. Learning the language and translating or localizing the approach is an important step, but so is understanding the customs and etiquette of that market.

Increasingly today the slow pace and underdevelopment of the African continent can be traced to the gradual degradation and loss of "African" culture. It's said that the so-called contemporary development called values, norms and morals does not take place in a vacuum, but in what the human does with his/ her immediate habitat.

We must note that values, norms and morals are universal assets in understanding and defining culture; which do not change easily. In Africa we have specific values associated with some group of people, but these may solely be the material or visible culture, such as food, clothing, housing, drumming and dancing, and art. The values and morals are abstract and invisible (non-material) such as respect, love, marriage, taboos, laws, kindness and worship and is prevalent in the background, visible to a select few outsiders.

In Africa, social culture reflects the past colonial history, along with the civilization that existed centuries before. Broadly we can divide this vast land today into three groups, i.e. Anglophone countries (English speaking), Francophone countries (French speaking), and Lusophone countries (Portuguese speaking), excluding the Arab-influenced in North Africa.

At the same time, the old beliefs and witch craft, supernatural beings and ancestral spirits still practiced, promoted very strong and healthy relationships among the communities. For instance, in Nigeria, the belief in the role of the Ogun and the God of Lightning and Thunder are paramount in controlling crime and corruption.

The belief in witch-craft still influences the traditional healing and medication practices in the treatment of various ailments and diseases in society. The beliefs also promoted good kinship and cordial interpersonal relations and respect for elderly, kindness and habit of sharing, compliance with social norms, taboos and totems, and control of deviant behaviors in the society.

As a visitor in Africa, one is therefore broadly exposed to three distinctive components of the people inhabiting present-day Africa: (1) traditional Africans who are yet little affected by modernization (thereby socializing among the same ethnic people), (2) transitional Africans, and (3) modern Africans (foreign educated, well-travelled and socializing using modern tools). Hence, the social cultural set up in Africa is quite diverse and varied and not static, and has been impacted upon by both internal and external forces.

Conducting business in Africa requires the social cultural awareness and effective cross-cultural communication skills. What might be acceptable in SE Asia, for example, may be unacceptable in Africa. Do not expect French or Portuguese speaking business people to speak to you in English even if they understand it. Business objectives may be the same, but ways of implementation and communication differ greatly.

While in Singapore, they focus on producing quick and tangible results in their work; the experience in Africa, on the other hand, differs. The pace of doing things is slower and the outlook is often long-term. It's therefore normal, being used to the efficiency of Singapore system, to develop a sense of frustration by not understanding the local business practices. Do kindly note that the African approach to decision-making does not mean that local business people are unable to make quick decisions. Far from it; what it shows is the cultural significance of consensus and consultation, which tends to guide the decision-making process in Africa's group-oriented cultures.

BUILDING RELATIONSHIPS

As seen in SE Asia, socializing is key and builds personal trust, which is a prerequisite to doing business.

However, in Africa most of the time it's difficult to see the dividing line that determines where socializing ends and where business begins. Sometimes it takes a backyard barbeque or a couple of visits to the village for a meal or getting acquainted before you are offered any water or tea or even start discussing business. Some outsiders have misinterpreted these as being rude and viewed leisure to mean African laziness. Fact is leisure and socializing form the foundation that is key to group solidarity that is important to Africa.

Here are some examples:

- When entering a social function, shake hands with the person to your right and then continue around the room going from right to left. Say good-bye to each person individually when leaving;

- The West African handshake - where the middle finger snaps the middle finger of the person you are shaking. The louder the snap, the better, and it is acceptable to try the snap a second time if you miss it;

- The most common greeting is "How are you?" or "Bonjour", "Jambo", or in the country's local language, which is generally said immediately prior to the handshake;

- Always greet people first when you enter an area. Otherwise, you may wonder why people are just looking at you when you enter a room. They are waiting for you to offer a greeting, which will be received with a big smile and a warm reply;

- Direct, "let's get to business" conversation is considered rude. Always exchange pleasantries and inquire about family before beginning to transact any business. Even if you are just purchasing vegetables!

- When in rural areas and small villages, a visit to the local chief is the first stop you should make. When in the presence of the chief, remove your hat, keep your hands out of your pockets and do not cross your legs;

- In the countries with colonial pasts, European etiquette is socially acceptable. For example, English manners in Kenya and Nigeria and Dutch manners in various parts of South Africa;

- Soft handshakes are common across Africa. In Muslim countries, such as Morocco, men may hold handshakes so long that they become handholds.

CONCLUSION

Understanding cultural differences is critical to the success of companies engaging in international business. A society's culture affects the political, economic, social and ethical rules a company must follow in its business dealings within that country.

A society or country's culture reflects its values, beliefs, behaviors, customs and attitudes. Culture is learned behavior that is transmitted among people within a country to another. The elements of culture are interrelated and reinforce each other. It's important to note that these elements are adaptive, changing as outside forces influences the country. Hence, there are many factors that must be considered to successfully conduct business in Africa.

Religion influence attitudes towards work, investments, consumption, laws and responsibility for one's behavior. Language is another cultural element since it allows people to communicate with each other. Learning the language and translating or localizing the approach is an important step that can be noted.

So, like I mentioned before, for the time being fasten your seatbelts because in Africa you will be a while on Airplane mode waiting for things to happen, while you become a Master of Patience.

Hopefully in a near future our millennials generation will bring better leaders to become Presidents and Prime Ministers so we can see countries making that Giant leap that is needed in today's world, so Africa can become more interconnected and it jumps from the Airplane Mode into a full Operational Mode.

Take the example of Dubai. There is no country where they value culture more than the United Arab Emirates. They have managed to make a Culture Fusion when it comes to doing business that business grows fast and it moves at the speed of light when it comes to decision making and Foreign Investment. Culture is not a wall barrier for Foreign Investment.

So, African Leaders, while our generation of the Crazy Minds prepare for the transition into Power, which we are not at all interested, please take a look at the Top 20 easiest countries to do business, according to the World Bank Doing Business Ranking, with strong culture that have managed to adapt themselves to the world economy so you can attract more Foreign Direct Investment and not lose opportunities due to cultural barriers.

"Time is free, but it's priceless. You can't own it, but you can use it. You can't keep it, but you can spend it. Once you have lost it you can never get it back." Harvey Mackay

CHAPTER 8: Is Time not valued in Africa? Or is it valued differently?

Whenever you hear someone talking about time most of the time you hear people saying that time is more valuable than money. You can make money always, but you cannot get more time or buy it even if you are the richest billionaire in the world.

The old adage "time is money" is wrong. Time and money are very different. Time is irreplaceable. Money can be accumulated into massive piles and spent whenever you choose, but your stockpile of time is being depleted at a rate of one day per day. You can always make more money, but you can never make more time. And it's easy to trade time for money but very hard to do the reverse. So we should have a bias toward favoring time over money.

Once I was watching FashionTV channel and it was the weekend special about the luxury fashion designer Roberto Cavalli. And on an interview they asked him what was the most valuable thing to him. He said, and I quote: "Time, because time is the ultimate luxury."

Bill Gates & Melinda Gates in their 2016 Annual letter for the Bill & Melinda Gates Foundation named "If you could have one superpower, what would it be?" More Time was one of the Superpowers they chose! If you want to read it go to gatesnotes.com and you will find it, along with other great posts on various subjects written by Bill Gates himself.

IS TIME THE MOST VALUABLE THING IN THE WORLD?

I think so. Everything is acquired in time and all of man's business is conducted by time. You can have food, clothing, fabulous homes, wisdom - have all you want, but if you do not have time, it means - you have nothing.

A large segment of people live as if by guesswork, according to the accepted custom, day by day, year by year, not at all concerned about what they did with their days and years or how they lived their lives. Sometimes we mourn over the loss of some existing trifles, but we have no regrets at all, nor are we sorry, when we foolishly lose not just some petty cash, but the most precious minutes of our time.

DO WE HAVE UNLIMITED TIME?

We do not, but many people seem to believe we have unlimited time and they will never die. We all die one day, rich, and poor, religious or not, the Pope, everyone will die one day. So why don't most of us don't value our time?

Sunrise is a magical portion of our day when most dreams are still possible and the illusion of "enough" time to achieve them still exists.

No matter how bad was your day today, if you see the sunrise tomorrow it will give you a boost of energy and a daily opportunity to commit to a "New Day's Resolution". Each day in year is a 365 opportunity you will have.

Carl Sandburg once said "Time is the coin of your life. It is the only coin you have, and only you can determine how it will be spent. Be careful lest you let other people spend it for you."

You hear among different cultures, people saying "Your time is a gift from God. What you decide to do with your time is your gift back to God."

Yet, it is a common complaint that we don't get enough time to do all that we wanted to do today, this week, this month, this year, and this life. Every being receives 24 hours every day, to accomplish, enjoy, fritter, ignore, waste, ignore, prepare, or appreciate the time we receive. The daily challenge is to live like there is no tomorrow, plan for a thousand more tomorrows, take responsibility for the requirements of life (family, work, school, eating, sleeping, and money) and produce a fulfilled day with no regrets.

HOW DO WE VALUE TIME?

Not all uses of time are equal and this simple truth can make a big difference in life. Whether you want more wealth, more friendship, more freedom, or more impact, it all comes down to how you spend your time.

Understanding how to get the most out of your time starts with knowing in exact terms what your time is worth to you. Because you cannot compare the value of your time with the value of someone else.

Most people never calculate what their time is actually worth. Everyone has an hourly value, but very few people can actually tell you what that number is. The same happens to companies since they are managed by people.

All the time management techniques in the world will not help you if you cannot get this one fundamental down, that your time is valuable.

IS TIME NOT VALUED IN AFRICA?

From my experience most of businesses done with Governments, they tend to believe that since time is free there shouldn't be a rush in taking decisions or moving forward before they take as much time as they need to decide. Which in business is nonsense because if you are an investor and you want your money to keep producing more wealth you would rather applied to any type of secure financial investments (commercial banks deposits with interest, government bonds) while you wait for a decision to be issued. But it is not the same case across Africa. There are countries that time is valued more than money. I had the pleasure to live in Mauritius for three (3) years, promoting Foreign Direct Investment and it is amazing the level of professionalism and the way they conduct business that makes you want to keep doing business with the country. No wonder is among the Top 50 countries in the World. Mauritius occupies rank 49 in the 2017 World Bank Doing Business Ranking.

MAURITIUS SUCCESS STORY

Not sure if you ever been in Mauritius or if you have done business with the Country or anyone in the private sector there. If not then just give it a try and you will see that it is no different than doing business in Europe or USA.

The success of Mauritius has been so amazing that you won't believe you are in Africa.

Here are some facts about the country, as of 31st of December 2016, according the 2017 World Bank Doing Business Ranking and the Central Intelligence Agency (CIA) The World Factbook:

- Income category: upper middle income;
- Population: 1.2million;
- GDP (purchasing power parity): Usd25.8 billion;
- GDP (official exchange rate): Usd11.7 billion;
- GNI Per Capita: Usd9.610;
- GDP per capita PPP: Usd20.500;
- Doing Business Rank: 49;
- GDP composition by sector:
  - 4% Agriculture;
  - 22% Industry;
  - 74% Services;

- No Natural resources such as gold, oil, diamond;

- Agriculture products: sugarcane, tea, corn, potatoes, bananas, fish;

- Industries: food processing, clothing, chemicals, metal products, tourism, transport equipment, machinery;

- Labor force: 624.700;

- Unemployment: 7%;

- Public Debt: 66% of GDP;

- Stock of narrow money: Usd2.7 billion;

- Stock of domestic credit: Usd13.9 billion;

- Exports: Usd2.6 billion;

- Reserves of Foreign Exchange and gold: Usd4.5 billion;

- Currency: Mauritian rupee (MUR);

- Exchange rate of MUR to the USD: 35.5;

Let me share with you the data of Cape Verde so you can see the difference, beside Cape Verde being a success story in Africa in terms of Governance and has always showed up on the Top 3 best Governed Countries in Africa along with Mauritius, on the annual lists that the Mo Ibrahim Foundation publishes every year about Africa Governance. In 2016 Mo Ibrahim Africa

Governance Index, Cape Verde came on 3rd place and Mauritius on 1st place.

So, if Cape Verde is so advanced in Governance and other millennials goals established by the United Nations, why haven't we achieved similar success like Mauritius?

Well, here are the facts of Cape Verde Economy, as of 31st of December 2016, according to the 2017 World Bank Doing Business Ranking and the Central Intelligence Agency (CIA) The World Factbook:

- Income category: lower middle income;
- Population: 520.502;
- GDP (purchasing power parity): Usd3.5 billion;
- GDP (official exchange rate): Usd1.6 billion;
- GNI Per Capita: Usd3.290;
- GDP per capita PPP: Usd6.700;
- Doing Business Rank: 129;
- GDP composition by sector:
  - 7% Agriculture;
  - 17% Industry;
  - 76% Services;

- No Natural resources such as gold, oil, diamond;

- Agriculture products: sugarcane, coffee, corn, potatoes, bananas, fish;

- Industries: food processing, beverage, fish processing, shoes and garments, salt mining, ship repair;

- Labor force: 196.100;

- Unemployment: 15%;
- Public Debt: 128% of GDP;

- Stock of narrow money: Usd576 million;

- Stock of domestic credit: Usd1.3 billion;

- Exports: Usd148 million;

- Reserves of Foreign Exchange and gold: Usd447 million;

- Currency: Cape Verde Escudos (CVE);

- Exchange rate of CVE to the USD: 102;

Why is Mauritius performing better then Cape Verde?

The reasons have been mentioned before in different chapters in the book but here they are:

- Bad Leadership from the Prime Minister;
- Lack of Leadership from Government Leaders;
- Bureaucracy from Government Agencies;
- No business experience from Ministers;

- Limited access to financing;
- Operating environment; not easy to do business;
- Corruption; and the believe that Government should control everything;
- Unattractive tax policies and financial incentives;

How can you make a country with Usd1.6 billion GDP reach a Public debt of 128% of GDP?

Only a Magician can believe that the country can pay back its debt by not attracting foreign investment and by not supporting the Private Sector to contribute to the country's growth so everyone can pay more taxes to help the State borrow more money abroad. This is basic economics Mr. Prime Minister. By the way, this Magician name is Jose Maria Neves. The Prime Minister that was schooled by the Ambassador of the European Union about the bad business environment for doing business in Cape Verde. So, in a nutshell Good Governance does not automatically mean a country will see economic development, great business leadership by Government Leaders is the key to help countries move from bad economic situation into prosperity. FACTS! Not Politics.

IS TIME VALUED DIFFERENTLY IN AFRICA?

My perception from my experience is that the success of one country against the other is not just the reasons mentioned on the differences between Mauritius and Cape Verde cases but also the perception of value different Governments have of the time.

Politicians as soon as they are in Power they normally think they have all the time in the world and most really don't tend to act considering a business mindset but a political mindset which is very simple: How can we win votes in the next election with this project? Once you have this kind of mentality by Government leaders then you have countries losing a lot of opportunities, being Cape Verde an example. So don't be fooled by the Governance Index that makes you believe that the country is business friendly.

Entrepreneurs don't have time to wait. Either you decide to act fast so money can keep following and making more money, or it will flow elsewhere.

There are many economies to choose from. Why should you wait too long when there are many other countries offering similar or better conditions to attract foreign investment?

CONCLUSION

Please value your time and kindly make sure no matter the country you decide to invest in, people understand that your time is priceless and not unlimited.

"The biggest risk is not taking any risk. In a world that is changing really quickly, the only strategy that is guaranteed to fail is not taking risks."
Mark Zuckerberg

CHAPTER 9: Africa FDI Experiences and Lessons Learned.

Like they say, you learn from experience. It either makes you learn a lesson or it breaks you up in a thousand pieces if your spirit is not strong enough to understand that it was all about learning something. In business you either win or learn. Never is considered a loss. You always learn something new.

On this chapter I will share some of my Foreign Direct Investment experience with you. Some nice, some funny, and some really bad experiences but at the end they made me who I am today, and I am glad to all of them.

Like Mark Zuckerberg said once, the biggest risk is not taking any risk. I guess our generation doesn't really care about risks. We love risks. If there is none it doesn't excites us. My journey has been an amazing one so far and I hope, in GOD´s willing there will be more to come as I get old. I am still 37 years old as I write this book to you now, so I guess I still have a long way to go if GOD have something great planned for me, for this lifetime.

Before I started my company, I used to work for an Italian Entrepreneur named Andrea Stefanina. Even though life has separated us to go each one on its path he was one of my business mentors. Stefania is one of the first foreign investors that in 1991 decided to invest in Cape Verde tourism sector and had the balls to build the first resort to bring European tourists on vacation to a desert island destination in the middle of the Atlantic Ocean with no basic infrastructure. He became friends with my father because my father use to work back then at the National Airline and he was commercial Director in charge of developing new partnerships.

With Stefanina investment in a Eur15million resort hotel the National Airline of Cape Verde was able to have the courage to lease their first Boeing 757 to begin international operations from Cape Verde to Italy to transport the tourists that Stefanina Tour Operator company, named Cabo Verde Time Spa, based in a city named Brescia, marketing Sal Island in Cape Verde to Italian Tourists.

When I returned to Cape Verde in 2002, from University in Europe, after graduating in Business Administration from Evora University, at the amazing City of Evora which is a UNESCO World Heritage Site, I started my first working experience with Stefanina Group. In 2002 Stefanina was already a Corporation with many businesses under the Group with operations in Cape Verde and Italy. From Hotels, Tour Operator, Construction, Engineering, Salt Mining, Cement Factory, and Shipping line, the group was one of the biggest groups operating in Cape Verde.

After 4 years of learning as CEO of Real estate Division, CFO of the Group, and advisor to Stefanina investments in Cape Verde, I have learned a lot from the man himself. He was a great mentor from whom I can say that today as given me part of my business DNA, which allowed me to achieve some of the milestones you will read on this chapter.

After 4 years working at Stefanina Group I decided it was time to leave to set up my own company. So I decided since day one that what I wanted to do was promote foreign direct investment into Cape Verde by helping investors invest in Cape Verde and help them with the process of investing in the Country, structuring their project, and acquire all Government related licenses before their investments could be given green light to start.

Since Tourism and Real estate sectors were the main sectors that were booming, with Cape Verde becoming one of the favorite holiday destination for European tourists and a hotspot for second home buyers, I decided to focus initially on Tourism and Real estate.

After 4 months I got my first client. A Dubai based group with many projects in Dubai Real estate sector, which was developing Island Resorts with the Dubai Developer of Palm Jumeirah, Nakheel Properties, and other international Real estate projects in India, Morocco, and Cuba.

My life was turned upside down. I started my small company with Eur2000 which I borrowed from my parents and in less than 1 year I was managing Eur1.5billion portfolio for a Dubai Foreign Investor and flying business class and on private jets all around the world to meet with companies, design teams, investors, and Government leaders in Dubai, Europe, and Morocco.

I even had to become a resident of Dubai and set up base there to promote Foreign Investment from the GCC into Cape Verde. My life was basically meetings, traveling, meeting people at the Burj Al Arab Jumeirah 7 Star hotel in Dubai (one of the most exclusive and expensive hotels in the world).

Then in 2008 the Perfect Global Financial Tsunami hit us all, to what everyone thought was impossible to happen again after the 1929 financial crisis.

Below I will share a great publication from Manoj K. Singh, in Investopedia, about the Tsunami that the 2007-2008 Financial Crisis was. Like all previous cycles of booms and busts, the seeds of the subprime meltdown were sown during unusual times.

In 2003, the Fed lowered interest rates to 1%, the lowest rate in 45 years. The whole financial market started resembling a candy shop where everything was selling at a huge discount and without any down payment. "Lick your candy now and pay for it later" - the entire subprime mortgage market seemed to encourage those with a sweet tooth for have-it-now investments.

Unfortunately, no one was there to warn about the tummy aches that would follow.

But the bankers thought that it just wasn't enough to lend the candies lying on their shelves. They decided to repackage candy loans into collateralized debt obligations (CDOs) and pass on the debt to another candy shop. Hurrah! Soon a big secondary market for originating and distributing subprime loans developed. To make things merrier, in October 2004, the Securities Exchange Commission (SEC) relaxed the net capital requirement for five investment banks - Goldman Sachs (NYSE:GS), Merrill Lynch (NYSE:MER), Lehman Brothers, Bear Stearns and Morgan Stanley (NYSE:MS) - which freed them to leverage up to 30-times or even 40-times their initial investment. Everybody was on a sugar high, feeling as if the cavities were never going to come.

According to 2007 news reports, financial firms and hedge funds owned more than Usd1 trillion in securities backed by these now-failing subprime mortgages - enough to start a global financial tsunami if more subprime borrowers started defaulting. By June, Bear Stearns stopped redemptions in two of its hedge funds and Merrill Lynch seized Usd800 million in assets from two Bear Stearns hedge funds. But even this large move was only a small affair in comparison to what was to happen in the months ahead.

It became apparent in August 2007 that the financial market could not solve the subprime crisis on its own and the problems spread beyond the United States borders. The interbank market froze completely, largely due to prevailing fear of the unknown amidst banks. Northern Rock, a British bank, had to approach the Bank of England for emergency funding due to a liquidity problem. By that time, central banks and governments around the world had started coming together to prevent further financial catastrophe.

The subprime crisis's unique issues called for both conventional and unconventional methods, which were employed by governments worldwide. In a unanimous move, central banks of several countries resorted to coordinated action to provide liquidity support to financial institutions. The idea was to put the interbank market back on its feet.

The Fed started slashing the discount rate as well as the funds rate, but bad news continued to pour in from all sides. Lehman Brothers filed for bankruptcy, Indymac bank collapsed, Bear Stearns was acquired by JP Morgan Chase (NYSE:JPM), Merrill Lynch was sold to Bank of America, and Fannie Mae and Freddie Mac were put under the control of the U.S. federal government.

By October 2008, the Federal funds rate and the discount rate were reduced to 1% and 1.75%, respectively. Central banks in England, China,

Canada, Sweden, Switzerland and the European Central Bank (ECB) also resorted to rate cuts to aid the world economy. But rate cuts and liquidity support in itself were not enough to stop such a widespread financial meltdown.

The U.S. Government then came out with National Economic Stabilization Act of 2008, which created a corpus of Usd700 billion to purchase distressed assets, especially mortgage-backed securities. Different governments came out with their own versions of bailout packages, government guarantees and outright nationalization.

The financial crisis of 2007-08 has taught us that the confidence of the financial market, once shattered, can't be quickly restored. In an interconnected world, a seeming liquidity crisis can very quickly turn into a solvency crisis for financial institutions, a balance of payment crisis for sovereign countries and a full-blown crisis of confidence for the entire world. But the silver lining is that, after every crisis in the past, markets have come out strong to forge new beginnings.

When the dust settled from the collapse, Usd5 trillion in pension money, real estate value, savings and bonds disappeared

During this financial tsunami, Capital Consulting, has diversified into an investment company with Eur5 Billion investment portfolio under management and business interests spanning from consultancy, brokerage, Real estate development and management, Private equity, asset management across a wide range of economic sectors in Cape Verde Islands and other international markets.

Our focus for promotion of Foreign Direct Investment is Africa. For this reason we focus all our energy to attract capital from our investor's network in various markets (USA, GCC, Europe, and Asia) for investment opportunities in Africa.

Remember: Roses are beautiful but they have spikes!

Even though we were very successful, prior to the financial crisis and during the crisis, there have been a lot of lemons and bad experiences which I will share with you so you cannot experience the same when you decide to invest in any country in Africa.

Below I will share just three (3) of the projects we have project managed and the challenges and barriers we have come across:

1. CESARIA RESORT

This project is a resort that was master planned and designed by some of the best designers, architects, and engineers the world knows.

Our company had the pleasure to work on the development of the master plan and design of a 130 million square foot beachfront resort along with big companies like ARUP Engineering, Davis

Langdon Everest, Lab Architecture Australia, Atelier Ten USA, CBRE Richard Ellis, Echarris UK, Woods Bagot Architects, Dxb Lab Arichitects, Dwp Architects Dubai, Corporate Edge, Infoterra 3D, Mac Capital Advisors, and Urbis JHD.

The project was branded after a renown Cape Verdean singer named Cesaria Evora. She is in heaven now. She is the most famous Cape Verdean singer. She has won a Grammy Awards. Among her declared fans are Madonna, US President Bill Clinton, and other celebrities. If you have never heard of Cesaria Evora please look for her music on Youtube and share it with your friends. Her voice is like listening to an angel singing.

At her house once, after drinking a Cognac, she told me after looking at the 3D renderings of the Master Plan of the Resort that she hoped that she would be alive to see it completely built and contributing to the development of our country and our people. Well, the sad thing is that after all the hard work, passion, and years of work, and Eur20million worth of master development costs, marketing, hospitality, offices, and payments to the Government treasury, none of us still haven't seen it being built yet.

Such a beautiful project and with all the right ingredients to make Cape Verde one of the biggest tourism destinations known to Europeans and other tourists. What really happen? Who fault it was?

Again, sadly, the Government of Cape Verde lack of Leadership from the Prime Minister has made it possible for a Government to sign all the agreements that you can possibly think about and given the Foreign Investor all the guarantees that you can think about, and still take 10 years without transferring the title of the land to the investors company.

Case is today with lawyers filling a case against the Cape Verde Government to refund the investor its money back.

Moral of the story, we all worked hard, commit to everything we have signed to with the Government and at the end we are still waiting to see our money back and profits not made.

There is a new Government in power now. They will probably will say oh, it was the previous Government fault. Well, we honestly don't care what you think. We just want our money back and period!

2. FOGO COFFEE / STARBUCKS RESERVE

This project came up as a dream to me and a dear friend of mine named Josephine Sturiale, who lives in the Netherlands, and was born from a Cape Verdean mom and an Italian Dad from Sicily.

Once we were in a business trip in Paris and we went to the Louvre Museum for a visit. At the Louvre there is a Starbucks were we decided to have a coffee after a long walk. After having three different coffees we said to one another: "we should put Fogo Island coffee one day at Starbucks, because these coffees don't taste that good for being one of the special reserve coffees."

Since our company main focus was promoting foreign direct investment into Cape Verde, from that day at Starbucks Louvre we decided to find a company that had the know how to farm, process and export coffee to the international market.

Funny thing is, Josephine found a company in Amsterdam, named Trabocca that was doing a project in Ethiopia with farmers there to farm, process and export organic Arabica coffee.

So I flew from Dubai to Amsterdam one day to meet with the founder of Trabocca and we decided to move ahead with an inspection visit to the Island of Fogo in Cape Verde. Fogo Island is the island I was born and where most of my family is from.

After visiting Fogo Island, and after a meeting with the coffee association that had a factory closed and abandoned for many years, with a coffee industry that was already in coma for many decades, we decided to launch a company named Fogo Coffee Spirit to help revive a 300 year old coffee industry and promote Fogo coffee internationally and eventually export it to Starbucks one day.

In just 3 years we have managed to install all the manufacturing facilities on the island and restructure the industry. On the fourth year we have successfully exported the first 7ton of green coffee to Starbucks Reserve.

Today there is a special Starbucks Reserve Cape Verde as one of the most exclusive coffee Starbucks sells to its clients at its Starbucks Reserve Roastery and Tasting Room, in Seattle - Washington, USA.

WHAT IS STARBUCKS RESERVE?

Starbucks Reserve is Starbucks brand for their rarest, small batch coffees roasted in Seattle. In constant search of great coffee, Starbucks every so often find something special in the most unlikely places - something they can't wait to bring home and share. For these unique, small-lot coffees, they created Starbucks Reserve, an ongoing series of Starbucks rarest and most exotic coffees. Our coffee is among them.

Guess we were right that day at that Starbucks at Louvre Museum in Paris. Today Starbucks Reserve sells our coffee at Usd55/kg.

The factors that make a coffee unique are many, and discovering the extraordinary terroir where they all align - often as small as a single hillside - is something we cherish sharing. Coffee, like wine grapes, gets much of its flavor from specific growing conditions like soil, temperature, elevation, rainfall and sunshine.

Starbucks Reserve coffees often come from remote and rugged places, with limited harvests from lots as small as a family backyard. Whether they purchase a single bag or several, each is extremely limited and can often last only a matter of weeks.

Remember the roses? Well this story too has spikes.

Even though we have managed to achieve all of this our partner on the company, managed to double cross us by hiding profits in Europe while the company in Cape Verde loses a lot of money and it's at financial bankruptcy.

So, today we are in court fighting for what we think is right, to change the business model of the company since they think that we can make all the hard work in Cape Verde to export to Starbucks and to other clients in Japan, Germany, UK, while we export at Eur10/kg (when Eur5 is to pay the farmers and the other Eur5 is for operations of the company and harvest) so they resell our coffee from Europe to Starbucks and buyers in Japan between Eur25-Eur35/kg.

Just to illustrated this on a simple case: imagine you and another partner you owned Mercedes Benz, brand and factory, and that you had a factory and all of your production were sold to one of the partners at a price that the company was not sustainable and was at risk of bankruptcy, while your partner is making profit from its trading and you are not making anything. When you request your partner to change the business model so it can benefit the company and all parties involved they say that they cannot change it because that's the way they have worked for their other projects in Africa. Well, this is Africa too but this is SMART Africa. Same school they went too we went too. So, unless business is done fair to all we will fight until our last breath and really don't care how long it takes to fight in court. May take 100 years, we will still fight for what we think is right and fair.

By the way, in the UK our coffee is sold by a high end roaster named Franco Anglo Coffee that sells it at Harrods Luxury chain on a nice 200gr bottle at GBP50 per unit (yes, that's Usd62 per each 200gr) as one of their line of the top 10 most exclusive coffees in the world, our coffee is branded as Number 6 Cape Verde Fogo.

You are probably saying. Wow! Unbelievable.

3. WEST AFRICA AVIATION HUB & GROUP / CABO VERDE AVIATION HUB

This project came up as a result of my passion for aviation by growing up in an Island that its entire economy for decades depended on the Aviation sector and more particularly to South Africa Airways. When I was a boy our house use to be right next to Sal International Airport and since a young boy I use to see 4 South African Airways Boeing 747 take off daily from Sal International Airport to Atlanta and New York City. This was during the time South Africa was under the apartheid regime. Planes use to take off and the roof of our house would shake all the time while one of the biggest and most beautiful plane

(Boeing 747) ever made would go above our house at a village named Lomba Branca located at the end of Sal International Airport 4km runway.

My experience in Dubai by experiencing the success case of Dubai Aviation business model by Emirates Airlines and Dubai International Airport, as also influence me in designing this project as part of our company´s vision for Cape Verde aviation sector and tourism future.

After seeing how Dubai has successfully developed its aviation market in 2011 we have proposed to the Cape Verde Government to develop a similar project by blueprinting Dubai Aviation success model.

The Government accepted our proposal and we set up a big team of advisors, with companies such as American Appraisal, Lufthansa Consulting, PLMJ Lawyers, with a major European Airline Group as our aviation partners to help transform Cape Verde Islands into the Aviation HUB in West Africa to connect 50million passengers and 5million tons of cargo between three continents (Africa, Americas, and Europe) in a 25 years period.

Cape Verde Islands strategic location within the Atlantic Ocean makes it a perfect air & sea hub for the cross road of West Africa to Europe, North America and South America to Europe, giving Cape Verde the ability through is Special Partnership with Europe and being a World Trade

Organization & ECOWAS Member to have access to more than 2 Billion potential consumer.

At 450 km of the African Western Coast, in the middle of the Atlantic Ocean, Cape Verde benefits of a strategic geographical location, between the African, European and American continents, at 4 hours of flight to Europe, 3 hours and a half to South America, 6 hours to USA, and 2 hours to the West coast of Africa.

Our mission for this investment opportunity as the promoters and consulting company specialized in promoting Foreign Direct Investment into Africa was to attract foreign investors, international airline partners to become Airline Equity partners of a major holding controlled by the Cape Verde Government, and attract Private Equity Investors with interest in being part of this lucrative aviation investment opportunity for Africa.

We had received support letters from the Minister of Infrastructure, President of the Investment Agency, President of the Airports of Cape Verde. So we decided to spend a lot of our own funds to promote investment road shows in Dubai, Abu Dhabi and Europe, which has received a lot of interest from many investors in the GCC, as well as infrastructure development banks such as DEG Invest from KFW Bank group, and expression of interest from one of the biggest Airport management company in the world – Munich Airport FMG.

After all the success in marketing the project internationally, it was time to move ahead with phase 1 of the project which was the feasibility of the international operations of the Airline that would become the major airline of the Aviation HUB. Since the Government wanted to become part of it, they decided to include the National Airline as part of the project. So we requested them to fund the feasibility studies for the international airlines routes and they said it was not in their interest to progress with the studies. Reallyyyyy? Amazing.

As I mentioned on a previous chapter we decided to put the project on hold back them. Well, the rest of the story you know because I have mentioned on a previous chapter when the new Government that came into power contacted us to support with the Privatization of the National Airline, TACV Cabo Verde Airlines, and we decided to rebrand the project to Cabo Verde Aviation HUB.

The story end up the same. Government after Government trying to use us and use our network to get what they want, for free.

You are probably thinking now, so give up on Cape Verde. There must be a real problem of leadership there. Well, history showed us that Cape Verde is not a single case. Let me share Zambia's case with you.

ZAMBIA GOVERNMENT ON AIRPLANE MODE

In 2014 we were invited by the Government of Zambia to fly there and meet the Minister of Transport, his entire team, Civil Aviation Authority, and the Chief of the Cabinet of the President of the Country.

The invitation was to come and support the Government with the setup of their National Airline and to help transform Zambia into an Aviation HUB for the Southern region of Africa.

After a couple of days of meetings and introducing a solution to the Government here is what the Minister of Transport of Zambia wrote to us, which I literally transcript, from his letter dated March 31st 2014:

****

Mr. Saidy Andrade
Group Chairman & CEO
Capital Consulting

Subject: Establishment of Zambia National Airline & SADC Aviation Hub

I refer to your presentation at our Ministry on 7th of February 2014 on your proposal to work with the Zambian Government to establish a National Airline and Regional Aviation Hub serving the Southern African Region.

As per your offer, we are interested to have preferential access to a leading European Aviation

Group to develop a Joint Venture Airline Partnership (as a Private Public Partnership project) with our Government in order to launch the Zambian National Airline and allow Zambia to have direct access to Europe and America within 2014.

While we are proud of our past achievements, our airports infrastructure plans for the region are ambitious. Our current efforts in developing international airports to connect Zambia to the world are a testament to our Government´s vision in our Aviation Industry. These airports are further proof that we are delivering on our key strategic pillars of providing a safe, secure and responsible airport environment; capacity to meet airline and economic growth plans; world class service and innovation; revenue and value, all underpinned by great people, effective systems and processes with sound corporate governance systems.

Having a strong national airline carrier is vital for the country's long term development in the SADC region. We believe the establishment of a National Airline will boost our Aviation and Tourism industries, which will contribute to accelerate GDP growth and create employment for our citizens. As you demonstrated in your presentation, we believe this is a viable project which will not only generate new income but also save the country from loss of foreign currency.

In this regard, we are currently going through the normal project processing. Once concluded we will get back to you.

Yours sincerely,

Minister of Transport, Works, Supply &
Communications
Government of Zambia

****

Guess what? We are in 2017, three (3) years later, and we still haven't heard back from the Government. The Government has changed, there is a new Minister of Transport and even a new President in the Cabinet.

Like I mentioned on the chapter about Patience and Airplane mode, I guess Zambia is still on Airplane mode. Perhaps they will get in touch when they decide to unlock the country and take advantage of the possibilities that they have for being one of the richest and largest exporters of copper in the world.

How the hell can you not have your own Airline when you are one of the biggest copper exporters in the World? Seriously! Unbelievable is all we can say.

Let me share more about a different issue when it comes to promote Foreign Direct Investment into Africa.

GOVERNMENTS & PRIVATE SECTOR BIGGEST ISSUES IN FDI

The reason we have too many Governments and private companies looking for our services is because two key ingredients are the biggest barriers for Governments and Private sector developers in Africa. These barriers are:

1. Promotion of the country and projects in the international market to attract investors;

2. Access to capital from different sources in the international market;

It seems marketing and attracting capital it is something magical to most people. To me it all depends on how you see the world and understanding where money is flowing to.

Stefanina once taught me a great lesson. He said and I quote: "money will always flow to where it feels safe and not stressed." This has been one of the greatest lessons I have learned and so far it has helped me be a better business man and understand much better how the world works.

There will always be money flowing all over the world, no matter how many financial crises happen over the years. So you just need to learn how to follow the flow of money and go after it to attract it to invest where you want. Investors do not like uncertainty and instability, uncertainty around central bank policies and elevated geopolitical risks all weight on decision to invest more on FDI.

That said, it must seem easy but without a network is impossible even for Governments to convince investors that their country and their projects are the right opportunity for their money.

This is where we have focused a lot for the last 10 years. Building a strong network will help you find money even in the Moon.

There is a brilliant quote that says "your network is your net worth!"

For many years we have promoted investment opportunities from Africa in markets such as Saudi Arabia, Dubai, Abu Dhabi, Europe, Singapore, and China.

Because of our coffee success story in Africa, beside the spikes, we have just received an invitation to go to Sao Tome & Principe to help the Government revive the coffee and cocoa industry. This country is like Eden garden on earth. I am going to fly there for the first time but from pictures you can really tell that it is so beautiful that it is impossible to exist such a place on planet Earth.

Before I met my wife, Maria Andrade, the mother of Zion, she went there and for years she has been telling me we should go to Sao Tome & Principe one day because I would love it.

So, next month I will fly to Sao Tome & Principe to meet with the Minister of Agriculture, the Prime Minister, and some other people to discuss a public private partnership to set up a holding between our company and the Government to resuscitate old farms that use to produce more than 10.000 tons of coffee and cocoa all together. All it needs is factories, people to understand about farming, which they have, harvest, and process, store the processed beans in jute bags, and export the dam bags to clients internationally. In terms of annual revenues we are talking about Usd150 million worth of trading. Hopefully we will not end up in the same Airplane mode as other cases we have experienced.

You should check it out. Sao Tome & Principe. China is going to spend Usd800 million to build a new deep sea water port there. Countries from all over the world are flying there now to try to seat with the Government to develop partnerships. Guess why? They just found Oil a couple of years ago, and beside Oil there is a huge potential for Agribusiness, Fishing, and Tourism.

Hopefully in a couple of years we will hear about Sao Tome & Principe as a success story in Africa. And hopefully we will be one of the game changers helping the people of Sao Tome & Principe develop into a great economy so they can become happier and more hopeful about their future and their children's future.

TITANIUM SPIRIT

Being an entrepreneur is never easy. Especially in Africa. But we have always found strengthen to keep going and keep fighting for what we believe.

To succeed in Africa you must be patient but also have a Spirit made of Titanium so you can keep your focus on the future and have faith the future will be much better than the entire struggle.

To finish this chapter let me share a story about a Titanium Spirit that is one of those stories that gives me strength to keep going forward. This story is about someone we all know, his brand is ridiculously famous worldwide, but most people probably don't know what storms he had gone through to reach to where his company and brand is today.

It's Phil Knight, the founder of Nike. In his recent book Shoe Dog, Phil Knight's memoir about the creation of Nike. He explains in an honest way what the path to business success really looks like. It's messy, and chaotic journey riddled with mistakes, endless struggles, and sacrifice. In fact, the only thing that seems inevitable when reading Knight's story is that his company will end in failure before you finish reading the book.

He started his shoe import business, known then as Blue Ribbon Sports, with Usd50 he borrowed from his father. It was the beginning of many years of living in debt. Year after year, he would go on his knees to his bankers to beg for more credit so he could import shoes from a Japanese supplier. He rarely had any savings in the bank because he would plow all of his profits back into the company to order more shoes from Japan. Even as sales of his shoes took off, his business was constantly on life support. Well, we know how it feels like to be on Survival mode and waiting for great things to happen.

Failure, of course, is about the last thing people would associate with Nike. The company's sales top Usd30 billion and Nike is today one of the most globally recognized brands across planet earth. If Aliens come one day they will definitely buy Nikes and take some as gifts for their families.

Congratulations for all the achievements Phil. Only a Titanium Spirit can handle so many struggles and have faith that at the end you will be successful no matter what.

A research done by Jim Collins, and his team as he mentions it, on a book named Good to Great, Why some Companies Make the Leap and others Don't, they found out that successful companies that have achieved Greatness and their clients love their brands, are all companies that the founders have always believed that no matter how big the struggles and the storms they had to go through, they had always faith that at the end they would prevail.

ADVICE WHEN IT COMES TO FOREIGN INVESTMENT IN AFRICA

Despite all of our hardships we have experienced in Africa along the way, we don't regret any of our experiences. They are just lessons learned, from which we have learned a lot. So, my advice is even if it takes 100 years for your company to be successful, Never, Ever Give Up, and keep fighting until your last breath! If you don't achieve greatness your sons will keep up with the fight until one day they can say my dad or my mom made this possible. How cool is that? So, Have faith, Patience, and have fun while you try to develop some crazy projects to make this world a better place to us all. And off course, please make sure you do most of them in Africa.

Like Thomas Edison once said brilliantly about success, and I quote: "I have not failed 10.000 times. I've successfully found 10.000 ways that will not work."

"Always bear in mind that people are not fighting for ideas, or for the things in anyone's mind. They are fighting to win material benefits, to live better and in peace, to see their lives move forward, to guarantee the future of their children." Amilcar Cabral

CHAPTER 10: Africa Brain Export – why does everyone want immigration?

Beside the people that really don't have a choice but to leave their country due to political instability, war, and other circumstances that force them to leave their country to search for a better life in a country abroad, this chapter of the book I will speak about only the part of our generation that is willing to leave everything behind to search for a life with more meaning than just waiting at their country for a miracle to happen while they get old.

Immigration Statistics

- There is significant migration from Africa to Europe. There is an estimated 7 million African migrants living in OECD countries. Of these, about half are of North African origin, mostly residing in France, Italy, Belgium, Spain and the Netherlands, while the other half are of Sub-Saharan African origin, present throughout Western Europe, with significant concentrations in Belgium, France, Italy, the Netherlands, Portugal, Spain and the United Kingdom;

- African immigration to the United States has been comparatively slight, totaling around 3.5million individuals;

AFRICAN POPULATION IN EUROPE

Approximate populations of African origin in Europe:

- Arabs and Berbers (including North African and Middle Eastern Arabs): approx. 5 million, mostly in France, Italy, the Netherlands, Belgium, Germany, United Kingdom, Sweden, Spain, Norway, Denmark, Switzerland, Greece and Russia;

- Sub-Equatorial Africans: approx. 5 million; mostly in Italy, France, the United Kingdom, Germany, Spain, the Netherlands and Portugal;

- Horn Africans: approx. 1 million, mostly Somalis and Eritreans, mostly in United Kingdom, Germany, Sweden, the Netherlands, Norway, Denmark, Finland;

- Ethnic Europeans with colonial roots: approx. 8 million; mostly in France, United Kingdom, Greece and Belgium;

- North African Jews: approx. 500 thousands; mostly in France;

MIGRATION FLOWS

From 2000-2005, an estimated 440.000 people per year emigrated from Africa, most of them to Europe.

According to Hein de Haas, the director of the International Migration Institute at the University of Oxford, public discourse on African migration to Europe portrays the phenomenon as an "exodus", largely composed of irregular migrants, driven by conflict and poverty. He criticizes this portrayal, arguing that the irregular migrants are often well educated and able to afford the considerable cost of the journey to Europe. Migration from Africa to Europe, he argues, "is fueled by a structural demand for cheap migrant labour in informal sectors". Most migrate on their own initiative, rather than being the victims of traffickers. Furthermore, he argues that whereas the media and popular perceptions see irregular migrants as mostly arriving by sea, most actually arrive on tourist visas or with false documentation, or enter via the Spanish enclaves, Ceuta and Melilla. He states that "the majority of irregular African migrants enters Europe legally and subsequently overstays their visas".

Similarly, migration expert Stephen Castles argues that "Despite the media hysteria on the growth of African migration to Europe, actual numbers seem quite small - although there is a surprising lack of precision in the data".

According to the Organization for Economic Co-operation & Development (OECD), migration from African countries to more developed states is small in comparison to overall migration worldwide.

ILLEGAL IMMIGRATION

Illegal immigration from Africa to Europe is significant. Many people from poor African countries embark on the dangerous journey for Europe, in hopes of a better life. In parts of Africa, particularly Mauritania and Morocco, trafficking of immigrants to Europe has become more lucrative than drug trafficking. But some illegal immigrants die during the journey and most of them who do not get asylum awe deported back to Africa. Libya is also a major departure point for irregular migrants setting off for Europe.

Between October 2013 and October 2014, the Italian government ran Operation Mare Nostrum, a naval and air operation intended to reduce irregular immigration to Europe and the incidence of migratory ship wreckages off the coast of Lampedusa. The Italian government ceased the operation as it was judged to be unsustainable, involving a large proportion of the Italian navy. The operation was replaced by a more limited joint EU border protection operation, named Operation Triton managed by the EU border agency, Frontex.

Some other European governments, including Britain's, argued that the operations such as Mare Nostrum and Triton serve to provide an "unintended pull factor" encouraging further migration.

EUROPEAN MIGRATION POLICIES

The European Union does not have a common immigration policy regarding nationals of third countries. Some countries, such as Spain and Malta, have called for other EU member states to share the responsibility of dealing with migration flows from Africa. Spain has also created legal migration routes for African migrants, recruiting workers from countries including Senegal. Other states, such as France under the presidency of Nicolas Sarkozy, have adopted more restrictive policies, and tried to offer incentives for migrants to return to Africa. While adopting a more liberal approach than France, Spain has also, according to a Council on Foreign Relations report, "attempted to forge broad bilateral accords with African countries that would exchange repatriation for funding to help the returned migrants".

Spain has also run regularization programs in order to grant employment rights to previously irregular immigrants, most notably in 2005, but this has been the subject of criticism from other EU Governments, which argue that it encourages further irregular migration and that regularized migrants are likely to move within the EU to richer states once they have status in Spain.

De Haas argues that restrictive European immigration policies have generally failed to reduce migration flows from Africa because they do not address the underlying structural demand for labor in European states.

Dirk Kohnert argues that EU countries' policies on migration from Africa are focused mainly on security and the closing of borders. He is also skeptical that the EU's programs that are designed to promote economic development in West Africa will result in reduced migration.

Stephen Castles argues that there is a "sedentary bias" in developed states' migration policies towards Africa. He argues that "it has become the conventional wisdom to argue that promoting economic development in the Global South has the potential to reduce migration to the North. This carries the clear implication that such migration is a bad thing, and poor people should stay put".

Wow! Now let's reverse the facts back to Africa.

Did you know that there are more Europeans in Africa, than Africans in Europe?

Reallyyyyy! Hahahahaha! Nice. I have to share the following facts I have just read about Mawuna Koutonin named The Truth about Africa Immigration: Where do they Go?

Mawuna Koutonin is a world peace activist who relentlessly works to empower people to express their full potential and pursue their dreams, regardless of their background. He is the Editor of SiliconAfrica.com, Founder of Goodbuzz.net, and Social activist for Africa Renaissance. Koutonin's ultimate dream is to open a world-class human potential development school in Africa in 2017.

Here are some facts from Mawuna Koutonin research:

- In South Africa only, there are over 6 million Europeans;

- In Zimbabwe only there are more than half a million British;

- Also, did you know that there are more Arabs in Africa than in the Middle East. And, there are more Indians, Pakistanis and Bangladeshis in Africa than in UK and all Europeans countries combined;

- Africans welcome all those people without ever committing a Genocide or racist crime on them. In contrary, most of those immigrants have very good positions and social status;

- If Africa has to chase Europeans, Asians back home, like some are talking about Africans in Europe, those who will suffer the most are the Europeans;

- Contrary to what you hear on BBC, CNN, RFI, Africans are not desperate folks seeking prosperity in Europe;

- The World Bank estimates that Africa has about 30 million international migrants, but the size of its diaspora, including unrecorded migrants and second- and third-generation migrants, is significantly larger;

- Regardless of the "poverty porn" of the western Medias depicting Africa as a place of despair forcing its hungry and uneducated kids to invade Europe, the reality is far from the truth. A recent data crunch by the awesome guys at Peoplemov.in clearly shows that not a single African country is in the list of the world top emigration countries, but the vast majority of African migrants just go to another African country.

Check out his research, as it also shows data from every single country in Africa where there top destinations for immigration is.

THE DREAM OF A BETTER LIFE

If you look at different researches of why people decide to immigrate to a foreign country, you will find that the most common reasons are as follow, contrary to what you may think:

- Crime, government corruption, and a better future for their children;

- People don't want to leave their country, but feel they have to leave. The push factor is a better future for their children;

- ongoing disruption to life and business working environment;

- Feed up with life and the way their country works;

It's sad when you hear young graduated university students saying "I have no hope for my future, there is no jobs, no money and nothing for myself and my family here in my Country".

Why do young people lose hope?

Well, it brings us back to the subject of corruption and government leaders not caring for them citizens, and only focusing on their own political gang, by giving jobs to their boys and family members. This is the reality all over Africa. Political Patronage. No matter how Good Governance you read about in the media about how successful a country is, the reality is that the country does not work the same for everyone. If you know someone, you will get a job, if you don't know anyone then you are on your own. Unfortunately that's the reality still in Africa in the 21st century. There should be a universal law states that Political Patronage should be considered as a way of corruption in the eyes of any Democracy.

AFRICA BRAIN DRAINAGE

Sadly there is a huge number of graduated young people that went to university in Europe, USA, Brazil, China, Russia, and other countries that are returning back to find out that their country really don't have any plans for them.

So the result is a huge number of youth trying to find a better life elsewhere. Normally most don't really care if it is USA or Europe because they would need to go on a working via or try the illegal way, which is getting a tourist visa fly there and then stay illegally hoping that things will work out eventually.

When you feel sad in your own country you will do anything to go anywhere that gives you hope of a better life. This is pure human nature. No one wants to stay stuck without any hope for the future and without any means to support its family. It breaks your heart and your soul.

So the best brains and the youngest people from my generation (the Crazy Millennials) are all looking to fly and live elsewhere (especially across Africa) beside their own country. Unfortunately this is a sad reality.

AFRICAN MIGRANTS: WHAT REALLY DRIVES THEM TO EUROPE?

Try to watch a special coverage that the media channel Aljazeera made about Africa   migration to Europe, named African migrants: What really drives them to Europe? This short coverage will make you cry from your soul, because it shows how thousands of Africans are putting their lives at risk as they go on boat journeys in search of what they think would be a better and easier living. It is a journey that begins with hope, but often ends in despair.

IF EVERYONE LEAVES WHO WILL BE PART OF FUTURE GOVERNMENTS?

Well, I guess this is the whole idea from the African leaders that are Corrupt and don't want to leave power ever. If they leave one day they want to make sure that their family members stay in Power. How is this considered Democracy? Guess is not, and they don't really care, unless the African Union, the United Nations, and all the international agencies that really care about fighting for freedom so people around the world can have a better future decide to step forward and make these corrupt leaders get out of Power.

My next chapter is about these basterds, who they are exactly, and how many decades they have been in Power.

"The world will not be destroyed by those who do evil, but by those who watch them without doing anything." Albert Einstein

CHAPTER 11: Corrupt Africa Leaders. Why are they still in Power?

I will probably go into so many black lists to ban me from entering the following countries in Africa that I will mention after I write this chapter, because I will mention the most corrupt Presidents and what they are doing to their people and their own country. But honestly I really don't care. Like Kurt Cobain once said: "the duty of youth is to challenge corruption."

So, I Challenge the following Corrupt Presidents and Countries to prove the world wrong about themselves and their family members wealth. If you are not corrupt disclose to your people and to the world how did you, your gang of ministers and your families managed to become millionaires after going into power and your people still leave with Usd1 a day to survive.

Coup d'état's, violence characterizes leadership in Africa, and dictatorship and some scholars have argued that Democracy is not an African ideology. Historically, leadership in Africa was based on conquest and monarchy and then colonialism. Following colonialism, dictatorship continued in many parts of Africa.

Regardless of how they came to power, these people are regarded as the worst dictators in Africa.

The regime of most of these African dictators was marked by horror, terror, chaos and bloodshed. Some of these dictators were notorious leaders, and some have led their country towards economic prosperity while others started on the right path and lost their way.

Below is the Corrupt Gang that has been in power more than 2 to 3 decades:

EQUATORIAL GUINEA

Being one of the wealthiest nations in the world beating Saudi Arabia, Korea and Italy combined. Equatorial Guinea has also managed to become one of African most corrupt countries. It is one thing to take bribes, but to put the entire nation below 60% poverty rate is almost Ludicrous. As most citizens of Equatorial Guinea survive under Usd1 per day, it has truly managed to become a prominent addition to the list of 10 most corrupt countries in Africa.

Teodoro Obiang Nguema Mbasogo has been President of Equatorial Guinea since 1979 when he ousted his uncle, Francisco Macias Nguema, in a bloody military coup and sentenced him to death by firing squad. President Obiang is one of the oldest and longest serving dictators in Africa.

Years in power: 38 years.

Equatorial Guinea's has emerged as a significant oil producer under Obiang. He also served as the Chairperson of the African Union from 31 January 2011 to 29 January 2012.

State-operated radio declared President Obiang "the country's god" with "all power over men and things," and thereby he "can decide to kill without anyone calling him to account and without going to hell." Unlawful killings, government-sanctioned kidnappings; torture of prisoners by security forces, and even accusations of cannibalism has trailed President Obiang's regime. Forbes estimates his wealth to be around Usd600 million; he has used an oil boom to enrich his family at the expense of the citizens of Equatorial Guinea.

ANGOLA

Jose Eduardo dos Santos, the father of Africa's richest woman Isabel dos Santos, is Africa's second longest-serving head of state, behind Equatorial Guinea's Teodoro Obiang Nguema Mbasogo. He has been in power since 1979, and in 2017, he announced that he would finally step down and end his dictatorship over Angola.

Years in power: 38 years.

The Angolan economy has grown to become the third-largest economy in Sub-Saharan Africa, after South Africa and Nigeria.

Strong allegations of corruption, misuse, and diversion of public funds for personal gain, human rights abuses, and political oppression. 70% of the population of Angola lives on less than Usd2 a day and yet the Dos Santos family has amassed a massive sum of personal wealth with Angola's oil proceeds.

Having corrupt officials in the government has become a norm for many countries, but the entire government swindling few hundred million dollars for personal gain is unheard of. Angola is one African country which has managed to gain quite a reputation for itself as one of the most corrupt countries in the world. Since not being able to account for more than Usd5 billion in the past 10 years, Angola has managed to become the 4th most corrupt country in Africa and is also on the world's top ten most corrupt countries list.

CAMEROON

Paul Biya has been the President of Cameroon since 6 November 1982. He consolidated power in a 1983 –1984 power struggle with his predecessor and he remains a powerhouse in Africa and the president of Cameroon till today.

Years in power: 35 years.

Cameroon has enjoyed peace and stability for the past 30 years. Paul Biya's regime has also overseen one of the strongest diplomatic relations in Africa.

Paul Biya has kept himself in power by organizing sham elections and paying international observers to certify them free of irregularities, the top African leader, and dictator who has been accused of constant human right abuse, was ranked 19th in Parade Magazine's Top 20 list of "The World's Worst Dictators."

Surveys show that 62% of Cameroonians paid a bribe in the last year. Of the respondents, 81% felt that the judiciary is very corrupt, and 71% felt that corruption was rife in academic institutions. More disappointing is that 46% of the respondents feel that corruption has increased over the last 2 years; only 30% felt that corruption had decreased.

UGANDA

Yoweri Kaguta Museveni is a Ugandan politician who has been President of Uganda since 29 January 1986.

Years in power: 31 years.

Museveni was involved in rebellions that toppled Ugandan leaders Idi Amin (1971–79) and Milton Obote (1980–85). With the notable exception of the north, Museveni has brought relative stability and economic growth to a country that has endured decades of rebel activity and civil war. His tenure has also witnessed one of the most effective national responses to HIV/AIDS in Africa.

In the mid to late 1990s, Museveni was celebrated by the west as part of a new generation of African leaders. His presidency has been marred, however, by involvement in civil war in the Democratic Republic of Congo and other Great Lakes region conflicts. Rebellion in the north by the Lord's Resistance Army had perpetuated a drastic humanitarian emergency.

President Museveni and his government have repeatedly promised to stamp out corruption, but major corruption scandals resurface in government departments and ministries.

Many rural schools in Uganda remain in a poor state and there are regular teachers' strikes over low pay. The health system is ailing, with more doctors preferring to work in foreign countries where they can receive better salaries. The country loses up to Usd258.6 million per year due to corruption, according to the African Peer Review Mechanism report.

ZIMBABWE

Robert Gabriel Mugabe is the current President of Zimbabwe and one of the oldest dictators in Africa. He has been in power since 1980 when he was prime minister of Zimbabwe before he consolidated his power to become president on 31st December 1987.

Years in power: 30 years.

The United Nations estimates Unemployment in Zimbabwe to be as high as 80%. The economy of Zimbabwe is in ruins, and life expectancy for both male and females is a little above 50 years. Massive hyperinflation has made the local currency of Zimbabwe worthless, the exchange rate of Zimbabwe dollar is 36 quadrillion to Usd1. The local currency has been retired and replaced with the US dollar and South African rand, and this has led to the near collapse of the manufacturing industry in Zimbabwe.

Zimbabwe boasts of one of the most impressive education systems in Africa.

Zimbabwe also has a very high literacy rate, one of Zimbabwe's pride.

At 90 Mugabe leads Zimbabwe, he still has a spring in his stride, and he is very eloquent. Coming to the English language the man speaks the Queen's language better than the rest of the World.

Dictator, thug, thief, murderer, ruthless, demented, ferocious, the most dangerous person, destroyer, die hard, diamond thief, selfish are some of the words used to describe the man.

SUDAN

Sudanese President, Omar al-Bashir has been the leader of Sudan since 1989 when he took power in a military coup. Al-Bashir is one of the most brutal dictators in Africa and despite ICC's warrant against him; he remains the president of Sudan.

Years in power: 28 years.

The International Criminal Court wants Omar al-Bashir for genocide, war crimes, murder, torture, and other crimes against humanity for his crimes in Darfur.

CHAD

In December 1990, Idriss Deby and his Patriotic Salvation Movement, an insurgent group, backed by Libya and Sudan sacked the incumbent government, and Deby became the President of Chad.

Years in power: 27 years.

Deby has used oil proceeds and funds that could have been used to develop Chad to purchase weapons and strengthen his Army. Forbes named Chad the world's most corrupt nations in 2006. It described Deby's decision to buy weapons with the funds supposedly intended to counter famine as "what may turn out to be the single most piggish use of philanthropic funds."

GAMBIA

Yahya Jammeh took power in a bloodless military coup in 1994. Jammeh got re-elected as the 2016 general elections to Adama Barrow, and surprisingly, he conceded defeat. Only to reject the results few weeks after, he finally left Gambia on exile to Equatorial Guinea after sustained pressure by the African Union, ECOWAS, and UN.

Years in power: 23 years.

Strong human rights abuses have marked Yahya Jammeh's regime, he also claims to have a cure for HIV Aids and his hate for homosexuality is well documented, recently, he threatened to slit the throats of any homosexual in Gambia.

Africa has come a long way, and it continues to overcome setbacks and rewrite its history. These dictators represent the worst moments in post-colonial African history. I wonder if during colonial time these African countries were better off.

So why are these Presidents still in Power? Isn't there anyone in their country better off than these guys? Fear is their power over their people. Military power.

Kofi Annan once said that "Many African leaders refuse to send their troops on peace keeping missions abroad because they probably need their armies to intimidate their own populations."

So this is what have been happening in most of the countries were Presidents are in power more than 3 decades stilling all the country wealth from their people and enriching their family members and politicians which are part of their gang.

How can Africa keep moving forward and how can these countries see a brighter day one day?

Like Einstein said once "The world will not be destroyed by those who do evil, but by those who watch them without doing anything." So, African Union, the United Nations, European Union, USA, please do something to take this greed politicians out of power.

I am quite sure all the international agencies and countries that have signed the Universal Declaration of Human Rights can choose out of the following Humans Rights to invoke a mix of rights to protect a country that has been under dictatorship, tyranny and oppression by its Leaders for decades:

1. Right to Life, Liberty, Personal Security.

2. Right to Equality.

3. Freedom of Discrimination.

4. Freedom from Slavery.

5. Freedom from torture and degrading treatment.

6. Right to Recognition as a Person before the Law.

7. Right to Equality before the Law.

8. Freedom from Arbitrary Arrest and Exile.

9. Right to Asylum in other Countries from Persecution.

10. Freedom of Belief and Religion.

11. Freedom of Opinion and Information.

12. Right to Participate in Government and in Free Elections

Otherwise what's the point having an African Union and a United Nations to protect the weaker against the strongest from their abuse of Power?

The Universal Declaration of Human Rights (UDHR) is a milestone document in the history of human rights. Drafted by representatives with different legal and cultural backgrounds from all regions of the world, the Declaration was proclaimed by the United Nations General Assembly in Paris on 10 December 1948 (General Assembly resolution 217 A) as a common standard of achievements for all peoples and all nations. It sets out, for the first time, fundamental human rights to be universally protected and it has been translated into over 500 languages.

Bellow I share with you the transcript of the Universal Declaration of Human Rights just like it was approved by the United Nations:

PREAMBLE

Whereas recognition of the inherent dignity and of the equal and inalienable rights of all members of the human family is the foundation of freedom, justice and peace in the world,

Whereas disregard and contempt for human rights have resulted in barbarous acts which have outraged the conscience of mankind, and the advent of a world in which human beings shall enjoy freedom of speech and belief and freedom from fear and want has been proclaimed as the highest aspiration of the common people,

Whereas it is essential, if man is not to be compelled to have recourse, as a last resort, to rebellion against tyranny and oppression, that human rights should be protected by the rule of law,

Whereas it is essential to promote the development of friendly relations between nations,

Whereas the peoples of the United Nations have in the Charter reaffirmed their faith in fundamental human rights, in the dignity and worth of the human person and in the equal rights of men and women and have determined to promote social progress and better standards of life in larger freedom,

Whereas Member States have pledged themselves to achieve, in co-operation with the United Nations, the promotion of universal respect for and observance of human rights and fundamental freedoms,

Whereas a common understanding of these rights and freedoms is of the greatest importance for the full realization of this pledge,

Now, Therefore THE GENERAL ASSEMBLY proclaims THIS UNIVERSAL DECLARATION OF HUMAN RIGHTS as a common standard of achievement for all peoples and all nations, to the end that every individual and every organ of society, keeping this Declaration constantly in mind, shall strive by teaching and education to promote respect for these rights and freedoms and by progressive measures, national and international, to secure their universal and effective recognition and observance, both among the peoples of Member States themselves and among the peoples of territories under their jurisdiction.

ARTICLE 1

All human beings are born free and equal in dignity and rights. They are endowed with reason and conscience and should act towards one another in a spirit of brotherhood.

ARTICLE 2

Everyone is entitled to all the rights and freedoms set forth in this Declaration, without distinction of any kind, such as race, colour, sex, language, religion, political or other opinion, national or social origin, property, birth or other status. Furthermore, no distinction shall be made on the basis of the political, jurisdictional or international status of the country or territory to which a person belongs, whether it be independent, trust, non-self-governing or under any other limitation of sovereignty.

ARTICLE 3

Everyone has the right to life, liberty and security of person.

ARTICLE 4

No one shall be held in slavery or servitude; slavery and the slave trade shall be prohibited in all their forms.

ARTICLE 5

No one shall be subjected to torture or to cruel, inhuman or degrading treatment or punishment.

ARTICLE 6

Everyone has the right to recognition everywhere as a person before the law.

ARTICLE 7

All are equal before the law and are entitled without any discrimination to equal protection of the law. All are entitled to equal protection against any discrimination in violation of this Declaration and against any incitement to such discrimination.

ARTICLE 8

Everyone has the right to an effective remedy by the competent national tribunals for acts violating the fundamental rights granted him by the constitution or by law.

ARTICLE 9

No one shall be subjected to arbitrary arrest, detention or exile.

ARTICLE 10

Everyone is entitled in full equality to a fair and public hearing by an independent and impartial tribunal, in the determination of his rights and obligations and of any criminal charge against him.

ARTICLE 11

(1) Everyone charged with a penal offence has the right to be presumed innocent until proved guilty

according to law in a public trial at which he has had all the guarantees necessary for his defense.

(2) No one shall be held guilty of any penal offence on account of any act or omission which did not constitute a penal offence, under national or international law, at the time when it was committed. Nor shall a heavier penalty be imposed than the one that was applicable at the time the penal offence was committed.

ARTICLE 12

No one shall be subjected to arbitrary interference with his privacy, family, home or correspondence, nor to attacks upon his honor and reputation. Everyone has the right to the protection of the law against such interference or attacks.

ARTICLE 13

(1) Everyone has the right to freedom of movement and residence within the borders of each state.

(2) Everyone has the right to leave any country, including his own, and to return to his country.

ARTICLE 14

(1) Everyone has the right to seek and to enjoy in other countries asylum from persecution.

(2) This right may not be invoked in the case of prosecutions genuinely arising from non-political crimes or from acts contrary to the purposes and principles of the United Nations.

ARTICLE 15

(1) Everyone has the right to a nationality.

(2) No one shall be arbitrarily deprived of his nationality nor denied the right to change his nationality.

ARTICLE 16

(1) Men and women of full age, without any limitation due to race, nationality or religion, have the right to marry and to found a family. They are entitled to equal rights as to marriage, during marriage and at its dissolution.

(2) Marriage shall be entered into only with the free and full consent of the intending spouses.

(3) The family is the natural and fundamental group unit of society and is entitled to protection by society and the State.

ARTICLE 17

(1) Everyone has the right to own property alone as well as in association with others.

(2) No one shall be arbitrarily deprived of his property.

ARTICLE 18

Everyone has the right to freedom of thought, conscience and religion; this right includes freedom to change his religion or belief, and freedom, either alone or in community with others and in public or private, to manifest his religion or belief in teaching, practice, worship and observance.

ARTICLE 19

Everyone has the right to freedom of opinion and expression; this right includes freedom to hold opinions without interference and to seek, receive and impart information and ideas through any media and regardless of frontiers.

ARTICLE 20

(1) Everyone has the right to freedom of peaceful assembly and association.

(2) No one may be compelled to belong to an association.

ARTICLE 21

(1) Everyone has the right to take part in the government of his country, directly or through freely chosen representatives.

(2) Everyone has the right of equal access to public service in his country.

(3) The will of the people shall be the basis of the authority of government; this will shall be expressed in periodic and genuine elections which shall be by universal and equal suffrage and shall be held by secret vote or by equivalent free voting procedures.

ARTICLE 22

Everyone, as a member of society, has the right to social security and is entitled to realization, through national effort and international co-operation and in accordance with the organization and resources of each State, of the economic, social and cultural rights indispensable for his dignity and the free development of his personality.

ARTICLE 23

(1) Everyone has the right to work, to free choice of employment, to just and favorable conditions of work and to protection against unemployment.

(2) Everyone, without any discrimination, has the right to equal pay for equal work.

(3) Everyone who works has the right to just and favorable remuneration ensuring for himself and his family an existence worthy of human dignity, and supplemented, if necessary, by other means of social protection.

(4) Everyone has the right to form and to join trade unions for the protection of his interests.

ARTICLE 24

Everyone has the right to rest and leisure, including reasonable limitation of working hours and periodic holidays with pay.

ARTICLE 25

(1) Everyone has the right to a standard of living adequate for the health and well-being of himself and of his family, including food, clothing, housing and medical care and necessary social services, and the right to security in the event of unemployment, sickness, disability, widowhood, old age or other lack of livelihood in circumstances beyond his control.

(2) Motherhood and childhood are entitled to special care and assistance. All children, whether born in or out of wedlock, shall enjoy the same social protection.

ARTICLE 26

(1) Everyone has the right to education. Education shall be free, at least in the elementary and fundamental stages. Elementary education shall be compulsory. Technical and professional education shall be made generally available and higher education shall be equally accessible to all on the basis of merit.

(2) Education shall be directed to the full development of the human personality and to the strengthening of respect for human rights and fundamental freedoms. It shall promote understanding, tolerance and friendship among all nations, racial or religious groups, and shall further the activities of the United Nations for the maintenance of peace.

(3) Parents have a prior right to choose the kind of education that shall be given to their children.

ARTICLE 27

(1) Everyone has the right freely to participate in the cultural life of the community, to enjoy the arts and to share in scientific advancement and its benefits.

(2) Everyone has the right to the protection of the moral and material interests resulting from any scientific, literary or artistic production of which he is the author.

ARTICLE 28

Everyone is entitled to a social and international order in which the rights and freedoms set forth in this Declaration can be fully realized.

ARTICLE 29

(1) Everyone has duties to the community in which alone the free and full development of his personality is possible.

(2) In the exercise of his rights and freedoms, everyone shall be subject only to such limitations as are determined by law solely for the purpose of securing due recognition and respect for the rights and freedoms of others and of meeting the just requirements of morality, public order and the general welfare in a democratic society.

(3) These rights and freedoms may in no case be exercised contrary to the purposes and principles of the United Nations.

ARTICLE 30

Nothing in this Declaration may be interpreted as implying for any State, group or person any right to engage in any activity or to perform any act aimed at the destruction of any of the rights and freedoms set forth herein.

THE END OF THE DECLARATION.

CONCLUSION:

I guess we can now start thinking about how to do something about taking this basterds out of power, because in their country this important document seems to have the same value as toilet paper for its leaders not taking most of its article that serious.

So, if you want to fight for change and make Africa great, start doing something today even if it is small. Like Norman Sykes beautifully said: "If a butterfly flaps its wings in Venezuela, there will be a Tsunami in Asia."

We are the connected generation (Facebook, Twitter, Instagram, Snapchat, Pinterest, and LinkedIn), so start a *butterfly effect* today and make a Tsunami come to bring change and happiness for the countries in Africa that are still under dictatorship, tyranny and oppression by its Corrupt Leaders.

"Yes We Can." President Barack Obama

CHAPTER 12: When will Africa Wake Up to an Obama Trump Cocktail mix?

Before we go into this chapter let me explain the reason I choose the title of this chapter and why I have used the rainbow word on the title of this book.

The rainbow, a natural phenomenon noted for its beauty and its place in the sky, has been a favorite component of art and religion throughout history.

The rainbow has a place in legend owing to its beauty and the historical difficulty in explaining the phenomenon.

In Greco-Roman mythology, the rainbow was considered to be a path made by a messenger (Iris) between Earth and Heaven.

In Chinese mythology, the rainbow was a slit in the sky sealed by goddess Nuwa using stones of five different colours.

In Hindu religion, the rainbow is called Indradhanush, meaning "the bow (Sanskrit and Hindi: dhanush is bow) of Indra, the God of lightning, thunder and rain". Another Indian mythology says the rainbow is the bow of Rama, the incarnation of Vishnu. It is called Ramdhonu in Bengali, dhonu (dhanush) meaning bow. Likewise, in mythology of Arabian Peninsula, the rainbow, called Qaus Quzaħ in Arabic, is the war bow of the God Quzaħ.

In New Age and Hindu philosophy, the seven colours of the rainbow represent the seven chakras, from the first chakra (red) to the seventh chakra (violet).

In Armenian mythology the rainbow is a belt of Tir, the Sun god.

In Norse Mythology, a rainbow called the Bifrost Bridge connects the realms of Asgard and Midgard, homes of the Gods and humans, respectively.

In The Bible Study site biblestudy.org you will find the following meaning for what does a rainbow mean in the Bible?

Interestingly, we only need to look in three places in the Bible to discover the meaning of a rainbow and what certain colors mean. These places to study are found in the books of Genesis, Ezekiel and Revelation.

In the Genesis account, a rainbow appears right after the great worldwide flood brought in order to remove sinful and evil-minded man from the earth. It symbolized God's mercy and the covenant He made with Noah (representing mankind) not to destroy the world in such a way again.

12. And God said, "This is the sign of the covenant which I make between Me and you and every living creature with you, for everlasting generations: 13. I set my rainbow in the cloud, and it shall be the sign of the covenant between

me and the earth . . . and the waters shall no more become a flood to destroy all flesh. (Genesis 9:12, 15, HBFV)

In a way, a cloud which has the bow in it pictures God, as Exodus 13 states.

"And the Lord went before them by day in a pillar of CLOUD to lead the way . . ." (Exodus 13:21)

In his first vision from God, known as the "wheel in the middle of a wheel" vision, the prophet Ezekiel compares the glory of God to what he saw.

As the rainbow appears that is in the cloud in the day of rain, so was the appearance of His brightness all around (Ezekiel 1:28)

Bows appear again in the prophetic book of Revelation, which foretell the end of man's rule on the earth and the coming of Jesus to set up his Kingdom. The first mention in Revelation appears when the apostle John uses it to describe the glory and power of God on his throne.

1. After these things I looked, and behold, a door opened in heaven . . . 3. And He who was sitting was in appearance like a jasper stone and a sardius stone; and a rainbow was around the throne . . . (Revelation 4:1, 3)

The second mention of a rainbow occurs when John describes the look of a mighty angel.

1. Then I saw another strong angel coming down out of heaven, clothed with a cloud, and with a rainbow on his head; and his face was like the

sun, and his feet were like pillars of fire; (Revelation 10:1)

The most common colors seen by the naked eye are as listed by Isaac Newton: Red, Orange, Yellow, Green, Blue, Indigo, and Violet. In English, a popular way of remembering these colors is to memorize the name "ROY G. BIV." The primary colors are red, yellow, green, blue and violet.

The rainbow colors red, purple (which is a mix of red and blue), and scarlet (a bright red) and crimson (a cooler hue of the color red) were used extensively in the tabernacle Moses made in the wilderness. They were also a part of the temple later constructed, and in the garments for the High Priest and other priests (Exodus 25:3-5, 36:8, 19, 27:16, 28:4-8, 39:1-2, etc.). These colors were types or shadows of atonement.

The colors purple and scarlet can mean or represent iniquity or sinfulness (Revelation 17:3-4, 18:16, etc.). Purple itself was used as a symbol of royalty (Judges 8:26). Scarlet by itself can represent prosperity (Proverbs 31:21, Lamentations 4:5).

The color blue, referred to directly or when scripture states something is like the appearance of a sapphire or sapphire stone, can be a symbol of deity or royalty (Numbers 4:5-12; Ezekiel 1:26, Esther 8:15, etc.). Blue was also the color God commanded some threads in the fringes of Israelite garments be colored in order to remind them of the commandments and living a godly way of life (Numbers 15:38 - 39).

The color white found in a rainbow can mean holiness, righteousness and dedication to serving the true God (Leviticus 16:4, 2Chronicles 5:12, etc.). In vision, Jesus first appears to the apostle John with hair that is white (Revelation 1:12 - 14). All believers throughout history who die in the faith will, according to the Bible, be resurrected and given white robes to wear (Revelation 7:13 - 14, 19:7 - 8).

AFRICA RAINBOW

Within North African indigenous cultures, the rainbow is associated with hope and a bright future.

In the Genesis a rainbow appears right after the great worldwide flood brought in order to remove sinful and evil-minded man from the earth. How cool is this?

Amazing how an ancient book like the bible has this message by connecting it to a rainbow sign.

So, this is one of the main reasons I have associated the word rainbow to the title of the book.

It signifies that no matter the suffering and bad experiences there is still hope that one day we will see the evil minded man thrown out of Power, so prosperity and peace can be lived by every human being in their own country.

THE COCKTAIL MIX

Why do we need a mix of Obama and Trump to help Africa wake up for Greatness?

Because no matter what people may like of Obama or Trump, America is still one of the greatest country on Earth and every country wants to reach its level of development, freedom and respect of human rights, and most importantly the opportunity that the country provides to anyone willing to fight for a better life.

If you mix both Presidents famous campaign messages it will end up something like this: "Yes We Can Make America Great Again." How about that?

So, Yes We Can Make Africa Great!

WHY OBAMA?

Because no generation taught we could see a black President become President of the United States of America during our lifetime. He has made history and left a brilliant legacy of amazing achievements no matter who likes him or not.

I wish Africa leaders could at least try to learn what Obama legacy is instead of just trying to show off themselves in pictures with him and be thankful that he is USA first black President. Well, he is half black half white. Why do we tend to focus only on the black side and picture him as being 100% black? Isn't that racist? Think about it.

So, Mr. Presidents from Africa Countries, below are some of the most outstanding President Obama achievements, which are part of his Presidency Legacy. Please make sure you try to do at list 20% of this list in your country instead of seating there for decades stilling from your people:

HEALTHCARE REFORM

After five presidents over the course of a century failed to create universal health insurance, signed the Affordable Care Act in 2010. More than twenty million Americans have gained coverage since the passage of the law, which provides subsidies for Americans to buy coverage, expands Medicaid eligibility, and prohibits insurers from denying coverage to people with preexisting conditions. The uninsured rate has dropped from 16% in 2010 to 9% in 2015. The law also mandates free preventive care, allows young people to stay on their parents' policies up to age twenty-six, and imposes a ban on annual and lifetime caps on benefits.

RESCUED THE ECONOMY

Signed the Usd787 billion American Recovery and Reinvestment Act in 2009 to spur economic growth amid the most severe downturn since the Great Depression. As of October 2016, the economy had added 15.5 million new jobs since early 2010 and set a record with seventy-three straight months of private-sector job growth. The unemployment rate, which hit a sustained peak of about 10% in 2009, has dropped to 4.6% as of November 2016.

WALL STREET REFORM

Signed the Dodd-Frank Wall Street Reform and Consumer Protection Act in 2010 to re-regulate the financial sector after its practices that caused the 2008 Recession. The law tightens capital requirements on large banks and other financial institutions, allows the government to take them into receivership if they pose a threat to the economy, and limits their ability to trade with customers' money for their own profit. Dodd-Frank also created the Consumer Financial Protection Bureau to crack down on abusive lending and financial services.

GLOBAL AGREEMENT ON CLIMATE CHANGE

Provided key leadership to the United Nations Framework Convention on Climate Change, which produced the 2015 Paris Agreement, a commitment by 197 nations to reduce global carbon emissions and limit the global rise in temperatures to below 2 degrees Celsius.

TURNED AROUND THE U.S. AUTO INDUSTRY

In 2009, injected Usd62 billion (on top of the Usd13.4 billion in loans from the George W. Bush administration) into ailing GM and Chrysler in return for equity stakes and agreements for massive restructuring. By December 2014, the car companies had repaid Usd70.4 billion of the funds, and the Center for Automotive Research estimated that 2.5 million jobs were saved.

LIMIT CARBON EMISSIONS FROM POWER PLANTS

Finalized a "Clean Power Plan" in 2015 through new EPA regulations, setting the first-ever carbon pollution standards for existing power plants. When fully implemented in 2030, the new rules will result in a 32% reduction in carbon emissions compared to 2005.

NORMALIZED RELATIONS WITH CUBA

In 2014, took steps to open diplomatic and commercial ties with Cuba, ending the failed Cold War policy of isolation. In March 2016, direct mail flights to Cuba resumed for the first time in 50 years. American tourists may also now freely visit the country.

PROTECTED DREAMERS FROM DEPORTATION

Took executive action in June 2012 to protect undocumented young people brought to the U.S. as children (so-called DREAMers) from deportation and allow them to apply for work permits.

ESTABLISHED NET NEUTRALITY

Directed the Federal Communications Commission to issue a rule classifying internet service providers as a public utility and forcing them to treat all web traffic the same, regardless of source. After years of litigation, a federal court upheld the FCC's rule, meaning providers can't favor certain websites or block others.

IMPROVED AMERICA'S IMAGE ABROAD

With new policies, diplomacy, and rhetoric, reversed a sharp decline in world opinion toward the U.S. (and the corresponding loss of "soft power") during the Bush years.

CLEAN ENERGY INVESTMENT

As part of the 2009 stimulus, invested Usd90 billion in research on smart grids, energy - efficient electric cars, renewable electricity generation, cleaner coal, and biofuels. Launched a clean energy incubator within the Argonne National Laboratory and encouraged Usd4 billion in commitments by foundations, institutional investors, and other private-sector stakeholders to boost their investments in clean energy technology.

REDUCED THE THREAT FROM NUCLEAR WEAPONS

Initiated the biannual Nuclear Security Summit to address the global threat posed by nuclear terrorism and advance a common approach to strengthening nuclear security. As a result, weapons-usable highly enriched uranium has been removed from sixteen countries. Signed and won ratification of a 2011 treaty with Russia to limit each country to 1.550 strategic warheads (down from 2.200) and 700 launchers (down from more than 1.400). The treaty also reestablished a monitory and transparency program that had lapsed in 2009.

CREDIT CARD REFORMS

Signed the Credit Card Accountability Responsibility and Disclosure Act of 2009, which prohibits credit card companies from raising rates without advance notification, mandates a grace period on interest rate increases, and strictly limits overdraft and other fees.

IMPROVED SCHOOL NUTRITION

Signed the Healthy Hunger-Free Kids Act in 2010, championed by Michelle Obama, mandating an Usd4.5 billion spending boost and higher nutritional standards for school lunches. New rules double the amount of fruits and vegetables, and require only whole grains, in foods served to students.

EXPANDED THE DEFINITION OF HATE CRIMES

Signed the Hate Crimes Prevention Act in 2009, applying existing hate crime laws to crimes based on a victim's sexual orientation, gender, or disability, in addition to race, religion, or national origin.

PROTECTED LGBTQ AMERICANS FROM EMPLOYMENT DISCRIMINATION

Signed an executive order in 2014 prohibiting federal contractors and subcontractors from discriminating against their workers on the basis of sexual orientation or gender identity.

MAJOR VICTORIES AGAINST HOUSING AND MORTGAGE DISCRIMINATION

Through the Justice Department, reached a record Usd335 million settlement against Countrywide Financial Corporation and an Usd175 million settlement against Wells Fargo for their practices of charging higher interest and fees to African American and Latino borrowers prior to the financial crisis, in addition to numerous other suits pursued on behalf of borrowers. In 2015, the administration successfully argued before the Supreme Court that victims of housing discrimination suing for bias only need to show "disparate impact", not an intent to discriminate, to win their case.

EXPANDED BROADBAND COVERAGE

Obtained approval from the FCC to shift Usd8 billion in subsidies away from landlines and toward broadband internet access for lower-income rural families. By 2016, 98% of Americans had access to fast 4G/LTE broadband.

EXPANDED HEALTH COVERAGE FOR CHILDREN

Signed the Children's Health Insurance Program Reauthorization Act in 2009, expanding the Children's Health Insurance Program (CHIP) to cover an additional four million children, paid for by a tax increase on tobacco products.

IMPROVED FOOD SAFETY

Signed the 2011 FDA Food Safety Modernization Act, which increased the Food and Drug Administration's budget by Usd1.4 billion and expanded its regulatory responsibilities to include increasing the number of food inspections, issuing direct food recalls, and reviewing the safety practices of countries exporting food products to the U.S.

AVOIDED SCANDAL

Became the first President since Dwight Eisenhower to serve two terms with no serious personal or political scandal.

WHY TRUMP?

Because no generation taught they could see a President so open like Trump is. Beside most of his policies that most of us don't agree with, he has a passion to send a powerful message that he is protecting America's interest. Isn't that what every leader of any Country should do?

I am not saying I agree with him building a wall between USA and Mexico, or banning Muslim people from entering USA, or even worst ideas of deporting people to protect the American jobs and Americans, but in a way he has a point. What if African Presidents decided to do the same by protecting their economy from multinationals doing unfair business practices, and fighting so their people can have a job and dream for a better future for their families? Where is the wrong in that?

I guess what the media shows us today about all the mess that is going on with US Foreign Policy and the message that comes out is that the President is not thinking about the world. Well, he is not supposed to think about it. That's the job of the United Nations. He is supposed to think about American citizens.

I wish some African leaders had the same balls he has. Now imagine a Cocktail mix between President Obama and President Trump. This is what Africa needs to wake up. A Crazy mix that will have the courage, the wisdom, and the balls to develop the continent beyond their own country borders.

"When I look into the future, it's so bright it burns my eyes." Oprah Winfrey

CHAPTER 13: Africa Countries to invest for the future.

Africa is home to 11 of the 20 most rapidly growing countries in the world. That's 55% of the world fastest growing economies.

As stated by international reports 7 of the 10 most rapidly developing economic powers are expected to emerge from Africa over the next decade. That's 70% of the top 10.

Africa, once considered 'a sleeping giant', with a narrative of backwardness, abject poverty and conflicts, now holds what many believe to be the future of the world. Though accompanied by the sound of guns in some parts the continent, there already began miraculous economic growth here and there.

The Grand Ethiopian Renaissance Dam, Ethiopia's 6.000 MW hydro-power plant, Egypt's ultra-modern connection of 900kms of high-speed rail between Alexandria and Aswan and the democratic transitions of power in Ghana, Cape Verde, Senegal, Nigeria, Seychelles, and Sao Tom & Principe are few of the reasons why a skeptic can count on Africa's future.

The narrative of black continent has already begun to flicker a ray of development. There has never been a time with such a period for the world to believe in the African continent.

Countries are working around the clock to materialize iconic mega projects across the four corners of the continent. To mention just a few, in the west, the West African rail network that connects Benin, Burkina Faso, Niger, Ivory Coast, Ghana, Nigeria, and Togo. West African is in full swing. Mining companies in the region are investing in a massive rail project, when completed, will be 3.000kms long and link Benin, Burkina Faso, Niger, Ivory Coast, Ghana, Nigeria, and Togo.

Spearheaded by Ethiopia, East African Region is also at the disposal. The Grand Ethiopian Renaissance Dam which is under construction on the Blue Nile River in Ethiopia is a flagship project in the region. The Mombasa-Kigali Railway Project stretching almost 3.000kms and connecting three East African states will pass through Kampala, Uganda.

Ethiopia, Democratic Republic of Congo, Ivory Coast, Mozambique, Tanzania and Rwanda are recording the fastest compound growth in the continent, and are amongst the fastest-growing economies in the world. These countries, along with those who set the target of reaching middle-income status in the coming decade, are contributing towards eradicating poverty in one generation.

Many countries are displaying commitment towards creating free continental trade. Botswana, Ivory Coast, Ethiopia, Ghana, Kenya, Lesotho, Nigeria, Rwanda, Senegal and others on industrialization, value addition, as well as the initiatives to build regional value chains, as the

Continent poised to start the Continental Free Trade Area.

Following the launch of the African Passport in Kigali last year, good examples of progress on free movement of persons by countries such as Benin, Comoros, Ghana, Madagascar, Mozambique, Namibia, Rwanda, Seychelles, Togo and Uganda, who are already offering visa-free access or visa on arrival for all Africans.

The Economic Community of West African States (ECOWAS) responded to the situation in the recent Gambia elections, with the support of the African Union and the support of the United Nations, has been something exemplary that he hope could be copied in many other parts of the world.

Sure deficits remain, but what's important is that investors realize there is money to be made for those bold enough to help close the gaps. As that takes place, the promise of greater prosperity for Africans and African businesses will be realized.

Still not convinced Africa is the place to be for the future? Here are more reasons why you should invest in Africa.

As recently published in the World Economic Forum on Africa, the following are reasons why it is a good time to invest in Africa:

1. Africa needs connectors

Missing across much of Sub-Saharan Africa are roads, rails, ports, airports, power grids and IT backbone needed to lift African economies. This lack of infrastructure hinders the growth of imports, exports, and regional business.

Companies that can connect Africans and markets can prosper. Sub-Saharan Africa is plagued by power outages – almost 700 hours a year on average – sapping productivity, adding cost and leaving businesses captive to back-up with alternative power options. Massive investment is leading to major upgrades and expansion at African ports and airports, but much of Africa's growth potential depends on in-country and intra-African road, rail and air connections.

Roads and rail lines are sparse, decrepit and over-burdened. A lack of aviation agreements has limited intra-African air connections. Africa's lack of efficient storage and distribution infrastructure hinders businesses, entrepreneurs and farmers. Up to 50% of African fruit and vegetables spoil before reaching markets.

There's a soft infrastructure deficit, as well. Outside of South Africa, the data and information critical to decision-making by businesses is missing or hard to obtain – credit and risk information, market data, consumption patterns, you name it. Lessons from Dubai and Singapore tell us that once an infrastructure race is on in a rapidly expanding market, being the first-mover is a significant advantage for investors.

2. African trade barriers are falling and intra-African trade holds enormous potential

With the 54 nation Continental Free Trade Area – Africa's own mega-trade deal – even the smallest African economies could see a lift. If duties are lowered and incentives introduced, manufacturers could see benefit from setting up production and assembly operations in multiple African countries. That could lead to development in electronics, machinery, chemicals, textile production and processed foods.

As a first step, free trade between and within the African economic blocs would make a huge difference. Africa's share of global trade – a meager 3% – can only increase if the continent's commodity and consumption-led economies begin to produce a broad array of goods for home markets and export.

And an increase in local beneficiation in the commodities sector could be a driver of growth – processing local commodities (such as minerals, coffee, cocoa, cotton) in the country rather than exporting them in raw form. That said, it will continue to be a challenge for regions with poor power and infrastructure to compete as global manufacturers.

3. Customers are changing

With the growth of Africa's middle class, we're seeing development of new expectations. Educated, urban professionals are young, brand-aware and sophisticated in terms of their consumption. Retailers and consumer brands want to anticipate and drive buying preferences in fashion, home and lifestyle products, but they know they need international standard supply chains if they are to meet demand. The largest economic forces in Africa are small to medium enterprises, working to meet this new demand and competing with global brands.

4. Digital transformation

Africa leads the world in mobile adoption, which continues to offer the biggest cross-sectoral economic opportunities. Mobile payment networks, pioneered in East Africa, opened the wired, global economy to poor, unbanked city and rural dwellers. Companies such as Novartis are using mobile communications to manage their supply chain; Olam has used mobile to reach out to new African suppliers and farmers. These mobile initiatives have achieved huge successes.

5. Africa is diversifying

African economies are finally beginning to diversify beyond commodities, though this is still in the early stages. Africa is seeing a returning diaspora that recognizes the potential and opportunities in their own countries. This population supports local economic growth with their skills and talent, by acting as "first movers", investing back in their communities.

At the same time, African countries are beginning to place bets on non-commodity areas where they can be competitive. And they are packaging themselves to appeal to a broader set of investors. Recognizing they can no longer count on growing investment from China, every country has Investment Promotion Agencies, which act as one-stop shops for investors, assisting with registration, taxes, and other steps to establish foreign investment in the country.

6. Africa can lead in sustainable development

In energy, technology, supply chain design and other areas, Africa has the ability to look at what works elsewhere then fashion its own answers. It can openly embrace new technology and ideas, with no historical imprint from which to break free. It can develop flexible fuel grids that generate power with a mix of abundant wind, solar, hydro and bio energy, alongside conventional fuels such as oil and gas, which are also abundant. Nowhere on Earth is there as much unused or poorly used arable land, so look for big agricultural breakthroughs and productivity gains in food production in Africa.

IS AFRICA'S INVESTMENT DREAM STILL ON TRACK?

In many countries across Africa the real GDP is growing higher than the global average and more than double that of the Euro area, making Africa the second fastest growing region in the world, behind East Asia.

Abraaj Group, Dubai based Private equity Group, CEO Arif Naqvi said on the sidelines of the World Economic Forum this year that Africa was core to the firm's investment strategy, as it bets the continent's rising middle class will consume more goods. Naqvi said he continues to believe in the opportunities the continent offers.

"It's the consumption-driven economies that we focus on a lot," he said. "In those economies, as people emerge into the middle classes and move into cities, they're going to want more products, more infrastructures."

He noted there could be short-term problems in particular countries due to currency fluctuations or other things, but said the long-term trend of increased consumption would not stop.

WHAT MOST INVESTORS BELIEVES ABOUT INVESTING IN AFRICA?

Most investors we come across believe that just by having money they can solve anything when it comes to project development in Africa. But that's not the case in Africa. Even if you have Usd1 billion in cash you must have a great local team with the know-how on how to operate on that country and to execute the project on the ground. If there are barriers no amount of money will solve it. Only smart and practical minds working together can overcome bureaucracy and cultural barriers.

Successful implementation requires a thorough understanding of the regulatory frameworks. In many countries, these frameworks are improving and are more predictable than they were previously. Africa accounted for the highest number of reforms worldwide in the World Bank's latest Ease of Doing Business report, with five countries listed among the top 10 improvers globally, but challenges still remain.

Top 10 Countries we suggest you keep an eye to invest for the future

1. Mauritius
2. Botswana
3. South Africa
4. Kenya
5. Rwanda
6. Egypt
7. Seychelles
8. Ghana
9. Nigeria
10. Tanzania

FDI AFRICA INDEX COUNTRIES TO INVEST FOR THE FUTURE:

Why these countries?

Capital Consulting has developed a FDI Index by making a correlation of various Index, World Bank doing business ranking in sub-Saharan Africa, Transparency International Corruption Perceptions Index, the strongest economies in Africa and their resilience to shocks, diversification, infrastructures, business enablement, human development, as well as resilience to current macro-economic challenges, UNECA Africa Development Bank and Africa Union regional integration index, FDi Intelligence Countries of the future, Mo Ibrahim Africa

Governance Index, and Ernest & Young Africa Attractiveness Index.

The countries selected also have the potential to become greater economies from which you can trade and promote investment across different economic blocs in Africa, due to their regional integration and infrastructure to export easily to various international and regional markets.

We hope this helps support investors in adapting to a more uncertain environment, and to assess variable opportunities and risks across the continent.

Which sectors should you focus your investments in these countries?

1. MAURITIUS

By leveraging its strategic position at the crossroads of Africa, Asia and Australia, Mauritius is gradually transforming itself into a hub and an international jurisdiction for investors in search of security, transparent regulation and high value-addition. Over the years, the economy has been successfully metamorphosed following a smart shift from a mono-agricultural model to a diversified, innovation-driven and knowledge-based economy, underpinned by a broad spectrum of business activities.

They may just be a few tiny specs in the middle of the Indian Ocean, but the small island nation of Mauritius has made a big name for itself in financial services.

Traditionally seen as a route for investment into India, more recently Mauritius has been selling itself as a gateway to mainland Africa.

Some complain its low tax status is diverting much needed revenue away from governments in Africa, while others argue that Mauritius provides a secure and stable platform that enables more investment to take place.

The Mauritius International Financial Centre has been servicing the local and international business community for more than a decade. The country has a long history and a banking tradition, a share ownership and a corporate culture going back more than a century.

Mauritius has signed and ratified 38 Double Taxation Agreements (DTAA) to date with leading developed and emerging economies around the globe. With all its DTAAs based on the OECD model, the IFC is today recognized as the ideal hub for investing in the growing regional markets.

They currently have DTAAs with African nations including Botswana, Lesotho, Madagascar, Mozambique, Namibia, Rwanda, Senegal, South Africa, Swaziland, Uganda, Zambia and Tunisia.

Mauritius offers full protection of foreign investments in key African nations through its network of Investment Promotion Protection Agreements (IPPAs). As to date, Mauritius has signed IPPAs with 36 countries including 17 African countries. IPPAs signed with African countries include: Benin, Botswana, Burundi, Cameroon, Chad, Comoros, Ghana, Guinea, Madagascar, Mauritania, Mozambique, Rwanda, Senegal, South Africa, Swaziland, Zimbabwe and Tanzania.

The OECD classifies Mauritius as a jurisdiction that has substantially implemented internationally agreed tax and transparency standards. Since, this has proved very beneficial to Mauritius as an International Financial Centre as global investors' confidence and trust in the jurisdiction increased, thus allowing for more use of the platform by the international business community.

The Global Financial Centers Index (GFCI), on the other hand, has classified Mauritius as one of the top jurisdictions with regard to information exchange.

The reputation of Mauritius as a well-regulated and business friendly investment destination is also evidenced by its international recognition and signatory to the IOSCO, IAIS, OECD, FATF and IFSB.

Mauritius remains the jurisdiction of choice for many global investors looking to expand their operations from a safe, stable and secure platform. The country is a convenient GMT+4 location allowing trading and business to be done with major markets including Europe, USA and Asia, all in a single business day.

We recommend you to look at investments in Mauritius in the following sectors: financial services, agriculture, hospitality and property development, logistics, manufacturing, seafood.

2. BOTSWANA

Botswana is a land-locked country located in Southern Africa. Botswana has historically enjoyed high economic growth rates and its export - driven economy is highly correlated with global economic trends. Development has been driven mainly by revenue from the diamond industry, which has enabled Botswana to provide infrastructure and social services.

Botswana is stable, peaceful, and transparent. Botswana is the most transparent country in Africa, according to Transparency International. Botswana has an official policy of zero tolerance for corruption.

Botswana is increasingly becoming a popular business hub with many looking to expand their portfolios, into the country.

The country is ranked as the world's second most attractive investment location by New York University's Altman's Baseline Profitability Index (BPI).

They have the highest sovereign credit rating, and according to the Heritage Foundation and the Wall Street Journal's 2014 Index of Economic Freedom Botswana has been ranked the second freest economy in Sub-Saharan Africa after Mauritius and above countries such as Norway, Belgium and France.

Botswana provide investors with preferential access to the Southern African Development Community's (SADC) entire marketplace – over 230 million people; open up duty-free access to South Africa, Namibia, Lesotho and Swaziland; and duty-free and quota-free access to the European Union (EU) market.

The quality of Botswana's workforce is second to none in Africa. The workforce is well educated - 82% are literate - and most speak English.

Economic diversification has been the priority concern in recent and current national development plans.

Botswana is a Net Food Importing Developing Country (NFIDC) the opportunity to increase domestic production of basic foodstuffs, particularly cereals (grain sorghum and maize) and pulses. Cereal national demand stands at 200.000 tons per year, of which only 17% is supplied through local production. Investments in arable agriculture will stimulate private sector development, create employment, create value-addition opportunities, and enhance food security and ultimately exports.

The Zambezi River offers supply irrigation to help increase 20.000 hectares of agricultural development.

Similarly, recommendations from the National Master Plan for Arable Agricultural and Dairy Development (NAMPAADD) report identify projected irrigation in Mmadinare-Tobane (750 hectares), supplied by Shashe Dam, and in Selebi-Phikwe (1.019 hectares) supplied by

Letsibogo Dam. Spin off investment opportunities of these projects include horticulture packaging and gross sales to domestic and international markets at standardized rates. Tomato paste production is an existing opportunity, utilizing surplus tomato production, and opens the possibility to other food packing opportunities.

Botswana is renowned for cattle farming and potential exists to expand the rawhide processing and tanning industries. A study on the Economic Diversification of Selebi-Phikwe, in 2006 noted that Botswana produces around 360.000 cattle hides per year, with the majority being exported in raw form.

Botswana is a net importer of pork products. According to the 2011 LEA study on pork value chain development in Botswana, in 2008/09, local pork production stood at 441 million tons while imports were 952 million tons. Traditional suppliers of pork products are South Africa and Namibia. The Southern African Customs Union (SACU) Region has a net import demand currently met by supply from Brazil, offering a regional market for pork exports.

There are opportunities to invest in pig rearing, slaughter facilities, and grain/feed production. Botswana has exported fresh and frozen beef products to Europe since Independence.

Further investment opportunities exist in domestic production; fodder/feed production; transportation and processed meat for domestic and export markets.

Opportunities presented by the manufacturing sector covers a wide array of sectors such as food and beverages, textiles and garments, jewelry making, metal and metal products amongst others.

Opportunities for investment in the mining sector include; prospecting and surveys, expansion of existing mining projects, new mining projects, beneficiation of minerals and improved value chain benefits.

The beneficiation of diamonds represents one of the most promising areas of opportunity. The Botswana Diamond Hub was established to develop a sustainable secondary diamond industry in Botswana. To facilitate the establishment of diamond ancillary businesses, 28 licensed cutting and polishing companies are in operation, mainly centered in Gaborone. The potential exists to expand operations to other parts of the country.

Opportunities in the diamond mining sector include: diamond trading, cutting and polishing, ancillary support services; banking, security, insurance, certification and brokerage services; support and outsourcing; general security services, information technology and support, accounting and human resource services.

Targeted projects and policy interventions in the transport sector have been established with the goal of developing Botswana as a transport hub within the SADC region. It is hoped that the transport and logistics industry become a major growth sector, stimulating economic diversification.

In 2009, the Botswana Export Development and Investment Authority (BEDIA) conducted a feasibility study on cargo and logistics facilities, identifying opportunities for an air cargo hub at Sir Seretse Khama International Airport (SSKIA) in Gaborone specifically to handle perishable goods. It is though that the hub could attract both freight and passenger airlines to provide cargo capacity at SSKIA. Such a hub would add value to logistics, transport and secondary storage facilities, for both export and import. Further the hub would eventually provide, air cargo transport (on freighters and passenger airlines), ground handling services, imports and exports, customs, health inspections, agricultural inspections, trucking, general and specialized storage (including cold storage), and value-added logistics.

Botswana is well known for having some of the best wilderness and wildlife areas on the African continent. With a full 38% of its total land area devoted to national parks, reserves and wildlife management areas - for the most part unfenced, allowing animals to roam wild and free - travel through many parts of the country has the feeling of moving through an immense Nature wonderland.

Botswana is a rarity in our overpopulated, over-developed world. Untamed and untamable, it is one of the last great refuges for Nature's magnificent pageantry of life.

Experience here the stunning beauty of the world's largest intact inland Delta - the Okavango; the unimaginable vastness of the world's second largest game reserve - the Central Kalahari Game Reserve; the isolation and other - worldliness of the Makgadikgadi - uninhabited pans the size of Portugal; and the astoundingly prolific wildlife of the Chobe National Park.

Botswana is the last stronghold for a number of endangered bird and mammal species, including Wild Dog, Cheetah, Brown Hyena, Cape Vulture, Wattled

Crane, Kori Bustard, and Pel's Fishing Owl. This makes your safari experience even more memorable, and at times you will feel simply surrounded by wild animals.

The first - and most lasting impressions - will be of vast expanses of uninhabited wilderness stretching from horizon to horizon, the sensation of limitless space, astoundingly rich wildlife and bird viewing, night skies littered with stars and heavenly bodies of an unimaginable brilliance, and stunning sunsets of unearthly beauty.

We recommend you to look at investments in Botswana in the following sectors: tourism, diamond mining, ICT, energy, agriculture, livestock value chains, manufacturing, transport and logistics hub.

3. SOUTH AFRICA

With the most advanced, broad-based economy on the continent, South Africa offers investors a diverse and mature economy with a vibrant financial and service sector, as well as preferential access to export markets in United States, European Union, and Southern Africa. Standards are generally similar to those in most developed economies, investors find local courts generally fair and consistent, and infrastructure is well-developed.

South Africa's Democracy is well-established with transparent and contested elections, and an appreciation for the rule of law.

South Africa is one of the most sophisticated, diverse and promising emerging markets globally. Strategically located at the tip of the African continent, South Africa is a key investment location, both for the market opportunities that lie within its borders and as a gateway to the rest of the continent, a market of about 1 billion people.

South Africa is the economic powerhouse of Africa and forms part of the BRICS group of countries with Brazil, Russia, India and China. It has a favorable demographic profile and its rapidly expanding middle class has growing spending power.

South Africa has a wealth of natural resources (including coal, platinum, coal, gold, iron ore, manganese nickel, uranium and chromium) and it enjoys increased attention from international exploration companies, particularly in the oil and gas sector.

It has world-class infrastructure, exciting innovation, research and development capabilities and an established manufacturing base. It is at the forefront of the development and rollout of new green technologies and industries, creating new and sustainable jobs in the process and reducing environmental impact.

South Africa has sophisticated financial, legal and telecommunications sectors, and a number of global business process outsourcing (BPO) operations are located in the country.

It has political and macro-economic stability, an abundant supply of semiskilled and unskilled labor, and it compares favorably to other emerging markets in terms of the overall cost of doing business.

The South African Government has introduced wide-ranging legislation to promote training and skills development and fast-track the building of world-class skills and competences.
One of the main reasons for South Africa becoming one of the most popular trade and investment destinations in the world is due to the country ensuring that it can meet specific trade and investment requirements of prospective investors.

South Africa has a host of investment incentives and industrial financing interventions that are aimed at encouraging commercial activity and its trade rules favor a further expansion in South Africa's burgeoning levels of international trade.

South Africa's unrivalled scenic beauty and reputation for delivering value-for money make it an attractive leisure and business travel destination.

South Africa produces 14% of the world's gold, and has 41% of the world's known reserves. It is estimated that 21.000 tons of undeveloped resources - about one fifth of the world's unmined gold - still remains. Over the past few years, South African mining houses have transformed into large, focused mining companies that include Anglo Platinum, Anglogold, De Beers Group, Implats and Iscor. South Africa is the world's largest producer of gold (after China) and platinum. The country is one of the leading producers of base metals and coal, accounting for a significant proportion of both world production and reserves. The country's diamond industry is the third largest by value, and the sixth largest by volume in the world, with Russia and Botswana leading in both categories.

The agricultural sector is well developed, and secondary manufacturing in the agro-processing industries is pervasive, evidenced by many locally-produced food items found in food retail outlets.

Today, South Africa is not only self-sufficient in virtually all major agricultural products, but in a normal year, it is also a net food exporter. Major import products include wheat, rice and vegetable oils. Despite the farming industry's declining share of GDP, it remains vital to the economy, and development and stability of the Southern African region.

South Africa boasts one of the most modern and extensive transport infrastructures in Africa. This infrastructure plays a crucial role in the country's economy and is depended on by many neighboring states. Its airline, South African Airways (SAA), is an incorporated public company owned by the South African government.

Technology is one of the most dynamic, innovative and growing sectors in South Africa. Local consumers are converging technology with their everyday purchases and experiences, largely for convenience. According to a recent study by global market research company Ipsos, 70% of South African consumers do their shopping online.

We recommend you to look at investments in South Africa in the following sectors: agro processing, aviation, banking, asset management, tourism and hospitality, real estate, diamond, gold and platinum mining, business process outsourcing and

IT-enabled services, green economy industries, advanced manufacturing, bio-manufacturing, chemicals, plastic fabrication and pharmaceuticals, creative and design industry, jewelry manufacturing and design, fashion design, infrastructure development, transport and logistics hub.

4. KENYA

East Africa's largest economy, Kenya, is one of the leading destinations for foreign direct investment (FDI) in Africa.

Kenya has the region best performing currency and constitutes 40% of East Africa community's GDP.

As the leading economy in East Africa, Kenya's strategic location and its well-developed business infrastructure make it a natural choice for investors, with many international firms making it their regional hub. Kenya grants investor's access to the larger East African Community and regional markets with access to over 385 million consumers. Nairobi is also a major transport Hub in East Africa with connections from Jomo Kenyatta International Airport to major destinations around the world.

Kenya has a steadily improving environment for foreign direct investment

(FDI). Foreign investors seeking to establish a presence in Kenya generally receive the same treatment as local investors, and multinational companies make up a large percentage of Kenya's industrial sector. There is no discrimination against foreigners in investment, ownership, or access to government-financed research, and the government's export promotion programs do not distinguish between local and foreign-owned goods.

Kenya is a signatory to a large and growing number of tax treaties and investment promotion and protection Agreements such as the Multilateral Trade System (MTS) ACP Cotonou Agreement, and the Africa Growth and Opportunities Act (AGOA). This allows exports from Kenya to enjoy preferential access to world markets under a number of special access and duty reduction programs.

Since independence, Kenya has maintained remarkable stability despite changes in its political system since the re-emergence of multiparty Democracy and promulgation of a new constitution in 2011, Kenyans have enjoyed an increased degree of freedom.

Kenya is making efforts to lower the cost of doing business by conducting extensive business regulatory reforms intended to substantially reduce the number of licensing requirements and to make the licensing regimes more simple and transparent and focused on legitimate regulatory purposes.

Kenya prides itself in its large pool of highly educated, skilled and sought after work force in Africa, trained from within the country and in institutions in around the world.

Kenya affords a pleasant and quality standard of living with its spectacular and diverse natural resources. Ranging from wildlife and sceneries. Including the world famous Masai Mara. The country also boasts of high quality social amenities such as restaurants, hospitals, and entertainment spots. A good reason why the country has the highest number of expatriates living and working in Kenya.

Kenya fully liberalized its economy by removing all obstacles that previously hampered the free flow of trade and private investment. These include exchange controls, import and export licensing, as well as restrictions on remittances of profits and dividends.

Kenya is signatory to a number of multilateral and bilateral trade agreements as part of its trade policy. Kenya is a member of the World Trade Organization (WTO) making her products access more than 90% of world markets at Most Favored Nation (MFN) treatment. In addition, Kenya is member to several trade arrangements and beneficiary to trade-enhancing schemes that include the Africa Growth and opportunity act (AGOA); ACP-EU Trade Agreement and Common Market of Eastern and Southern Africa (COMESA).

Kenya has adopted cluster development as part of regional and national competitiveness strategies with plans underway to develop industry clusters in strategic locations across the country. Investors can take advantage on existing arrangements with attractive incentives and simple investment procedures.

Kenya has a population of about 47.2 million people of which 47.5% constitute the working population. The country also has the highest 15 + literacy rate in the region (90%). Investors have access to a large pool of highly qualified professionals in diverse sectors at competitive rates within a very flexible legal framework.
Kenya envisages a massive upgrading and extension of the country's infrastructure. In this regard, the country has highlighted a number of infrastructure projects that present significant opportunities for investors in the coming years.

Manufacturing sector is mainly agro based at the moment and plays an important role in adding value to agricultural output by providing forward and backward linkages with agricultural sector. However, there is a shift to export oriented manufacturing as the main thrust of Kenya's industrial policy since the country aims to raise the share of products in the regional market from 7% to 15%.

Agriculture is the mainstay of the Kenyan economy directly contributing 26% of the GDP annually, and another 25% indirectly. The sector accounts for 65% of Kenya's total exports and provides more than 70% of informal employment in the rural areas. The sector comprises of crops, livestock, fisheries, land, water, cooperatives, environment, regional development and forestry sub sectors.

Financial services are expected to play critical in the next years by providing better intermediation between saving and investments.

Tourism is one of Kenya's leading foreign exchange earner and third largest contributor to the GDP after agriculture and manufacturing.

The auto industry, as well as the agriculture, logistics, infrastructure, and

ICT sectors are the top areas for FDI in Kenya. The 10 countries with the highest investments in Kenya are U.S., India, UK, Mauritius, Israel, Japan, Netherlands, Belgium, China, and South Africa.

Kenya has become one of Africa's hotbeds of innovation in recent years. The government has a five year strategic plan to transform the country into a high-tech hub in Africa. Nairobi is currently the most advanced city in Africa in terms of ICT use. According to a survey by the GSMA, entitled "The Mobile Economy in Sub-Saharan Africa 2015", access to financial services more than doubled over seven years, reaching two-thirds of the population in 2013, helped by the presence of mobile financial services in Kenya. The survey also stated that Kenya is one of the biggest countries in Africa for app downloads, and it has the highest mobile penetration rate in East Africa, at 42%. The GSMA describes Kenya's Nairobi as a Silicon Savannah, stating it has been the epicenter of the country's innovation.

Ernst & Young ranks Kenya as one of the 'rising stars' in Africa in terms of its attractiveness for renewable energy investment. The country possesses more than 7.000 MW of undeveloped geothermal energy resources in the Rift Valley area. The government plans to increase its generation capacity by 23.000 MW by 2030.

Kenya is the leading growth and investment hotspot in Africa. It is expected that this economic growth will continue in the long term. The government, is committed to improving the investment landscape. Tech innovations and renewables are the most promising sectors, having gained momentum in Kenya in recent years. Agriculture, Real estate, tourism, and infrastructure projects are the leading areas for investment. Most forecasts show investor confidence in the country's business climate to be strong.

We recommend you to look at investments in Kenya in the following sectors: infrastructure development, Real estate, manufacturing, mining, ICT, banking, tourism, agriculture, agro processing, and renewable energy.

5. RWANDA

Rwanda is a small market, with a population of 11.5 million people and a Gross Domestic Product (GDP) of Usd7.8 billion.

Rwanda's economy grew by an average of 8% annually from 2002 to 2012, before slowing to 4.6% in 2013, in the aftermath of international donor aid cuts and suspensions. The economy has since rebounded with 6.9% growth in 2015.

The International Monetary Fund (IMF) expects Rwanda's GDP growth to moderate to 6%-6.5% in 2016/2017. There are many positive big picture economic signs: inflation remains below 5%, the country maintains a well-deserved reputation for low corruption, Rwanda's debt-to-GDP ratio, at 20%, is low, and the percentage of foreign assistance in the country's annual budget has dropped from over 80% a decade ago to under 35% in 2015.

Rwanda enjoys relatively high rankings in the World Bank's Ease of Doing Business Index, which ranked Rwanda 62nd out of 189 economies in the 2016 report – second best in Africa behind Mauritius. It takes less than 24 hours, on average, to set up a company.

Rwanda is one of the 10 most attractive nations in Africa for investors, according to the 2016 Ernst & Young (EY) Africa Attractiveness Index. The country was ranked ninth and the second most preferred investment destination in East Africa after Kenya, which came fourth on the continental ranking and first in the region.

Leading sectors include agriculture, trade, hospitality, and financial services. Rwanda's economy is overwhelmingly rural and heavily dependent on agriculture.

The government's economic priority is turning Rwanda into a regional trade, logistics, and conference hub. Pillars of this strategy include the construction of two new international business class hotels and a convention center in downtown Kigali and investing in the fleet for the national carrier Rwandair.

Commodities, particularly tin, tantalum, tungsten, tea, and coffee, generated over 47% of Rwanda's export revenue.

Major markets for coffee exports are the United States and Europe, while the Middle East and Pakistan are the main buyers of Rwandan tea.

Tourism is the country's leading foreign exchange earner, with total revenues of Usd319 million in 2015, according to the National Bank of Rwanda. This is due to successes in leisure tourism, which is the highest income generating sector, and followed by business tourism – Meetings, Incentives, Conferences and Events (MICE). The country targets annual tourism revenues of Usd860 million in 2017 due to significant expansion in this sector.

Rwanda's small industrial sector contributes around 14% to GDP and employs less than 3% of the population. The services sector generates almost half of GDP (47%) and has grown at an average annual rate of 9%.

Market of 11.5 million people with a rapidly growing middle class, a market and customs union with a market potential of 162 million consumers in East Africa Community (EAC).

In 2009, Rwanda became the newest member of The Commonwealth. Rwanda is also a member of the Common Market for Eastern and Southern Africa (COMESA), which has a total population of 470 million.

Rwanda is playing a leading role in the Northern Corridor initiative, which includes Kenya, Uganda, South Sudan, and Ethiopia as core members and the DRC, Burundi, and Tanzania as observers. Rwanda is also at the forefront of the Central Corridor initiative, which includes Burundi, DRC, Rwanda, Tanzania, and Uganda. Unlocking some of the larger infrastructure projects, especially transportation, envisioned under the Central and Northern Corridor initiatives would help to substantially reduce the cost of conducting business and transporting goods across borders in the region.

Low corruption reputation, Rwanda is one of Africa's five least corrupt nations and in the world according to the Transparency International's Corruption Perception Index.

Domestic and regional energy demands far outweigh Rwanda's supply. The government has outlined a strategy to increase electricity generation capacity from around 186 megawatts currently to 563 MW by mid-2018.

Rwanda offers opportunities for independent power producers to invest in clean and renewable energy generation, methane, mini hydro, peat, and off-grid projects. The country is also positioned well to serve as a hub to wheel power from Ethiopia, Kenya, and Uganda to neighboring Burundi and eastern DRC.

The government, in pursuit of its goal to position Rwanda as a regional hub for tourism, services, and logistics, will commission a number of high-profile infrastructure projects, including a nearly-complete Convention Center and two new international business class hotels. The government has ambitious plans for future projects including, a new international airport (Bugesera), "Kigali Innovation City," tourist facilities, ring roads around Kigali, wastewater treatment and potable water facilities, and large ticket items such as railways to Uganda and Tanzania and regional oil pipelines.

The construction sector is booming, especially in Kigali. There is a significant gap in domestic production of concrete, steel, and other construction materials relative to demand.

Rwanda's agriculture sector contributes one-third of the country's national GDP. The government aims to boost that figure through the addition of high-value horticultural processing (including coffee washing, roasting, and packaging), expansion of irrigation and mechanization, and increased production and processing of value-added agriculture goods (e.g., dairy, tomato ketchup, mushrooms). Rwanda also aims to transition from subsistence crops to export oriented/commercial farming.

Rwanda continues to be one of the fastest growing African countries in ICT and there are several avenues for growth for the ICT sector - from ecommerce and e-services, mobile technologies, applications development and automation to becoming a regional center for the training of ICT professionals and research. The government has installed over 5.000 kilometers of fiber optic cable throughout Rwanda, with regional links to neighboring countries. Rwanda is also one of the few countries in Africa to have launched a high-speed 4G LTE wireless broadband network in Kigali, though uptake is slow due to high prices. Adequate numbers of skilled IT professionals are also still lacking.

The government forecast that tourism will grow at an average of 11% over the next two years. Opportunities exist in hospitality, entertainment, tour operations, and training services. Rwanda's growing list of business class hotels, soon to be joined by the Kigali Convention Center and two new international business class hotels will make it a prime destination for business, event, and conference tourism in the region.

The mining sector has expanded significantly since privatization in 2007. The Rwandan government has set a target of over Usd400 million in exports in 2017. Rwanda offers small-scale opportunities in exploration, extraction, and processing. Rwanda is a leading exporter of tantalum, a metal used in mobile phones.

Chinese businesses seem to have gotten the message. In Kigali's special economic zone, Chinese companies produce clothes, sanitary napkins, and wooden doors. A Chinese government-funded agricultural technology center to modernize Rwandan farmers is also focused on helping Chinese companies find new markets in the region. China emerged as Rwanda's largest investor.

We recommend you to look at investments in Rwanda in the following sectors: infrastructure, agriculture, energy, tourism, manufacturing, information and communication technology, mining, financial services, Real estate and construction.

6. EGYPT

With a population of over 91 million and a GDP of Usd1.1 trillion there are solid opportunities for investors in the medium-to-long term. Egypt's strategic location offers companies a platform for their commercial activities into the Middle East and Africa.

Egypt is now building its new political structure to fulfill the dreams of all Egyptians who called for change, dignity, freedom of speech and social, during the Arab Spring.

After the ratification of the new constitution in January 2014 through a public referendum with 98% approval rate and the election of a new President in June 2014 through direct elections. The Parliamentary election law; the final prerequisite for holding the elections, was ratified by President Abdel Fattah El-Sisi in December 2014.

The Egyptian Economy's resilience is capable of overcoming its economic challenges as it did in the 2008 financial crisis, and long-term investors will see many opportunities.

Egypt has started its transformation to a stable, democratic and modern economy, where the dividends of growth and prosperity will be shared by all who participated in its achievement.

The Egyptian economy's ability to post positive real economic growth rates amid the global economic downturn as well as during the political unrest that prevailed in 2011-2013 indicates how resilient economic activity is in Egypt.

At about 28 million, Egypt's labor pool is the largest in the region. For decades, Egypt has had a reputation as a net regional exporter of educated, skilled labor. However, as domestic demand for skilled labor rises, and the increase of youth searching for job opportunities, a national industrial training program is provided for labors through world-class universities.

Egypt has emerged as a consumer market of significant importance in the region, as witnessed by the arrival of dozens of global brands and the sharp expansion of retail sales in the past years. This is partly due to the sheer size of Egypt's population that put it as one of the most populated (91 million) country in Africa and the Middle East.

Egypt boasts a world class infrastructure base. Three independent mobile phone networks cover nearly 100% of the country's inhabited land. Wire line broadband is readily available in urban centers. The country's 15 commercial ports serve the nation's exporters and importers alike, while an expanding, upgrading airport network caters to both passengers and cargo traffic, Egypt's Air Cargo Airport, currently has three cargo terminals, dealing with textiles, vegetables and many industrial products. Also the country has a well-established network of railways and roads.

The road network has reached 108.784km, Railway network 9.570km and 20 Airports.

Egypt also provides competitive prices and reliable supplies of power, water and gas. Egypt possesses abundance in natural resources that can easily meet the needs of agricultural, industrial and mining activities.

Among the natural resources are Petroleum, iron ore, phosphate, limestone, manganese, talc, zinc, asbestos, gypsum, gold and the River Nile.

The renewable equipment market is worth several billion dollars.

The construction market has been growing rapidly at a rate of 15% a year since the 1980s, resulting in a substantial boom in residential and commercial real estate. There is strong demand for infrastructure projects due to rapid population growth and housing shortages. The sector is expected to grow 70% between 2015-2020 to reach Usd12 billion.

Egypt is the largest oil producer in Africa outside OPEC and is also the largest oil and natural gas consumer in Africa. Between October 2013 and January 2015, 53 agreements were signed, with minimum investments of roughly Usd2.9 billion and a total of Usd432 million in signing bonuses for the drilling of 228 wells. In May 2016, a new international bidding round was announced, including 11 blocks for the Gulf of Suez and the Western Desert.

Egypt's economy is among the most diverse in the Middle East and North Africa. Diversity is a key strength in the Egyptian economy where growth is driven by many sectors, helping ensure long-term growth prospects for all sectors.

FDI to Egypt increased substantially, signaling that government policies to increase foreign investment are working. In a 2016 FdiMarkets, a subsidiary of Financial Times Group, list the top 10 emerging markets recipients of Greenfield foreign direct investment, and Egypt came on 5th place, after India, China, Indonesia and USA. Egypt saw its ranking in global FDI inflows from increase from 15th globally the previous year to 5th place in 2016.

The primary growth drivers, and thus investment targets, were chiefly the financial industry, which has seen increased growth and expansion since a return to stability. Egypt's pharmaceutical industry, telecommunications sector, automotive, and raw materials also have become attractive targets for investment.

In June 2016 by UNCTAD reported that Egypt was one of the top five destinations for inbound FDI in Africa, receiving Usd6.9 billion in 2015, an increase of nearly 50% from 2014.

Recently, Russia's ministry of trade announced that a number of Russian companies were planning to invest Usd4.6 billion in a new industrial park in East Port Said, with construction slated to begin in 2018. Much of the investment is expected to come from the private sector, with energy companies Gazprom and Inter RAO among those interested, according to press reports. The park will also offer an attractive tax regime for foreign firms, including a 10% income tax and no sales tax, according to press reports.

Egypt has access to large key markets through various multilateral and bilateral trade agreements with the USA, European, Middle Eastern and African countries; which secures benefits to Egyptian-based producers supplying these markets.

Key global markets in Europe, the Middle East, Africa and the Indian Subcontinent are all readily accessible from Egypt. Closer to the European and North American markets than other major exporters including India, China and the Philippines, Egypt is also located on key international logistics routes.

Egypt enjoys the existence of the Suez Canal, which is considered to be the shortest link between the east and the west due to its unique geographic location.

Approximately 8% of the world's maritime shipping passes through the Suez Canal each year.

Vessels transiting through the canal from east to west or from west to east make significant savings in distance, time and operating costs. Moreover, the maritime transport is the cheapest means of transport, with more than 80% of world trade volume transported via waterways (seaborne trade).

We recommend you to look at investments in Egypt in the following sectors: infrastructure, logistics and transportation, tourism, manufacturing, information and communication technology, mining, petrochemicals, financial services, healthcare, pharmaceuticals, textiles, retail, real estate and construction.

7. SEYCHELLES

Seychelles is guided by a dynamic vision of economic growth and social well-being. In line with this strategy, the country has witnessed numerous investments in education, health, housing and other services and sectors over the years.

In spite of the many constraints related to its small size, Seychelles is doing its utmost to manage economic and social development with due regards to the environment, and may be considered as an exemplary country that has embarked on a sustainable development path. It is moving steadily and unstoppably forward, making the most of modern technology and its unique, vibrant, dynamic mix of people and cultures.

Over the years the tourism industry has contributed to more than 20% of the country's GDP and 60% of total foreign exchange receipts making it the single largest earner of foreign exchange in the economy. Over 15% of the total work force is directly employed in tourism related businesses including accommodation, restaurants, car hire businesses, airlines, tour operator, dive centers etc.

Today there are several leading international airlines, providing non-stop flights from London, Paris, Rome, Milan, Frankfurt, Dubai, Doha, Johannesburg, Nairobi, Mauritius, Reunion and Singapore.

Seychelles boasts some of the world's most prestigious names in the hospitality industry, including: Hilton, Four Seasons, Kempinski, and 31 new establishments are scheduled to appear on the scene in the near future including Emirates Holidays, Shangri-La and Oberoi.

With over 115 islands to sail to, each with their own distinctive features: granite sculptures, coral formations, reefs teeming with life and vibrant colors, exotic birds, beautiful sunsets and sunrises – what better way to explore than aboard a luxury mini cruise ship.

There is definite potential for the growth of the yachting industry in Seychelles. The seascape of the Seychelles Islands affords unlimited opportunity for the growth of the sailing industry. Mega-Yachts and Super Yachts, of the rich and famous often make their way to our shores, increasing the prospects to develop and offer infrastructural and logistical services to such clients.

Investment opportunities include sea based dive operations, live-aboard yachting experiences, mini-cruises, excursions, water-sports (in designated areas only) and other leisure marine activities.

Home to industrial fishing fleets from the European Union and Far East, Seychelles lies at the center of the western Indian Ocean tuna migratory routes, making it the region's most efficient hub from which to fish tuna and tuna-like species. It is therefore economical in light of the recent increase in international fuel prices, which have inflated the cost of sailing to and from fishing grounds. Seychelles, in fact, is the shortest distance to and from 90% of the tuna fishing grounds in the Indian Ocean. It is strategically located for fuel efficiency and the Seychelles port provides 24hr services with a very low turnaround time.

Today, a thriving, Seychellois-dominated, artisanal and semi industrial sector supplies the local market and sends high value-added fisheries products to the international market.

Industrial fisheries are led by European purse-seiner tuna fishing boats, which maintain a steady supply to the world's second largest tuna cannery, Indian Ocean Tuna (IOT), owned by MW Brands 60% and SSI 40% based in Victoria.

Aquaculture in Seychelles has great potential. The ambient environmental characteristics of Seychelles coupled with the new investment incentives on offer will make this sector irresistible to prospective investors.

A wide variety of opportunities exist in the processing and value addition of tuna, such as tuna loins, sashimi, sushi, and tuna steaks for the international market. Other tuna-like species have also been identified as having potential for processing and export.

In addition, the expected growth in the tourism sector will generate increased local demand for the supply of Seychelles' seafood.

We recommend you to look at investments in Seychelles in the following sectors: financial services, tourism, real estate resorts development, fishing, manufacturing of seafood, aquaculture, and marinas.

8. GHANA

Formerly known as the Gold Coast, Ghana gained independence from Britain in 1957, becoming the first Sub-Saharan nation to break free from colonial rule.

Gold, cocoa and more recently oil form the cornerstone of Ghana's economy and helped fuel an economic boom.

Ghana's wealth of resources, democratic political system and dynamic economy, makes it undoubtedly one of Africa's leading lights. Gaining the world's confidence with a peaceful political transition and a grounded and firm commitment to Democracy has helped in expediting Ghana's growth in foreign direct investment (FDI) in recent years.

Ghana has attracted the attention of well-known international businesses, investing in all sectors of the economy.

Ghana is considered one of the more stable countries in West Africa since its transition to multi-party Democracy in 1992, the country has made major strides towards consolidating its democratic achievements. There have been five free and fair elections in the past 20 years and two peaceful transfers of power, which is enough in itself to attract substantial investor interest.

Ghana ranks 26th globally and 2nd in Africa in the 2016 World Press Freedom Index which measures the pluralism, independence of the media, quality of legislative framework and safety of journalist in each of the 180 countries in the ranking. The broadcast media in Ghana is the strongest, with radio being the most far reaching medium of communication putting Ghana in an enviable political position and formidable social capital.

Ghana's governance has received significant progress through the strengthening of its democratic credentials. There are 24 registered political parties in Ghana according to the Electoral Commission. The landscape is dominated however by two parties. The longest traditional Democracy in Africa has been practiced by Ghana.

The Ibrahim Index of African Governance which assesses the performance of various countries by measuring the extent to which they meet the expectations of citizens politically, socially and economically has ranked Ghana 7th in the 2016 index.

Ghana has recently embarked on an ambitious but achievable reform program to improve the investment climate for both local and international investors. These efforts have paid off tremendously with Ghana being ranked the best place for doing business in West Africa, ahead of Nigeria and Ivory Coast, according to the 2017 Ease of Doing Business Report.

Ghana has a solid tradition of investments in agriculture and agro-processing. The financial services and telecommunications sectors are fast gaining ground, providing dynamic and innovative services to the most diverse customers in the world. Further opportunities exist in manufacturing, ICT, and Tourism. Mineral deposits including gold and diamond abound, and with the discovery of oil.

Ghana's medium term development framework, the Ghana Shared Growth and Development Agenda, pinpoints the critical and vital role infrastructure plays in propelling economic growth and sustainable poverty reduction, both key objectives of the Better Ghana Agenda.

In the specific context of improving the level of infrastructure in the country, the goal is to facilitate both intra-regional trade and to open up rural areas for investment, productivity enhancement and job creation, introduce/deepen competition and create an enabling environment for the private sector to spearhead the country's development.

We recommend you to look at investments in Ghana in the following sectors: Oil and Gas, agriculture, agro processing, horticulture, cotton and textiles, tourism, mineral processing, healthcare, and energy.

9. NIGERIA

Nigeria is the largest economy and most populous country in Africa with an estimated population of more than 180 million and an Usd1.089 trillion GDP in 2016. Although Nigeria's economy has become more diversified, crude oil sales have continued to be the main source of export earnings and government revenues.

Nigeria is Africa's most populous country, accounting for approximately one-sixth of the continent's people and 2.4% of the world's population. It is arguably one of the most culturally diverse societies in the world, with approximately 250 ethnic groups among its people. The dominant and most influential ethnic groups according to the National Population Commission (NPC) are: Hausa and Fulani in the north (29%), Yoruba in the southwest (21%), Igbo in the southeast (18%), Ijaw in the Niger Delta (10%), Kanuri in the north (4%), Ibibio in the Niger Delta (3.5%), and Tiv in the north-central (2.5%). While Nigeria's diverse nationalities and cultures offer incredible opportunities for business, they sometimes present challenges, especially in designing sales promotions and advertising that match various cultural perceptions, religious practices and traditional values. For instance, while the use of certain female portraits may not raise an eyebrow in the south, it may fuel a product/service boycott in the North.

Nigeria has a record of steady growth and improved political stability. Recent rebasing of Nigeria's GDP makes it the largest economy and market in Africa and the 26th largest in the world. Nigeria's annual growth rate averaged 7% over the past decade. Almost 40 million Nigerian live in consuming class households. As a result, the country is regarded as one of the fastest growing economies in the world. To sustain this annual growth rate, the Government of Nigeria is liberalizing Nigeria's economy, promoting public-private partnership and encouraging strategic alliances with foreign firms, especially for infrastructure development and technology acquisition in critical sectors such as security, power generation, transportation, and healthcare.

The considerable strides that Nigeria have made in the recent decade have not been fully recognized outside the country, because Nigeria's security challenges have gained more coverage in the media that its economic successes.

Nigeria is the key driver of international trade in all of West Africa. Market analysts from the National Association of Chambers of Commerce, Industry, Mines and Agriculture (NACCIMA) claim that Nigeria accounts for over 40% of imports in the sub-region and ranks among Africa's largest consumer markets.

Nigeria has enormous resources, most of which are yet to be fully exploited. Tremendous investment opportunity exists in the solid minerals sector. Mineral resources include coal, tin, iron ore and others. Agricultural products include, among others, groundnuts, palm oil, cocoa and coconut. Nigeria also has a booming leather and textile industry and is one of the largest oil producers on the continent creating huge inflows of foreign investment.

Since 2005 Nigeria has been considered to be among the "Next Eleven": the countries identified by Goldman Sachs investment bank as having a high potential of becoming, along with the BRICS, the world's largest economies. The growth is driven by a population of approximately 180 million (growing at over 3% per annum) and by an affluent and an increasing middle class. The "cosmopolitans" (higher middle class) and the affluent, together 10% of the population or 18 million people, account for 40% of total consumption. Another 21% of the population, or 36 million people, could be considered "rising strivers!" and are therefore of interest to multinationals. About 65% of the Nigerian population is younger than 25 years.

Nigeria is one of the top three destinations for foreign direct investment (FDI) in Africa, and the inflows have been increasing over the last years, according to UNCTAD, making Nigeria the 19th largest FDI recipient worldwide. While most of the investment is directed at the oil & gas sector, FDI flows are diversifying.

Nigeria has introduced a number of incentives to assist foreign investors. The Nigerian Investment Promotion Commission Act ensures that investors can repatriate 100% of profits and dividends, and that 100% ownership of companies is allowed in all sectors, apart from oil & gas.

Nigeria is the biggest oil exporter in Africa, with the largest natural gas reserves on the continent. Developments in key industry sectors such as Oil and Gas, Power Generation, and Construction indicate that Nigeria offers investors significant opportunities. Nigeria ranks as Africa's largest oil producer and the twelfth largest in the world, producing high-value, low-sulfur content crude oil.

Nigeria is rapidly developing its physical and industrial infrastructure, in terms of transportation, communications, electricity and water supply. Extensive road repairs and new construction activities are gradually being implemented as state governments, in particular, spend their portions of enhanced government revenue allocations. Four of Nigeria's airports– Lagos, Kano, Port Harcourt and Abuja– currently receive international flights and there are several domestic private Nigerian carriers.

The Government of Nigeria recently announced that Nigeria requires about Usd3.4 billion to upgrade its transmission grid to enable effective release of all generated power to increase capacity from less than 10.000 MW to 20.000 MW.

In the construction sector, the GON has identified a number of road and housing development projects. These present possibilities for construction and Real estate developers and heavy equipment manufacturers. Some of the projects involve construction of "new alignments" (green field projects) and improvement of "existing alignments" (brown field projects). Green field projects include the construction of a Golden Triangle Super Highway that will connect key hubs of economic activity and add an additional 5.000km to the national network of roads in Nigeria. Another is the construction of a Second Lagos Outer Ring Road to decongest traffic in the Lagos metropolitan area and improve movement of goods from the Lagos Sea Ports. The ongoing GON mandate to the Federal Housing Authority (FHA) to construct 800.000 housing units throughout Nigeria, with the Federal Mortgage Bank providing financing support, also offers opportunities to developers for exports of housing equipment and services.

Similar trade opportunities exist for exporters in other leading industry sectors such as aerospace (aircraft and parts); agricultural products (wheat, dairy, poultry, wines, and packaged food) and equipment; automobiles, trucks, buses, automotive parts, and accessories;

computer hardware and software; education; environmental services; security and safety equipment, accessories, and services; franchising; healthcare services and medical equipment; marine vessels; and telecommunications equipment and services.

Nigeria is also home to the most lucrative telecoms market in Africa, which is growing at twice the African average. The explosion of industries such as the mobile telecommunications market and the unparalleled success of foreign companies such as South Africa's MTN have demonstrated that potential can be turned into reality.

As the largest economy in Africa, and as a gateway to smaller West African countries and a net importer of most high precision equipment, Nigeria can be a very rewarding market for investors that take the time and effort to understand its market conditions and opportunities, find the right partners and clients, and take a long-term approach to market development.

We recommend you to look at investments in Nigeria in the following sectors: Oil, agriculture, agro-processing, mineral processing, healthcare, energy, telecom, infrastructure, real estate, retail and consumer goods.

10. TANZANIA

Tanzania enjoys an abundance of natural wealth, which offers tremendous investment opportunities for investors. These include an excellent geographical location (six land locked countries depend on Tanzania ports as their cheapest entry and exit ports); arable land; world renowned tourist attractions (Serengeti, Kilimanjaro, Ngorongoro, and the Spice islands of Zanzibar); natural resources; a sizeable domestic and sub regional market; a wide local raw materials supply base; abundant and inexpensive skills; assurance of personal safety; warm friendly people and a suitable market policy orientation.

Tanzania is an emerging economy with a very high growth potential. Whilst the economy is relatively diversified, a number of opportunities remain untapped in many sectors.

Following its liberalized trade regime and a sustained economic growth, Tanzania has enormous opportunities in both domestic and external markets. Currently, Tanzania exports coffee, cotton, manufactures cashew nuts, minerals, tea, sisal, tobacco, cloves and pyrethrum.

Business opportunities in Tanzania go beyond its borders, by considering the East African Community (with almost 90 million people), SADC (300 million people), EU (through Everything but Arms initiative), US market through the African Growth and Opportunity Act (AGOA) window, and Chinese market through Special Preferential Tariff Agreement with China. In all these markets products from Tanzania receive either relatively low tariff or tariff free treatment.

Tanzania offers high degree of investment security because of unparalleled political stability that is strife-free without ethnic division; democratic rule that respects diversity of opinion and a strong tradition of constitutionality and rule of law.

The country offers business-friendly macro-economic stability with low inflation, stable exchange rates supported by unrestricted and unconditional transferability of profits, loan repayments, emoluments, royalties and fees.

There is simplified bureaucracy, streamlined through the acclaimed services of the Tanzania Investment Centre which is a one-stop-facilitation agency of government serving registered investors and businesses.

Successful economic liberalization measures commended by both the World Bank and the IMF with business-supportive legislation continually being improved through genuine dialogue between government and the private sector.

Tanzania offers investors many lucrative investment opportunities in infrastructure, privatization and value adding facilities.

Investments in Tanzania are guaranteed against Political risks, Nationalization and Expropriation.

Tourism is a sector with enormous potential in Tanzania. Tourist's sites in Tanzania are indeed God sent gifts. Visitors to Tanzania do not only encounter the overwhelming force of nature but also enjoy a serene contact with it. Tourists observe and feel it at work in almost all the national parks and game reserves. Mountain climbers can also have a field training trying to reach the top of the highest mountain in Africa. For beach lovers, the palms on the sandy beaches of marking the western shores of the Indian Ocean do offer the peace and comfort for relaxation, while the Indian Ocean offers all sorts of opportunities ranging from swimming, angling, sailing and other water sports, as well as the opportunity to view its treasures, the colorful living and non-living resources. All this can be enjoyed in welcoming atmosphere of the friendly and hospitable Tanzanians.

Tanzania is proud to be the exclusive home of:

THE KILIMANJARO: This is a snow-capped mountain, just south of the Equator. At 5895 meters above sea level, the Kilimanjaro is the highest mountain in Africa and the tallest free standing in the world.

THE SERENGETI: The Serengeti is a national park with millions of wild life living together. It is indeed a garden of nature. The nature of this national park provoked a remark from the famous Prof. Grzimek that "Serengeti shall never die".

THE NGORONGORO CRATER: This is a World Heritage Site within the Ngorongoro Conservation Area. The Crater is the home of several species of wildlife. The famous Prof. Grzimek once observed that it was not possible to give a "fair description of the crater for, there is nothing with which to compare it". He concluded that the crater is one of the world wonders.

THE OLDUVAI GORGE: This is a place where remains of the earliest human, the

Nutcracker (Zinjathropus Boisei) were found by the Leakeys.

THE SEALDUS GAME RESERVE: This game reserve is the largest in Africa and one of the largest in the world.

ZANZIBAR: This is the spice island with abundant history, beautiful and white sandy beaches.

Tanzania is partly the owner of the following:

LAKE VICTORIA: The largest lake in Africa and the second largest fresh water lake in the world. It is the source of the River Nile. 66% of the lake lies within Tanzanian territory.

LAKE TANGANYIKA: The longest fresh water lake in the world and the second deepest. 41% of the lake lies within Tanzanian territory.

LAKE NYASA: Lake Nyasa located in the Great Rift Valley lies between Malawi on the west and Tanzania and Mozambique on the east. It is about 500 km (about 310 miles) long and an average of about 48 km (about 30 miles) wide. An outlet of Lake Nyasa flows into the Zambezi River.

We recommend you to look at investments in Tanzania in the following sectors:

tourism, agriculture and agro-based industries, mineral water bottling, mining, infrastructure development, energy, manufacturing, chemical industries, fishing, forestry, construction and real estate.

"Before you are a leader, success is all about growing yourself. When you become a leader, success is all about growing others." Jack Welch

CHAPTER 14: The Game Changers contributing to Africa Rising.

Like the great man, Nelson Mandela, once said, "It always seems impossible until it's done!" I just love this quote. It's so powerful if you truly believe it.

I honestly believe that our generation (*the crazy Millennials*) we grow up thinking that nothing is impossible and we have feed this into the brain of all living generation today. If you think about it, most of the revolutions in the tech sector as come out because our generation really loves the impossible and companies have invested billions to make sure they create the products and technology that our generation would end up buying and using in our daily lives.

That's one of the reasons you see too many startup tech hubs across the world today waking up every day thinking about the next billion dollar idea, such as things that haven't been done yet and we will try to make it happen during our lifetime. Like let's try to go live in Mars, Augmented reality, Artificial Intelligence search engines, tourism in space, self-driving cars, solar fuel, the cleanest energy source, cashless digital wallet payment systems, bitcoin currency, blockchain technology, transferring energy from one country to another, etc.

Beside all the game changers around the world, who are the biggest game changers contributing to the rise of Africa today?

They are the best and brightest minds who leverage emerging technology, global finance and sheer brainpower to upend entire industries and transform the everyday lives of millions.

To compile this list of the boldest businesses leaders we started by screening hundreds of companies, considering their innovation, global access, focus on Africa, and contributing to the future of the continent.

The list below, which according to facts, are companies whom are considered to be the most innovative and craziest ones bringing changes with their investment and creating real impact in 3 key areas (social, environmental, and financial returns). The list includes 30 companies from various sectors such as foundation, banking, agriculture, financial technology, telecom, airlines, manufacturing, fashion, entertainment, movies, hospitality, healthcare, e-commerce platforms, and Private equity.

The list is in no particular order. You will find a mix of the big boys and the little guys.

1. MO IBRAHIM FOUNDATION

The Mo Ibrahim Foundation (MIF) is an African foundation, established in 2006 with one focus: the critical importance of governance and leadership in Africa.

It is the Mo Ibrahim Foundation belief that governance and leadership lie at the heart of any tangible and shared improvement in the quality of life of African citizens.

Leadership is about making choices, defining priorities, and taking risks.

Governance is about properly documenting and effectively implementing these choices.

Africa has made considerable progress over the last decade. However, the continent still faces a number of complex and massive challenges in most areas. How can it translate its wealth of resources into improved quality of life for its citizens, in an equitable and sustainable way? What should governments do to make sure that their GDP growth is matched by employment gains? Why are political and human rights still lagging in many areas, despite significant economic progress?

These challenges pose a threat to Africa's success and potential transformation in the long-term. But all of these challenges can be met through sound leadership and governance on the continent.

African countries need to define a strategy - a 'business plan' - built on an inclusive vision which assesses and prioritizes challenges, makes the best use of human, natural and financial resources and closely monitors results in order to ensure efficient and tangible implementation.

The Foundation, which is a non-grant making organization, focuses on defining, assessing and enhancing governance and leadership in Africa through four main initiatives:

Ibrahim Index of African Governance (IIAG)

Ibrahim Forum

Ibrahim Prize for Achievement in African Leadership

Ibrahim Leadership Fellowships

2. AFREXIMBANK

The African Export Import Bank was established in Abuja, Nigeria in October, 1993 by African Governments, African private and institutional investors as well as non-African financial institutions and private investors for the purpose of financing, promoting and expanding intra-African and extra-African trade.

The Bank was established under the twin constitutive instruments of an Agreement signed by member States and multilateral organizations, and which confers on the Bank the status of an international multilateral organization; as well as a Charter, governing its corporate structure and operations, signed by all Shareholders. The authorized share capital of the Bank is Usd5 billion.

The Bank, headquartered in Cairo, the capital of the Arab Republic of Egypt, commenced operations on 30 September, 1994, following the signature of a Headquarters Agreement with the host Government in August, 1994. It has branch offices in Harare, Abuja, Abidjan and Nairobi.

3. DANGOTE GROUP

The Dangote Group is a Nigerian multinational industrial conglomerate, founded by billionaire Aliko Dangote. It is the largest conglomerate in West Africa and one of the largest on the African continent. It generated revenue in excess of Usd3billion. The group is one of the leading diversified business conglomerates in Africa, and employs more than 26.000 people.

The Group's activities encompass:

Cement - Manufacturing / Importing

Sugar - Manufacturing & Refining

Salt - Refining

Flour & Semolina - Milling

Pasta - Manufacturing

Noodles - Manufacturing

Poly Products - Manufacturing

Logistics - Port Management & Haulage

Real estate

Dangote Foundation

Since inception, the Group has experienced phenomenal growth on account of quality of its goods and services, its focus on cost leadership and efficiency of its human capital. Today, Dangote Group is a multi-billion Naira company poised to reach new heights, in every endeavor.

The Group's core business focus is to provide local, value added products and services that meet the 'basic needs' of the populace. Through the construction and operation of large scale manufacturing facilities in Nigeria and across Africa, the Group is focused on building local manufacturing capacity to generate employment and provide goods for the people.

4. ETHIOPIAN AIRLINES

Ethiopian Airlines (also known as Ethiopian) is the flag carrier of Ethiopia. During the past sixty five plus years, Ethiopian has become one of the continent's leading carriers, unrivalled in Africa for efficiency and operational success, turning profits for almost all the years of its existence.

Operating at the forefront of technology, the airline has also become one of Ethiopia's major industries and a veritable institution in Africa. It commands a lion's share of the pan African network including the daily and double daily east-west flight across the continent. Ethiopian currently serves 97 international and 20 domestic destinations operating the newest and youngest fleet.

The Addis Ababa Bole International Airport is the major hub for Ethiopian Airlines and one of the largest airports in Africa. The ultra-modern airport terminal was inaugurated on January 21, 2003. This spacious terminal handles all international flights with its 21st century facilities.

Addis Ababa Airport is the busiest airport in East Africa with a capacity of providing a world class passenger and cargo services to more than 6.5 million international and domestic passengers each year.

Ethiopian has an advanced maintenance base, which is fully operational for Airframe maintenance up to D-Checks, Engine, Overhaul, Components repair & overhaul, Light Aircraft maintenance and technical, and management assistance for other airlines. The maintenance base is certified by the US- Federal Aviation Administration (FAA).

5. SOUTH AFRICA AIRWAYS

South African Airways (SAA) is the flag carrier and largest airline of South Africa, with headquarters in Airways Park on the grounds of OR Tambo International Airport in Kempton Park, Ekurhuleni, Gauteng.

From Johannesburg, SAA's hub, the national carrier of South Africa flies to over 35 destinations across Africa, the Middle East, Asia, Europe, Australia and North and South America. From SAA first flight in February 1934 they have welcomed the world to South Africa by showing off the warm generous heart of the country.

SAA have become a global airline whose excellence - 14 Skytrax awards acknowledging SAA as the best African airline and Africa's first 4 star airline - has been built a dedication to excellence and embracing innovation.

Becoming the best airline in Africa does not happen overnight. SAA have more than 80 years of excellence and innovation to draw on.

The airline flies to many destinations worldwide, in partnership with SA Express, SA Airlink and its low cost carrier, Mango, within South Africa and across the continent, and nine intercontinental routes from its Johannesburg hub at OR Tambo International Airport.

SAA currently operates as a member of the Star Alliance.

6. WEFARM

There are an estimated 500 million smallholder farmers in the world today, most of them living on less than Usd1 a day. For rural farmers in the developing world, the challenges are amplified by a lack of access to information on farming practices that could improve their yields and profitability.

WeFarm, connects rural farmers in Africa - currently, Kenya and Uganda - and Latin America (Peru) through a simple mobile phone platform that allows them to ask and answer questions about agriculture, tapping into generations' worth of grassroots knowledge.

Relying mostly on print and radio advertising, WeFarm has acquired 141.000 users who have collectively asked some 210.000 questions and contributed more than 292.000 answers on topics ranging from controlling blossom end rot in tomatoes and the importance of pruning coffee plants, to the best ways to prepare farmland during dry season and the economics of raising rabbits.

Over the next five years, WeFarm aims to grow its user base to 1 million farmers and to keep the SMS service free, bringing in revenue by selling data gleaned from agricultural trends to corporate customers, governments, and NGOs.

WeFarm has been ranked among Africa's Top 10 Most Innovative Companies by Fast Company's innovation rankings.

7. ANDELA

Andela extends engineering teams with world-class software developers. They recruit the most talented developers on the African continent, shape them into technical leaders, and place them as full-time distributed team members with companies that range from Microsoft and IBM to dozens of high-growth startups. Backed by Chan Zuckerberg Initiative, GV (Google Ventures) and Spark Capital, Andela is building the next generation of global technology leaders.

Andela's motto: "Brilliance is evenly distributed; opportunity is not." In the U.S., there are five job openings for every software developer looking for work. In Africa, meanwhile, more young people will join the workforce over the next 20 years than the rest of the world combined. This young startup founded by entrepreneurs from North America and Africa aims to bridge the gap by recruiting high-potential developers in Africa, putting them through an intensive training program, and sending them to work for companies including Microsoft, IBM, Facebook, and dozens of high-growth startups around the world.

8. MFS AFRICA

With its huge "unbanked" population, Africa has seen some of the most rapid adoption of mobile payment systems in the world. While few people have a bank or credit card - or a formal bank account - most people have a mobile phone, and in places like Kenya, 70% of people with phones also use them as a "mobile wallet" for making payments via SMS. Sub-Saharan Africa (excluding South Africa) has fewer than 30 million bank cards in circulation, but more than 150 million mobile wallets, worth an estimated Usd90 billion.

There are mobile money services in nearly every market, but most are confined to domestic transactions, with almost no interoperability between networks or across borders.

To let customers send money to people outside their network or their country - and enable banks, mobile operators, merchants, utility providers, and employers to issue microloans, sell airtime, accept e-payments, and pay digital wages - all these systems need a way to talk to each other. That's what Port Louis, Mauritius-based MFS Africa does. Through partnerships with major mobile network operators like Airtel, Econet, MTN, Orange, Tigo, and Vodafone, this startup has become the largest mobile money gateway on the continent, connecting 120 million mobile wallets across Sub-Saharan Africa through its API platform.

Moving to monetize its position at the center of this vast and still largely untapped financial market, the company spent 2016 in strategic-expansion mode, forging a partnership with Wari, a popular Senegalese money transfer service, to build out its remittance and payments service popular with major employers in the region, and in July bought Sochitel, an international airtime "top-up" provider, to add airtime top-ups to its portfolio of services.

9. GRO INTELLIGENCE

Africa has more than half of the world's unused arable land, and 65% of the continent's workforce works in agriculture. Yet less than 1% of outstanding commercial bank loans actually go to the agricultural sector.

Gro Intelligence is changing the way the world understands agriculture. By structuring and contextualizing the world's agricultural data, they make complex analysis simple and accessible.

Under the company solutions is a cloud based software platform named Clews, which is a discovery engine for all data related to food and agriculture that lets you extract insights and access predictive modeling at a scale never possible before. They are enabling agriculture to enter the modern age. Agriculture data has, for far too long, remained hidden and too difficult to access. The roadblocks to a better understanding of our food have been the need to become an expert, a lack of access, a lack of reliability and the inability to look ahead. Gro Intelligence removes these institutional barriers for key agricultural players, from financial institutions to policy makers and physical traders, to create a comprehensive, holistic, and timely picture of agriculture.

Clews, sifts through a constantly updated stream of food and agriculture data never before accessible in one place - satellite imagery, government and industry reports, weather forecasts, and reports directly from small farmers.

In addition to helping financial industry customers analyze opportunities, Gro Intelligence helps government policy makers, farmers, buyers, food processors, and logistics providers to plan, invest, and forecast with unprecedented accuracy.

10. IROKO

IROKO is one of Nigeria's largest internet and entertainment companies. The company is the African equivalent of Netflix.

24 hours a day, 7 days a week, they showcase the very best of Nollywood, Africa's most popular, best

loved for entertainment, with movie fans tuning in from every single corner of the earth.

Nollywood is the most prolific film industry in the world, with an average of more than 2.500 releases in 2005, versus 485 in the United States and 1.091 in India.

With hit movies and awesome original TV series, playing on IROKO apps, TV channels and via their global distribution partnerships, the company is so far the best platform for African storytelling.

Iroko company vision is to expand the Iroko brand into in-flight movies, satellite television, music, and other forms of entertainment. So today they are diversifying into different businesses under the same brand such as IrokoTV, IrokoX, IrokoNetwork, IrokoGlobal, Iroking, Iroko+, RokStudios, and ROK.

11. ZUVAA

Zuvva is an e-commerce site that was launched with Usd500 investment and the simple idea that there was an unmet demand among people living outside Africa for authentic African styles.

Sourcing from a growing list of designers in Nigeria, Ghana, and South Africa as well as North America, Zuvaa has become the Amazon/Etsy of vibrant Ankara or Kente fabrics and cutting-edge clothing as seen on the streets of Lagos, Accra, and Johannesburg.

Launched in May 2014, Zuvaa currently features some 75 designers from Africa and North America, and rang up Usd2.3 million in sales of clothing and accessories in 2016.

12. SOLEREBELS

SoleRebels is one of the most disruptive innovative companies in the past few years. All the Ethiopian-born social entrepreneur wanted to do was provide her poor community in Addis Ababa (Zenabwork) with jobs, and the eco-friendly company remains the world's one and only World Fair Trade Organization (WTFO) certified footwear company.

Every single one of soleRebels' shoes is handcrafted and they spotlight the amazing artisan heritage of Ethiopia as well as the creative skills of the people in her local community. The Founder Bethlehem Tilahun Alemu is currently a United Nations (UN) Goodwill Ambassador for Entrepreneurship and is on the board of the United Nations Industrial Development Organization (UNIDO).

SoleRebels employees are among the highest paid workers in Ethiopia with full medical insurance which covers them and their families. This probably has something to do with why the brand, which relies solely (pun intended) on recycled car tires and inner tubes, hand-spun cotton and hand-woven fabrics, is the first of its kind to emerge from a developing nation and go global. Last year, Bethlehem launched 'Republic of

Leather', a new venture which offers custom made leather wears and accessories.

13. REKINDLE LEARNING

Rekindle Learning is an education technology company founded on the belief that every person should be able to develop their knowledge and learn. Computer and mobile internet devices are transformative in their capacity to overcome inefficiencies, socio-economic barriers and weak infrastructure. Now these benefits can be translated to education, training and development with Rekindle Learning.

Founder and CEO, Rapelang Rabana is a technology entrepreneur who co-founded her first company Yeigo after graduating from the University of Cape Town with a Bachelor of Business Science (Computer Science Honours). Yeigo is internationally recognized for its pioneering innovations in mobile VoIP and IP communications.

Rapelang is a Global Shaper of the World Economic Forum, was the Curator of the Cape Town Hub of Global Shapers 2013/2014 and was invited to the Annual Meeting of the Forum in Davos in 2012. Rapelang also serves an Ambassador for the UN World Summit Awards promoting the use of ICT, and was selected as an Endeavor Entrepreneur. She was listed by Forbes Africa as a '30 under 30 Best Young African Entrepreneur' and '20 Young Power Women in

Africa' for 2013 and graced the cover of Forbes Africa before the age of 30.

14. GROW AFRICA PARTNERSHIP

The Grow Africa Partnership was founded jointly by the African Union (AU), The New Partnership for Africa's Development (NEPAD) and the World Economic Forum in 2011. Grow Africa works to increase private sector investment in agriculture, and accelerate the execution and impact of investment commitments. The aim is to enable countries to realize the potential of the agriculture sector for economic growth and job creation, particularly among farmers, women and youth. Grow Africa brokers collaboration between governments, international and domestic agriculture companies, and smallholder farmers in order to lower the risk and cost of investing in agriculture, and improve the speed of return to all stakeholders.

Grow Africa is an African-owned, country-led, market-based and inclusive platform for cross-sector collaboration; to increase inclusive and responsible investment in to African agriculture; and thereby generate agriculture-driven economic growth that contributes to reducing poverty and hunger.

The Grow Africa Partnership comprises over 200 companies and governments in 12 countries. These companies have made formal commitments with the government in the respective country to invest in agriculture. Ten of these countries are part of the New Alliance for Food Security and Nutrition, a partnership in which stakeholders - public and private sectors, and donors - commit to specific policy reforms and investments, outlined in Cooperation Frameworks that accelerate implementation of African country food security strategies.

Grow Africa is supported by a Secretariat which during 2012-2015 has been designed and incubated by the World Economic Forum in Geneva, Switzerland. The Secretariat transitioned in 2016 to Johannesburg, South Africa and is now hosted by the NEPAD Agency.

Grow Africa is an autonomous entity, hosted by the NEPAD Agency and governed by a multi-stakeholder Steering Committee.

Additionally, Grow Africa's priorities are guided by a Leadership Council, an informal group of leaders committed to realizing the investment commitments pledged by the private sector, governments and development partners within the New Alliance and Grow Africa. It consists of high-level representatives from African governments, development partners, the African and multi-national private sector companies, civil society, and farmers' organizations that monitor, support and advance progress. Two co-conveners lead the Leadership Council. These are: African Union Commission, World Economic Forum.

Grow Africa is supported by grants from the following donors: United States Agency for

International Development (USAID) and Swiss Agency for Development and Cooperation (SDC).

15. HELIOS INVESTMENT PARTNERS

Helios Investment Partners is one of the largest Africa-focused investment firms, with a record that spans creating start-ups to providing established companies with growth capital and expertise.

Led and predominantly staffed by African professionals with the language skills and cultural affinity to engage with local entrepreneurs, managers and intermediaries on the continent, Helios leverages its local and global networks, identifying businesses opportunities and structuring proprietary transactions around them. The firm's unique combination of a deep knowledge of the Africa operating environment, a singular commitment to the region and a proven capability to manage complexity, is reflected in the firm's diverse portfolio of growing market leading businesses and its position as the partner of choice for multinational corporations.

16. ANALYSE AFRICA

Analyse Africa, a service from the Financial Times, is a digital database providing macroeconomic data from leading global sources. Gain instant access to thousands of professionally validated indicators in order to analyse, evaluate and spot opportunities in Africa.

Analyse Africa is used to analyse, understand and evaluate entire economies to inform critical business decisions by financial service organizations, corporations, government agencies, multilaterals, consultancies and research and academic institutions worldwide.

Analyse Africa features data from The World Bank, International Monetary Fund, UN agencies, national statistics and government offices.

Each data source is clearly referenced, so that you know exactly which source you are working with at each stage. This also allows accurate quotation in reports and presentations. The database features more than a decade's worth of data, dating from the year 2000 to the present day.

A dedicated team of researchers collate leading global and local data sources, across 54 African countries. The data goes through rigorous data cleansing and quality control checks.

Data are categorized into key groups: Banking and finance; Economic potential; Foreign direct investment; Infrastructure; Political stability; Social dynamics; Labour; Trade; Environment; and Education.

As soon as data sources are released, (typically at different times of the year, dependent on the source) our team of researchers runs the data through cleansing checks and quality control procedures before adding to the database.

All data can be exported quickly and easily into Excel, CSV and PDF format.

17. HEIRS HOLDINGS GROUP

Heirs Holdings is improving lives across Africa by investing in key sectors that are transforming the continent. They are creating a lasting legacy for all Africans who will tomorrow inherit the Africa that they are building today.

Heirs Holdings is an African proprietary investment company, with a track record of success and a firm belief in the opportunities that Africa offers. They are known for executing successful corporate turnarounds, and for their ability to identify growth opportunities, incubate new businesses and nurture them to maturity.

As active investors, they aim to transform the companies in which they invest in, and grow them into businesses that last - creating value for their shareholders and partners, as well as economic prosperity and social wealth for the continent.

Heirs Holdings is a partner in the US government's Power Africa Initiative, which is committed to trebling access to power in Sub-Saharan Africa, working with six power Africa partner countries: Ethiopia, Ghana, Kenya, Liberia, Nigeria and Tanzania.

18. AFRICAN RAINBOW MINERALS

African Rainbow Minerals (ARM) is a leading South African diversified mining and minerals company with long-life, low unit cost operations. ARM mines and beneficiates iron ore, manganese ore, chrome ore, platinum group metals (PGMs), copper, nickel and coal. ARM also produces manganese and chrome alloys, and has investment in gold through its shareholding in Harmony.

The ARM Platinum division comprises three operating mines, Modikwa, Two Rivers and Nkomati, and two exploration joint ventures in the Kalplats Project.

ARM's ferrous metals interests are held through wholly owned ARM Ferrous in partnership with Assmang, a long-established miner and processor of metals for the world's steel industries. Assmang's operating divisions are based on its three principal commodities: iron ore, manganese and chrome. ARM's attributable beneficial interest in Assmang's operations is 50%. The other 50% is held by Assore.

ARM Coal was formed in July 2006 in partnership with global diversified mining group Xstrata Coal South Africa. The joint venture includes an economic interest of 20.2% in Xstrata Coal Operations in South Africa, Participating Coal Business (PCB) and a 26% attributable beneficial interest in Goedgevonden (GGV).

ARM Copper holds an attributable beneficial interest of 40% in the Lubambe Copper Project. Vale owns 40% of the project and ZCCM 20%. ARM Copper holds the following: The Lubambe

Copper Project (previously Konkola North Copper Project); Lubambe Extension Area (previously known as Konkola North Area A).

The company Harmony operates and develops world-class gold assets in South Africa and Papua New Guinea. ARM owns 14.7% of Harmony's issued share capital.

19. FASHION DESIGNER LOZA MALEOMBHO

Brazil-born, Abidjan-raised Ivorian designer, Loza Maleombho, runs a fashion brand that takes creativity to the next level. Educated in the United States, Loza directed the artistic aspect of her Fine Arts in Animation degree into establishing a fashion career that has seen her work with ZARA, Diesel, Jill Stuart, Yigal Azrouël, and Cynthia Rowley in her early days in New York.

Loza's brand, which is now based in Abidjan, has been featured in VOGUE, ELLE Magazine, MARIE CLAIRE and a slew of other fashion magazines.

One of Loza's designs was featured in Beyonce's video for the song 'Formation' causing a lot of buzz for both the designer and her designs.

Presently, the Loza Maleombho team consists of six people but plans to grow into a larger team of solely women to promote female empowerment as well as social and economic development. Loza also plans to establish a training workshop for young women from unprivileged backgrounds to teach them sewing, pattern making and production so as to improve their economic situations.

20. MARA GROUP

Mara Group is a pan-African multi-sector business with extensive operating experience in both African and international markets. Mara's current investments and operations span from technology, financial services, manufacturing, real estate and agriculture. The Group is currently active in 22 African countries and 24 countries worldwide.

Mara possesses in-depth knowledge and unrivalled expertise in Africa. Its approach to business is built around creating value for its shareholders, whilst ensuring a genuine and lasting impact on the communities in which it operates.

21. DUBAI CHAMBER - AFRICA GLOBAL BUSINESS FORUM

Dubai Chamber of Commerce and Industry was established in 1965. It's a non-profit public organization whose mission is to represent, support and protect the interests of the business community in Dubai. It does so by creating a favorable environment; promoting Dubai as an international business hub and by supporting the development of business.

Dubai Chamber strategic goal is to create a favorable business environment in Dubai, promote Dubai as an international business hub, support the development of business, and achieve institutional excellence and efficient management of resources. By doing so, they have created a Global Business Forum (GBF) series that was initiated in 2013 as part of Dubai Chamber's strategy of international expansion, to position Dubai as the gateway to the world.

The GBF series is a platform to engage key business and government leaders in developing trade and exploring new investment opportunities in emerging markets. Over the years the GBFs have welcomed 10 heads of state, 74 ministers and dignitaries, 5.400 CEOs and other high-ranking delegates from 65 countries around the world.

The objective of the Africa Global Business Forum is to encourage international revenue flows into Africa by engaging leading decision-makers on the global investment scene. The Forum involves prominent African stakeholders to engage in a dialogue at the highest level of implementation, advising on key strategic directives related to Africa's economic outlook.

GBF Africa brings together a high profile audience of 1.000 top-level government and corporate decision-makers, including African heads of state, ministers and dignitaries, prominent CEOs operating globally, prominent entrepreneurs, heads of private banks, sovereign wealth funds, private equity firms, the UAE government and business elite, Heads of African Investment Promotion Agencies, Chief Executives representing African & multinational organizations and world-class leaders.

The Global Business Forum on Africa is at the core of Dubai Chamber's commitment to expand mutual business relations, identifying opportunities for trade, investment and partnership for GCC and African businesses. To realize this aim and ensure the GBF Africa agenda is at the forefront of business thinking in Africa, Dubai Chamber holds a series of roadshows, travelling to strategic African regions which would benefit from using Dubai as a hub to the continent. The Roadshows involves the participation of prominent Emirati business leaders, to promote the further development of UAE - Africa economic relations.

The Roadshows feature roundtable discussions with both the private and the public sector; networking with African Chambers of Commerce and the opportunity to learn first-hand from investors with direct market experience.

Via the Africa Global Business Forum, Dubai Chamber also promotes in partnership with the Economist Intelligence Unit an app named Africa Gateway to provide analysis, insights and commercial opportunities for companies looking to invest in key markets across Africa. The app combines authoritative country analysis from The Economist Intelligence Unit with exclusive resources from the Dubai Chamber of Commerce and Industry (DCCI) on how to engage with businesses in Africa.

22. JUMIA GROUP

Jumia aims at creating a connected digital Africa to improve people's lives on the continent thanks to the Internet. Jumia's mission is to connect African consumers and entrepreneurs to do better business together. Founded in 2012, with a presence across Africa, the group has MTN, Rocket Internet, Millicom, Orange, Axa, Goldman Sachs and CDC as investors. Jumia has created a sustainable ecosystem of digital services and infrastructures through online and mobile marketplaces and classifieds.

Jumia was founded in 2012 on the basis of a very strong belief: Internet can improve people's lives in Africa. Observing the challenges that people face every day (poor infrastructures, bad traffic, limited choice, limited information, expensive products and services just to name a few), they saw a huge opportunity to leverage Internet and use it to connect people and provide them with a solution to fulfill their daily needs.

Over 500.000 local African companies are making business on Jumia every day.

Among its brands are Jumia Market, Jumia Travel, Jumia Food, Jumia Deals, Jumia House, Jumia Jobs, Jumia Car, and Jumia Services.

23. THE BUSINESS YEAR

The Business Year (TBY) is a leading research firm and publisher of annual economic resources on national economies. Present in over 25 countries,

TBY provides first-hand access to the people and ideas shaping business and policy throughout the world. Each country-specific edition contains a comprehensive range of interviews and analysis, offering an inside looks at doing business in the world's most dynamic economies. TBY's interviewees, readers, and partners comprise an international network of thought-leaders who are helping to define the future of the global economy.

The Business Year (TBY) annual publications for each of the following countries: Azerbaijan, Kazakhstan, Turkey, Malaysia, Thailand, Mozambique, Tanzania, Nigeria, Zambia, Ghana, Colombia, Dominican Republic, Ecuador, Mexico, Panama, Peru, Costa Rica, Iran, Lebanon, Oman, Qatar, Kuwait, Saudi Arabia, UAE - Abu Dhabi, UAE – Dubai, UAE – Sharjah, UAE – Ras Al Khaimah.

24. MALAIK

Small and medium-sized enterprises (SME's) are the primary job creation engine in Africa, accounting for over 95% of firms and 60%-70% of employment. Yet, SME's on the continent report access to finance as the biggest obstacle to growth.

Malaik was founded because access to finance is a problem for entrepreneurs in Africa. So many inspiring African entrepreneurs that have amazing ideas that deserve to be scaled don't have funds because it's risky for banks to give out loans to start-up businesses. Malaik helps to close that gap by selling equity in start-up businesses to interested investors.

Malaik is a global portal for high impact investing in African businesses, offering opportunities for the crowd to invest in Africa's growth story. Malaik's impact-focused approach to equity crowdfunding is unique and focused on Africa. Malaik gives investors access to the continent's opportunities, and mediates its risks with a four step due diligence process. This combination is a fresh application of technology that can unlock massive potential in the world's most promising markets.

Malaik allows accredited investors to co-invest in high impact African businesses along with experienced lead investors. Companies listed on the platform will have to go through a four steps due diligence process.

Malaik focuses on companies that provide an impact with measurable metrics. Malaik uses IRIS metrics to create measureable goals to track the SDG goals that entrepreneurs who are successfully funded via the platform can use to report their progress in achieving these goals to their crowd of investors.

25. iHub KENYA

iHub believes that African innovation plays a critical role in shaping future technology globally. The iHub was the first such space in Kenya and has spurred a revolution in the tech ecosystem across the African continent over the last five years, constantly challenging and influencing technology development.

iHub provide a part open community space, a part vector for investors and VCs, and part incubator. This is a vibrant and collaborative environment for innovators and startups to think through their ideas, and develop their solutions, lowering the barriers to entry for many young would-be entrepreneurs.

Their commitment to spurring a vibrant community of innovators and entrepreneurs to build "best in the world" companies tailored to solving the myriad of problems in Africa and across the developing world motivates us. This community includes individual developers, designers, creatives, researchers, scientists, engineers, technologists, as well non-tech people looking to launch startups.

iHub goal is to continuously fuel an ecosystem of innovation and technology that allows people to develop enterprises that creatively solve problems around them using technology, while shaping the way African innovation is viewed by the world.

They are convinced that people are at the core of any successful company anywhere in the world, and that any country that diligently invests in its people (particularly for a young population such as Kenya's) is bound to reap huge benefits sooner or later. They want to help develop top-notch talent that can start or help build successful tech companies that can scale regionally and globally.

iHub include all parties in the ecosystem, supporting startups throughout their innovation journey and connecting them with opportunities through their initiatives. They want to be at the forefront of igniting the growth of successful company after successful company.

Since 2010, 152 companies have formed out of iHub. It has 15.000 members and on any day, numerous young Kenyans work in its labs and interact with global technologists.

iHub gave rise to Africa's innovation center movement, inspiring the upsurge in tech hubs across the continent.

26. FYODOR BIOTECHNOLOGIES CORPORATION

Fyodor is a US based biotechnology firm founded by Nigerian Eddy Agbo. Fyodor Biotechnologies Corporation is a privately held, socially-responsible company focused on the research, development and manufacture of innovative diagnostic and biopharmaceutical products, first targeted to large emerging economies in Africa, Asia and South America.

Fyodor's mission is to address certain urgent healthcare needs of people in target markets by developing and commercializing relevant and novel technologies capable of providing practical solutions to issues affecting patient care on a personal level, and economic development on a broader level.

Diseases such as malaria, sleeping sickness, meningitis and typhoid fever are leading causes of morbidities and deaths in most emerging economies around the world. Malaria is endemic in over 108 countries in Africa, Asia, South America, Mediterranean, and the Western Pacific. The most pronounced challenges in controlling these diseases is the limited availability of, and access to, accurate, rapid, point-of-care diagnostic tools and sustained effective treatment. To sustain the utility of any newer drugs and vaccines, diagnostic tools for monitoring the development of drug resistance in malaria is an important complement to an integrated approach.

Fyodor's specific goal is to expand the availability and affordability of rapid diagnostics and pharmaceuticals against infectious diseases, with an initial focus on malaria.

Malaria infects some 300 million to 600 million every year around the world, according to UNICEF. But Sub-Saharan Africa alone accounts for 90% of the world's 580.000 annual malaria deaths and Nigeria accounts for 18% of global infections.

Fyodor developed a urine malaria test which provides point-of-need diagnosis of the Plasmodium parasite using dipstick technology as used with manual pregnancy tests. The do-it-yourself solution delivers a diagnosis within 20 minutes of testing and can be done by people with little or no training.

This Urine Malaria Test won the inaugural 2015 Health Innovation Challenge Awards in Nigeria, backed by the Private Sector Health Alliance of Nigeria (PHN). The award comes with a grant of Usd100.000 and support for PHN from backers including Bill & Melinda Gates Foundation; Africa's wealthiest man, Aliko Dangote; and former Nigerian President Goodluck Jonathan.

The potential of offering accurate and early diagnosis of the malaria parasite can speed up the process of tackling malaria in rural areas lacking in healthcare infrastructure and also reduces the risk of the wrong treatment.

27. ONE ADVOCACY ORGANIZATION

ONE is a campaigning and advocacy organization of nearly 8 million people around the world taking action to end extreme poverty and preventable disease, particularly in Africa.

They believe the fight against poverty isn't about charity, but about justice and equality.

Whether lobbying political leaders in world capitals or running cutting-edge grassroots campaigns, ONE pressures governments to do more to fight AIDS and other preventable, treatable diseases in the poorest places on the planet, to empower small-holder farmers, to expand access to energy, and to combat corruption so governments are accountable to their citizens. Cofounded by Bono and other activists, ONE is strictly nonpartisan.

ONE's nearly 8 million members are critical to this work. They come from every walk of life and from across the political spectrum. They're artists and activists, faith and business leaders, students and scientists. They take action day in, day out - organizing, mobilizing, educating, and advocating so that people will have the chance not just to survive, but to thrive.

ONE teams in Washington D.C., New York, London, Johannesburg, Brussels, Berlin and Paris educate and lobby governments to shape policy solutions that save and improve millions of lives - and which every year are under threat from cuts and other priorities.

ONE is not a grant-making organization and they do not solicit funding from the public or receive government funds. ONE is funded almost entirely by foundations, individual philanthropists and corporations.

Some of ONE proudest accomplishment includes:

- Helping secure at least Usd37.5 billion in funding for historic health initiatives, including the Global Fund to Fight AIDS, TB and Malaria, and Gavi, the Vaccine Alliance;

- Helping secure legislation in the US, Canada and EU on transparency in the extractives sector to help fight corruption and ensure more money from oil and gas revenues in Africa is used to fight poverty;

- Successfully advocating for official development assistance, which has increased globally by Usd35.7 billion between 2005 and 2014;

- Helping to get new US legislation passed on energy poverty: the Electrify Africa Act of 2016.

RED a division of ONE, partners with some of the world's most iconic brands, such as Apple, Bank of America, Beats by Dr. Dre, Coca-Cola, Gap, HEAD and Starbucks, who contribute up to 50% of profits from RED branded goods and services to The Global Fund.

To date, RED has generated more than Usd465 million for The Global Fund to support HIV/AIDS grants in Ghana, Kenya, Lesotho, Rwanda, South Africa, Swaziland, Tanzania and Zambia. All of that money goes to work on the ground – no overhead is taken. The Global Fund grants that RED supports have impacted more than 90 million people with prevention, treatment, counseling, HIV testing and care services.

28. BILL & MELINDA GATES FOUNDATION

The foundation seeks to unlock the possibility inside every individual. They see equal value in all lives. And so they are dedicated to improving the quality of life for individuals around the world. From the education of students in Chicago, to the health of a young mother in Nigeria, they are catalysts of human promise everywhere.

The foundation is focused on the areas of greatest need, on the ways in which they can do the most good. From poverty to health, to education, the areas of focus offer the opportunity to dramatically improve the quality of life for billions of people. So they build partnerships that bring together resources, expertise, and vision—working with the best organizations around the globe to identify issues, find answers, and drive change.

They are focused on results. Those that can be measured. And those measured in ways beyond numbers. The Foundation sees individuals, not issues. They are inspired by passion, and compassion for the wellbeing of people. Their methods are based on logic, driven by rigor, results, issues, and outcomes. Their innovation means trying new things, learning from their mistakes, and consistently refining their approach. The Foundation strategies help them define their path to success, but their effectiveness is based in the aggregate power of their initiatives to impact holistic change.

They seek to drive change on a global scale. Their focus on economic empowerment unlocks possibility on the individual and communal level. Their work in the field of global health saves lives, helping families and communities thrive, both today, and tomorrow. Their efforts on education help ensure that individuals have the tools they need to achieve the promise in their own lives.

The Foundation considers itself for being impatient optimists. The problems they seek to solve are complex and demand the coordination and focus of many – leaders, governments, communities, and individuals around the world. Their work is challenging, but we know we can get there. They cannot succeed alone, but together they believe they can work for a world where all can thrive.

Bill & Melinda Gates Foundation believe:

THE PATH OUT OF POVERTY BEGINS WHEN THE NEXT GENERATION CAN ACCESS QUALITY HEALTHCARE AND A GREAT EDUCATION.

In developing countries, they focus on improving people's health and wellbeing, helping individuals lift themselves out of hunger and extreme poverty. In the United States, they seek to ensure that all people - especially those with the fewest resources - can access the opportunities they need to succeed in school and life.

THAT BY GIVING PEOPLE THE TOOLS TO LEAD HEALTHY, PRODUCTIVE LIVES, WE CAN HELP THEM LIFT THEMSELVES OUT OF POVERTY.

Every year, millions of people find ways to transition out of poverty - by adopting new farming technologies, investing in new business opportunities, or finding new jobs. The Foundation knows women and girls have a unique power to reshape societies. When you invest in a woman's health and empowerment, it has a ripple effect, helping families, communities, and countries achieve long-lasting benefits.

THEY CAN SAVE LIVES BY DELIVERING THE LATEST IN SCIENCE AND TECHNOLOGY TO THOSE WITH THE GREATEST NEEDS.

They work with partners to provide effective vaccines, drugs, and diagnostics and to develop innovative approaches to deliver health services to those who need it most. And they invest heavily in developing new vaccines to prevent infectious diseases that impose the greatest burden.

RESOURCES ALONE ARE NOT ENOUGH, SO THEY WORK TO CHANGE PUBLIC POLICIES, ATTITUDES, AND BEHAVIORS TO IMPROVE LIVES.

They partner with governments and the public and private sectors, and foster greater public awareness of urgent global issues.

29. M-PESA

M-Pesa (M for mobile, Pesa is Swahili for money) is a mobile phone-based money transfer, financing and microfinancing service, launched in 2007 by Vodafone for Safaricom and Vodacom, the largest mobile network operators in Kenya and Tanzania. It has since expanded to Afghanistan, South Africa, India and in 2014 to Romania and in 2015 to Albania.

M-Pesa was originally designed as a system to allow microfinance-loan repayments to be made by phone, reducing the costs associated with handling cash and thus making possible lower interest rates. But after pilot testing it was broadened to become a general money-transfer scheme. Once you have signed up, you pay money into the system by handing cash to one of Safaricom's 40.000 agents (typically in a corner shop selling airtime), who credits the money to your M-Pesa account. You withdraw money by visiting another agent, who checks that you have sufficient funds before debiting your account and handing over the cash. You can also transfer money to others using a menu on your phone. Cash can thus be sent one place to another more quickly, safely and easily than taking bundles of money in person, or asking others to carry it for you. This is particularly useful in a country where many workers in cities send money back home to their families in rural villages. Electronic transfers save people time, freeing them to do other, and more productive things instead.

M-Pesa is now branching into bank accounts, savings accounts, loans and insurance. That in turn is helping people rise out of poverty and invest in their future.

M-Pesa has spread quickly, and by 2010 had become the most successful mobile-phone-based financial service in the developing world.

M-Pesa is now used by about 17 million people in Kenya. By end of 2016, a total of 7 million M-Pesa accounts have been opened in Tanzania by Vodacom. The service has been lauded for giving millions of people access to the formal financial system and for reducing crime in an otherwise largely cash-based society.

30. USHAHIDI

Ushahidi, which translates to "testimony" in Swahili, was developed to map reports of violence in Kenya after the post-election violence in 2008. Since then, thousands have used Ushahidi crowdsourcing tools to raise their voice. The company is a technology leader in Africa, headquartered in Nairobi, with a global team.

Ushahidi design new products and initiatives with a global perspective. Their aim is to serve people with limited access in hard-to-reach places. In addition to their other products, they are proud to be a key catalyst of an innovation ecosystem that makes them leaders in East Africa and around the world. At Ushahidi they strive to create technology that solves global problems.

At Ushahidi they partner with leading foundations and organizations to increase access to information, empower citizens, and protect marginalized communities.

Ushahidi has been developed in partnership with renowned companies and brands such as OMIDYAR NETWORK, CISCO, FORD Foundation, Google.org, Humanity United, MacArthur Foundation, Rockefeller Foundation, Knight Foundation, and USAID.

Ushahidi has been used successfully in the Election monitoring on the Obama 2012 Campaign in USA, in Crises Response by Quakemap, in Advocacy & Human Rights by Syria Tracker.

Big names today uses Ushahidi on their international work such as World Vision, The World Bank, United Nations, Tufts University, USA Department of State, American Red Cross, BBC, The Huffington Post, Aljazeera, and Conversation International.

Among their products Ushahidi have different APPs such as:

- RollCall is a team check-in app that helps reach your people on any device, confirm they are OK, and get in touch. They built this tool so teams could be prepared and reach each other every day and in a crisis.

- BRCK makes accessing the internet simple and reliable wherever you are. It's a rugged, cloud managed, full-featured modem/router with built in fail-overs and programmable GPIO expansion. If there's a way for you to connect, BRCK will help you get up and stay up no matter where you are.

- SMSsync is a simple, yet powerful SMS to HTTP sync utility that turns any Android phone into a local SMS gateway by sending incoming messages (SMS) to a configured URL (web service).

- CrisisNET finds, formats and exposes crisis data in a simple, intuitive structure that's accessible anywhere. Now developers, journalists and analysts can skip the days of tedious data processing and get to work in minutes with only a few lines of code.

CONCLUSION

The businesses mentioned on this top 30 list, with the exception of the international organizations such as Bill & Melinda Gates Foundation, ONE and the big corporations, have not yet transformed the whole of Africa continent, but they show that African firms are capable of extraordinary innovation - if only they can be set free. We will get there. Africa Invictus!

"The growth of the Africa's middle class is one of the only economic bright spots across the world currently." George Soros

CHAPTER 15: Africa Invictus.

Growth in 11 African economies accounting for 60% of the continent's GDP has slowed sharply, a new McKinsey Global Institute report says.

The countries comprise the continent's oil exporters and the three countries involved in the Arab Spring - Egypt, Libya and Tunisia. But the economies generating the other 40% of Africa's GDP increased their annual growth rate from 4.1% between 2000-2010 to 4.4% between 2010-2015.

However, the report says that the overall outlook is positive, with the International Monetary Fund projecting that Africa will be the world's second fastest-growing region in the period to 2020.

The report, Lions on the Move II: Realizing the Potential of Africa's Economies, shows that between 2010 and 2015, GDP growth averaged just 3.3%, remarkably weaker than the 4.9% a year between 2000 and 2008.

"Despite recent shocks and challenges, spending by Africa's consumers and businesses totals Usd4 trillion annually, and is growing rapidly. Household consumption is expected to grow at 3.8% a year to total Usd2.1 trillion by 2025. African businesses are an even larger spender. From Usd2.6 trillion in 2015, business spending is expected to increase to Usd3.5 trillion by 2025," the report says

The continent has 700 companies with annual revenue of more than Usd500million, 400 of which generate more than Usd1 billion, says the new study from the McKinsey Global Institute (MGI). These large companies consist of both African-owned brands and foreign-based multinationals operating within the continent across a wide range of sectors.

Five years ago, African economies were accelerating, and the continent was home to 6 of the world's 10 fastest-growing economies. Yet that sunny confidence has waned due to the drop in oil and commodity prices, besides the sociopolitical instability that came along with the Arab Spring.

Despite that, African companies have become new drivers of economic growth, contributing not only to wages and taxes but also to innovation and technology dissemination. MGI estimates that the largest 100 companies by revenue contribute to an estimated 50% to 60% of corporate taxes in Africa.

Just over half of these large firms are African-owned, 27% are foreign-based multinationals, while the remaining 17% are state-owned enterprises.

The multinational corporations dominate in the food and agricultural sector, while state-owned companies play a bigger role in resources, utilities, and transportation sectors.

In contrast, state-owned companies operated mostly in their home countries, diversifying less and focusing heavily on resources and utilities. Family businesses make up only 10% to 20% by revenue of these companies, a sharp underrepresentation when compared to other global regions.

The report also shows that South Africa stands as a unique example of large company growth than the rest of the continent. The country is the only one that has a globally comparable prevalence of large companies and accounts for nearly half of all Africa's large companies. North African countries account for one-fifth of the continent's large companies.

However, despite the continuous growth, Africa is still heavily underrepresented in global business in both the number and size of large companies. The continent needs more of these companies, the report says, so as to drive growth and increase investment, corporate tax contributions, exports, and productivity.

"The fate of corporate Africa to a great extent lies in its own hands," MGI said, "but governments can strengthen dialogue with organized business, remove barriers, and enable large firms to grow and prosper."

On a recent publication by The Economist - Making Africa Work, the following interesting notes come out which I share with you:

- Afro-pessimists should remember two things about commodity busts. They don't last forever. And they don't hurt everyone:

17 African countries with a quarter of the region's population will show a net benefit from the current one, thanks to cheaper energy. More important, by focusing on the minerals markets it is easy to miss some big trends that are happening above ground - and these are mostly positive.

- The first is that Africa is far more peaceful than it was even a decade ago. The wars that ripped apart the Democratic Republic of Congo and sucked in its neighbors, causing millions of deaths, have largely been quelled. A few states, such as Somalia, South Sudan and the Central African Republic, are in chaos. But overall the risk of dying violently in Africa has tumbled. The latest ranking of the world's most violent countries by the Geneva Declaration includes just two African states (tiny Lesotho and Swaziland) among its top ten.

- Africa is also far more democratic than it was. In the 1960s, 1970s and 1980s, only one sub-Saharan government was peacefully voted out of office. Now nearly all face regular elections, which are harder to rig thanks to social media. Voters have real choices - one reason why policies have improved.

- Old-style governments favored nationalization, printing money and (in some cases) rounding peasants up at gunpoint and forcing them onto collective farms. Small wonder Africa grew poorer between 1980 and 2000. Now inflation has largely been tamed, most central banks are islands of excellence and many ministers boast of cutting red tape. Five of the ten fastest reformers in the World Bank's latest report on the ease of doing business are African. Better government has led to better results. The proportion of Africans living in absolute poverty has fallen from 58% to 41% since 2000. In that time primary-school enrolment has risen from 60% to 80%. Annual malaria deaths have fallen by more than 60%.

- Most countries in Africa are following sound economic policies, controlling government deficits and keeping inflation in check. Dig beneath the headlines, and even in countries that are making big errors there is momentum for reform: in South Africa once-taboo policies such as privatization are back on the table, and in Nigeria the government is clamping down on corruption and trimming a bloated civil service. Ethiopia is sucking in foreign investment, and smaller economies such as Ivory Coast and Rwanda are growing rapidly after making it easier to do business.

- The continent's future is in the balance. Whether it bounces back from this commodity slump or slips back into stagnation, war and autocracy will depend on whether enough of its leaders keep moving forward. Two goals stand out. The first is to recognize the new reality. Given the decline in its terms of trade, Africa's buying power has gone down. Currencies must fall and governments adjust. Those that relied on mineral royalties must broaden their revenue bases: taxes are just 10%-15% of GDP in most African countries. Second, African governments need to keep up the hard slog of improving the basics. Bad roads, grasping officials and tariff barriers still hobble trade between African countries, which are only 11% of total African exports and imports. Improving that means investing in infrastructure, fighting corruption and freer trade.

- Africa's past has long been defined by commodities, but its future rests on the productivity of its people. By 2050 the UN predicts that there will be 2.5 billion Africans - a quarter of the world's population. Given good governance, Africa will prosper.

As you have seen in previous chapters of this book, Investors and companies planning to open and develop businesses in the continent should be aware that Africa is a challenging market. But as facts shows too beside all the challenges and barriers the opportunities are too big to be ignored.

I have shared a lot of facts with you all over this book, and by it I believe Africa will be Invictus and become a beacon of Hope for future generations.

Invictus is a well-known poem by William Ernest Henley. It was Nelson Mandela's favorite poem. The poem basically talks about the undefeated and unconquerable soul of a hard worker, from an impoverished background, who will not give up. Like I like to call it: The Unbreakable Titanium Spirit.

CONCLUSION

As conclusion to this book a number of measures are necessary for many African countries to become more attractive to Foreign Direct Investment:

- Ease of Doing business has to be improve;

- Reduce corruption;

- Governments red tapes and bureaucracy must be eliminated;

- Countries must invest in energy powered by clean technology to lower the cost of production;

- Countries need to become more connected with their regional partners, with Africa so intra Africa trade can move without barriers, so they can increase their export markets;

- Restrictive legislation that leads to inefficiencies and low productivity must be withdrawn;

- Legislation that promotes both domestic and foreign investment must be encouraged, rather than discouraged;

- Improve access to capital for local investors;

- Countries infrastructure must be enhanced to support growth;

- Many Industries must be developed to reduce the dependence on import of manufactured products from industrialized countries;

- Many country's state assets, which are performing inadequately, must be privatized, and control handed to the private sector; specially Energy, Aviation, Airports and Ports;

- Incentives to help young entrepreneurs increase the number of Small and medium-sized enterprises (SMEs).

TO INVESTORS

Hope I could be of help in sharing facts and investment opportunities in Africa that may be of interest to your company and partners.

Just one last advice when you are considering investing in Africa, for the long term, please make sure your investment plans are considering impact investing with the intention to generate social and environmental impact alongside to your financial returns.

What is impact investing?

Impact investments are investments made into companies, organizations, and funds with the intention to generate social and environmental impact alongside a financial return. Impact investments can be made in both emerging and developed markets, and target a range of returns from below market to market rate, depending on investors' strategic goals.

The growing impact investment market provides capital to address the world's most pressing challenges in sectors such as sustainable agriculture, renewable energy, conservation, microfinance, and affordable and accessible basic services including housing, healthcare, and education.

Who is making impact investments?

Impact investment has attracted a wide variety of investors, both individual and institutional.

- Fund Managers
- Development finance institutions
- Diversified financial institutions/banks
- Private foundations
- Pension funds and insurance companies
- Family Offices
- Individual investors
- NGOs
- Religious institutions

To learn more about impact investing please visit the Global Impact Investing Network (GIIN) website: www.thegiin.org

ABOUT THE GLOBAL IMPACT INVESTING NETWORK

The Global Impact Investing Network is a nonprofit organization dedicated to increasing the scale and effectiveness of impact investing around the world. Impact investments are investments made into companies, organizations, and funds with the intention to generate social and environmental impact alongside a financial return.

INVICTUS POEM, by William Ernest Henley

Out of the night that covers me,

Black as the Pit from pole to pole,

I thank whatever gods may be

For my unconquerable soul.

In the fell clutch of circumstance

I have not winced nor cried aloud.

Under the bludgeoning's of chance

My head is bloody, but unbowed.

Beyond this place of wrath and tears

Looms but the Horror of the shade,

And yet the menace of the years

Finds, and shall find, me unafraid.

It matters not how strait the gate,

How charged with punishments the scroll.

I am the master of my fate:

I am the captain of my soul.

ABOUT THE AUTHOR

Saidy Andrade is major in Business Administration, with an extensive know how in Foreign Direct Investment, Capital Raising, Project Management, Business Model planning, and financial engineering of large scale projects.

Saidy Andrade has been a strong advocate in Promoting Foreign Direct Investment into Africa, and has been the driven force for the expansion of Capital Consulting internationally.

Capital Consulting is a Cape Verde Islands-based diversified investment company with a Eur5 Billion investment portfolio under management and business interests spanning from consultancy, brokerage, real estate development and management, private equity, asset management across a wide range of economic sectors in Cape Verde Islands and other international markets.

Capital Consulting focus for promotion of Foreign Direct Investment is Africa. For this reason we focus all our energy to attract capital from our investor's network in various markets (USA, GCC, Europe, and Asia) to investment opportunities in Africa. Capital Consulting Group Profile can be accessed at the following link: http://www.capital-consulting.net/CCG2017.pdf

Author can be contacted to the following emails:
andradesaidy@capital-consulting.net
andradesaidy@yahoo.com
andradesaidy@gmail.com

NOTES

The bulk of this book was drawn from researches made by the author, often done in concert with many collaborators across his international network, and Capital Consulting network.

The notes bellow shares the rankings from which the Index Capital Consulting FDI Africa Index Countries to invest for the future, mentioned on Chapter 13 - Africa Countries to invest for the future, was based on.

Capital Consulting FDI Africa Index Countries to invest for the future:

Top 10 Countries we suggest you keep an eye to invest for the future.

1. Mauritius
2. Botswana
3. South Africa
4. Kenya
5. Rwanda
6. Egypt
7. Seychelles
8. Ghana
9. Nigeria
10. Tanzania

Rankings used:

Most Advanced Economies in Africa

1. Nigeria
2. South Africa
3. Egypt

4. Algeria
5. Angola
6. Morocco
7. Ethiopia
8. Kenya
9. Tanzania
10. Tunisia

Ernest & Young Africa Attractiveness Index

1. South Africa
2. Morocco
3. Egypt
4. Kenya
5. Mauritius
6. Ghana
7. Botswana
8. Tunisia
9. Rwanda
10. Ivory Coast

World Bank 2017 Doing Business Ranking Sub-Saharan Africa

1. Mauritius
2. Rwanda
3. Botswana
4. South Africa
5. Kenya
6. Seychelles
7. Zambia
8. Lesotho
9. Namibia
10. Ghana

FDI Intelligence Country of the Future – Africa

1. South Africa
2. Morocco
3. Mauritius
4. Egypt
5. Kenya
6. Ghana
7. Nigeria
8. Botswana
9. Tunisia
10. Namibia

Mo Ibrahim Africa Governance Index

1. Mauritius
2. Botswana
3. Cape Verde
4. Seychelles
5. Namibia
6. South Africa
7. Tunisia
8. Ghana
9. Rwanda
10. Senegal

Africa Regional Integration Index
UNECA, Africa Development Bank & Africa Union

1. Ivory Coast
2. Kenya
3. Cameroon
4. South Africa
5. Morocco
6. Botswana

7. Senegal
8. Gabon
9. Uganda
10. Zambia

Corruption Perceptions Index

1. Botswana
2. Cape Verde
3. Mauritius
4. Rwanda
5. Namibia
6. Sao Tome & Principe
7. Senegal
8. South Africa
9. Ghana
10. Burkina Faso

ACKNOWLEDGMENTS

I would like to thank the following people and platforms that have made this book possible:

- Thank you God for giving me the strength to keep moving forward through all the storms that I have experienced in life and for giving me the strength to keep my Spirit like an Unbreakable Titanium;

- Thank You to my parents (Raul Andrade & Luzia Andrade) for giving me my life and for all their sacrifice towards making me and my brothers (Paulo Andrade & Nandixany Andrade) who we are today;

- Thank you to my amazing wife Maria Andrade and our son Zion J. Andrade for being patient and for all their support;

- Thank you to my uncles Ernesto Alves (lives in USA) and Joao Miguel Amado Alves (used to live in Germany but now living and chilling in Cape Verde) for always believing in me and for transferring knowledge and the love to read books;

- Thank you, Thank you, Thank you to Larry Page and Sergey Brin to invent Google and for making it possible for our generation to be able to access knowledge very fast at our fingertips; otherwise it would take me years to access all the data to write this book;

- Thank you to all the researches from financial institutions, books, and articles that I have referred to in this book;

- Special thanks to Leland Rice, Editor in Chief of The Business Year Magazine, for writing the Foreword of the book and for all his support;

- Thank you to all my family and all the teachers, mentors and kind people that I have had the pleasure to meet along the way from whom I have learned a lot of what I know today;

- Thank to you the free licensing of the high resolution Gold glitter background Created & Designed by Freepik which is part of the design background on the cover of the book inside the Africa Map.

- Thank you to Bill Gates and Microsoft for inventing Microsoft Word and Microsoft Excel software, without which it would take me years to finish this book;

SOURCES

Is blockchain the answer to building transparency and trust? By Uschi Schreiber
https://www.linkedin.com/pulse/blockchain-answer-building-transparency-trust-uschi-schreiber-1

African Natural Resources Center (ANRC)

https://www.afdb.org/en/topics-and-sectors/initiatives-

partnerships/african-natural-resources-center-anrc/

Aljazeera :: Mapping Africa's natural resources

http://www.aljazeera.com/indepth/interactive/2016/10/mapping-

africa-natural-resources-161020075811145.html

Aljazeera :: Shadow War in the Sahara

http://www.aljazeera.com/programmes/specialseries/2016/10/sha

dow-war-sahara-161009025023817.html

McKinsey Global Institute Report :: Lions on the move:

The progress and potential of African economies

http://www.mckinsey.com/global-themes/middle-east-and-

africa/lions-on-the-move

McKinsey Global Institute Report :: Lions go Digital

http://www.mckinsey.com/industries/high-tech/our-insights/lions-

go-digital-the-internets-transformative-potential-in-africa

African Economic Outlook 2016

https://www.afdb.org/fileadmin/uploads/afdb/Documents/Publicat

ions/AEO_2016_Report_Full_English.pdf

IMF Data

http://www.imf.org/external/data.htm

World Bank Data

http://data.worldbank.org/region/sub-saharan-africa

"The Looting Machine: Warlords, Oligarchs, Corporations, Smugglers, and the Theft of Africa's Wealth," by Tom Burgis;

https://www.amazon.com/The-Looting-Machine-Oligarchs-Corporations/dp/1610394399

"Which is Africa's most corrupt Country"?

http://www.bbc.com/news/world-africa-38749325

Transparency International

https://www.transparency.org/

Corruption Perceptions Index 2016

https://www.transparency.org/news/pressrelease/corruption_perce ptions_index_2016_vicious_circle_of_corruption_and_inequali

Sub Saharan Africa: corruption is a big issue in 2016 African elections

http://www.transparency.org/news/feature/africa_corruption_is_a_ big_issue_in_2016_african_elections

Mo Ibrahim Foundation :: A Decade of African
Governance :: 2006 - 2015
http://s.mo.ibrahim.foundation/u/2016/10/01184917/2016-
Index-Report.pdf?_ga=1.219151711.795854336.1484814156

The World Bank - Publications
http://www.worldbank.org/en/publication/reference

Bloomberg :: Where's the Growth? Africa
https://www.bloomberg.com/view/articles/2015-11-10/sub-
saharan-africa-thrills-investors-with-economic-growth

Private equity lines up $4.3 billion to snap up African
firms on the cheap
http://mgafrica.com/article/2016-02-29-what-crisis-private-equity-
lines-up-billions-to-snap-up-african-firms-on-the-cheap/

The Gold Standard
http://money.howstuffworks.com/currency7.htm

Fiat Money Definition | Investopedia
http://www.investopedia.com/terms/f/fiatmoney.asp#ixzz4WzCQTn
v9

Commodity Money
https://en.wikipedia.org/wiki/Commodity_money

Bitcoin
http://www.investopedia.com/terms/b/bitcoin.asp

Blockchain
http://www.investopedia.com/terms/b/blockchain.asp

Capitalism - Africa - Neoliberalism, Structural Adjustment, And The African Reaction
http://science.jrank.org/pages/8526/Capitalism-Africa-Neoliberalism-Structural-Adjustment-African-Reaction.html

Top 10 Countries with Largest Gold Reserves

http://www.usfunds.com/investor-library/frank-talk/top-10-

countries-with-largest-gold-reserves/#.WIx_jFOrTcc

African Development Report – The Paradox of Plenty
https://www.afdb.org/fileadmin/uploads/afdb/Documents/Publications/(E)%20AfricanBank%202007%20Ch4.pdf

Natural Resources in Africa
http://www.miningafrica.net/natural-resources-in-africa/

Mining Companies in Africa
http://www.miningafrica.net/mining-companies-africa/

Africa Natural Resources Center :: Africa Development Bank
https://www.afdb.org/fileadmin/uploads/afdb/Documents/Publications/anrc/AfDB_ANRC_BROCHURE_en.pdf

Placing Economic Value on Africa's Natural Resources
http://www.unep.org/newscentre/Default.aspx?DocumentId=2756&ArticleId=9718

African Natural Resources: The key to African growth
http://newafricanmagazine.com/resources-are-the-key/

Gold Exports by Country
http://www.worldstopexports.com/gold-exports-country/

The CIA World Factbook – Export Commodities
https://www.cia.gov/library/publications/the-world-factbook/fields/2049.html

Sub-Saharan Africa Trade at a Glance
http://wits.worldbank.org/CountrySnapshot/en/SSF/textview

US Geological Survey
https://minerals.usgs.gov/minerals/pubs/commodity/gold/goldmyb02.pdf

FORBES - 30 Most Promising Young Entrepreneurs In Africa 2016
http://www.forbes.com/sites/mfonobongnsehe/2016/04/25/30-most-promising-young-entrepreneurs-in-africa-2016/#31446fa11ef1

What is GDP and why is it so important to economists and investors?
http://www.investopedia.com/ask/answers/199.asp?utm_source=personalized&utm_campaign=www.investopedia.com&utm_term=8720956&utm_medium=email

Why Africa is poor despite resources!
http://theafricaneconomist.com/why-africa-is-poor-despite-resources/

Harvard Business Review: Africa Is The Greatest Continent For Opportunities
http://theafricaneconomist.com/harvard-business-review-africa-is-the-greatest-continent-for-opportunities/

United Nations Economic Commission for Africa – Publications
http://www.uneca.org/publications

Sub-Saharan Africa's Most and Least Resilient Economies
https://hbr.org/2016/02/sub-saharan-africas-most-and-least-resilient-economies

Journalists Resource – Africa
https://journalistsresource.org/studies/international/africa

Harvard University - Center for African Studies
http://africa.harvard.edu/about/background/

Sub-Saharan African Collection
http://hcl.harvard.edu/libraries/widener/collections/subsaharan.cfm

500 Years Later - independent documentary film
https://en.m.wikipedia.org/wiki/500_Years_Later

Meet the Tech Companies Creating Opportunity in Africa
https://hbr.org/2016/04/meet-the-tech-companies-creating-opportunity-in-africa&ab=Article-Links-End_of_Page_Recirculation

Africa's rising middle class – and why it matters
http://newafricanmagazine.com/11558-2/

G20 Members and participants
https://www.g20.org/Webs/G20/EN/G20/Participants/participants_node.html

Commodity Chains, Unequal Exchange and Uneven Development
http://erc.metu.edu/menu/series04/0411.pdf

Global Keynesianism: Critique of Unequal Exchange, Global Exploitation and Global Neoliberalism, Theory of World Income, Productivity, Grow
https://www.amazon.ca/Global-Keynesianism-Exploitation-Neoliberalism-Productivity/dp/1590330021

Priorities of the 2017 g20 summit - by Dr. Angela
Merkel - Berlin, 1 December 2016
https://www.g20.org/Content/DE/_Anlagen/G7_G20/2016-g20-
praesidentschaftspapier-en.pdf?__blob=publicationFile&v=2

Decision relating to the implementation of the
Yamoussoukro declaration concerning the
liberalization of access to air transport markets in
Africa
http://www.afcac.org/en/documents/conferences/July2012/yde.pd
f

Open Skies for Africa – Implementing the
Yamoussoukro Decision
http://www.worldbank.org/en/topic/transport/publication/open-
skies-for-africa

Open Skies for Africa - Implementing the
Yamoussoukro Decision
http://pubdocs.worldbank.org/en/849021434746549856/Air-
Transport-OpenSkiesForAfrica.pdf

Aluminum Ore Bauxite in Africa
http://www.miningafrica.net/natural-resources-africa/aluminium-
ore-bauxite-in-africa/

Mining Uranium in Africa
http://www.miningafrica.net/natural-resources-africa/mining-
uranium-in-africa/

Gas mining in Africa
http://www.miningafrica.net/natural-resources-africa/gas-mining-
in-africa/

Coal mining in Africa
http://www.miningafrica.net/natural-resources-africa/coal-mining-
in-africa/

Iron Ore in Africa
http://www.miningafrica.net/natural-resources-africa/iron-ore-in-africa/

Diamond mining in Africa
http://www.miningafrica.net/natural-resources-africa/diamond-mining-in-africa/

Cobalt mining in Africa
http://www.miningafrica.net/natural-resources-africa/cobalt-mining-in-africa/

AGROPOLY: A Handful of Corporations control World food production
http://www.econexus.info/sites/econexus/files/Agropoly_Econexus_BerneDeclaration.pdf

Oxford Economics :: Economic Impact of Aviation in Dubai
http://content.emirates.com/downloads/ek/pdfs/int_gov_affairs/Oxford_Economics_Quantifying_the_Economic_Impact_of_Aviation_in_Dubai_November_2014_Final_v1.pdf

Emirates Airlines Business Model
http://www.emirates.com/english/about/int-and-gov-affairs/our-business-model/our-business-model.aspx

Investment Corporation of Dubai
http://www.icd.gov.ae/

INVESTMENT CORPORATION OF DUBAI public register at DIFC
https://www.difc.ae/public-register/investment-corporation-dubai

Dubai: Growth through Diversification
http://www.investopedia.com/articles/investing/111014/dubai-growth-through-diversification.asp

Africa Competitiveness Report - Transforming Africa's Agriculture http://reports.weforum.org/africa-competitiveness-report-2015/chapter-2-1-transforming-africas-agriculture-to-improve-competitiveness/

Global Justice Now Report - From the roots up - How agroecology can feed Africa
http://www.globaljustice.org.uk/resources/roots-how-agroecology-can-feed-africa

Global Justice Now - Campaign on Trade issues
http://www.globaljustice.org.uk/campaigns/trade

African Countries Contemplate New Multinational Airline
http://www.ainonline.com/aviation-news/air-transport/2016-10-11/african-countries-contemplate-new-multinational-airline

Africa's struggles continue as economies weaken and competition intensifies
http://www.airlineleader.com/categories/regions/africas-struggles-continue-as-economies-weaken-and-competition-intensifies-322700

Airline Leader - Africa's international market: vision 2025
http://www.airlineleader.com/categories/regions/africas-international-market-vision-2025-294975

Bloomberg :: Is Emirates Airline Running Out of Sky?
https://www.bloomberg.com/news/features/2017-01-05/is-emirates-airline-running-out-of-sky

UN projects world population to reach 8.5 billion by 2030
http://www.un.org/sustainabledevelopment/blog/2015/07/un-projects-world-population-to-reach-8-5-billion-by-2030-driven-by-growth-in-developing-countries/

Dubai Ruler :: Sheikh Mohammed :: My Vision
Challenges in the Race for Excellence
https://www.amazon.com/My-Vision-Challenges-Race-Excellence/dp/1860633447

History Channel - The Industrial Revolution
http://www.history.com/topics/industrial-revolution

AfricaRenewal - A green path to industrialization
http://www.un.org/africarenewal/magazine/august-2016/green-path-industrialization

COP 22 - Greening Industrialization in Africa
http://www.wri.org/events/2016/11/cop-22-greening-industrialization-africa

Africa's New Climate Economy
http://newclimateeconomy.report/workingpapers/workingpaper/africas-new-climate-economy/

International Energy Agency - Number and share of
Africans without access to electricity
https://www.iea.org/newsroom/graphics/number-and-share-of-africans-without-access-to-electricity-by-country-in-2012.html

Africa Energy Outlook
http://www.iea.org/publications/freepublications/publication/weo-2014-special-report-africa-energy-outlook.html

Is the world's largest solar project a "green megawatt"
or a "green grab"?
https://www.equaltimes.org/is-the-world-s-largest-solar?lang=en#.WJMa4VOrTcc

Lake Turkana Wind Power Project: The largest wind farm project in Africa
https://www.afdb.org/en/projects-and-operations/selected-projects/lake-turkana-wind-power-project-the-largest-wind-farm-project-in-africa/

Africa's green energy challenge: mega projects, off-grid or somewhere in between?
https://ensia.com/features/africa-energy/

Vast Moroccan Solar Power Plant is Hard Act for Africa to follow
http://fortune.com/2016/11/05/moroccan-solar-plant-africa/

Power Africa Report - The Roadmap
https://www.usaid.gov/sites/default/files/documents/1860/USAID_PA_Roadmap_April_2016_TAG_508opt.pdf

Think Big and Ignore the Naysayers - Your idea could be good
https://medium.com/power-africa/think-big-and-ignore-the-naysayers-38afe0b09e5a#.scmp6e2t1

Scaling off Grid Energy
https://www.scalingoffgrid.org/

The Lights are turning on in Africa
https://medium.com/power-africa/the-lights-are-turning-on-in-africa-f78cbade63bb#.pubvuo89q

Decentralized Renewables: The Fast Track to Universal Energy Access
https://static1.squarespace.com/static/532f79fae4b07e365baf1c64/t/578d7f206b8f5bebe7f47444/1468890916501/Power_for_All_POV_May2016.pdf

Power People Planet :: Seizing Africa´s Energy and Climate Opportunities
http://www.africaprogresspanel.org/wp-content/uploads/2015/06/APP_REPORT_2015_FINAL_low1.pdf

Bill Gates Launches $1 Billion Breakthrough Energy Investment Fund
http://www.forbes.com/sites/kerryadolan/2016/12/12/bill-gates-launches-1-billion-breakthrough-energy-investment-fund/#61a6c47959a7

A New Model for Investing in Energy Innovation
https://www.gatesnotes.com/Energy/Breakthrough-Energy-Ventures

Bill Gates Launches $1 Billion Breakthrough Energy Investment Fund
http://www.forbes.com/sites/kerryadolan/2016/12/12/bill-gates-launches-1-billion-breakthrough-energy-investment-fund/#61a6c47959a7

Board & Investors of Breakthrough Energy Investment Fund
http://www.b-t.energy/ventures/board-investors/

Nzema solar project - Africa's largest solar (PV) power plant
http://www.blue-energyco.com/africas-largest-solar-pv-power-plant/

OPIC USA - Power Africa
https://www.opic.gov/opic-action/power-africa

Financial Times :: International banks ramp up presence in Africa
https://www.ft.com/content/600b6880-0fa0-11e1-a36b-00144feabdc0

The World Bank - Doing Business ranking
http://www.doingbusiness.org/rankings

How Companies Overcome Africa's Five Great Challenges
http://www.forbes.com/sites/baininsights/2012/04/05/how-companies-overcome-africas-five-great-challenges/#73053a3e5438

The biggest challenge facing new businesses in Africa is financing
https://venturesafrica.com/the-biggest-challenge-facing-new-businesses-in-africa-is-financing/

The 6 biggest obstacles startups face in Africa
http://ventureburn.com/2016/03/6-biggest-obstacles-startups-face-africa/

Challenges and opportunities facing African entrepreneurs and their small firms
http://www.freepatentsonline.com/article/International-Journal-Business-Research/208535102.html

The number of tech hubs across Africa has more than doubled in less than a year
https://qz.com/759666/the-number-of-tech-hubs-across-africa-has-more-than-doubled-in-less-than-a-year/

Innovators in an unconnected world
https://medium.com/bill-melinda-gates-foundation/innovators-in-an-unconnected-world-e3aef8fb261e#.1mkz77u5n

Facebook's latest plan for cheaper and faster internet in Africa is off to a good start
https://qz.com/825693/mtns-tests-of-facebooks-voyager-might-make-internet-cheaper-for-africans/

Why US tech giants are betting on Africa
https://thenextweb.com/africa/2016/06/29/us-tech-giants-betting-africa/#gref

Meet the Tech Companies Creating Opportunity in Africa
https://hbr.org/2016/04/meet-the-tech-companies-creating-opportunity-in-africa&ab=Article-Links-End_of_Page_Recirculation

Tech Talent War Moves to Africa
http://blogs.wsj.com/cio/2016/09/30/tech-talent-war-moves-to-africa/?utm_campaign=Media%20Coverage&utm_medium=Media%20Coverage%20CTA&utm_source=homepagev2

30 Most Promising Young Entrepreneurs in Africa2016
http://www.forbes.com/sites/mfonobongnsehe/2016/04/25/30-most-promising-young-entrepreneurs-in-africa-2016/#388fe71e1ef1

How we made it in Africa - Archive - Entrepreneur watch
http://www.howwemadeitinafrica.com/articles/entrepreneur-watch/

Meet The Kenyan Woman Who Has Dressed Oprah Winfrey up like a Maasai
https://mpasho.co.ke/meet-kenyan-woman-dressed-oprah-winfrey/

11 African Entrepreneurs Who Are Changing the Business Landscape
https://www.entrepreneur.com/article/283272

Best African Safari Tours: Our Top 10 Picks
http://www.go2africa.com/africa-travel-blog/11830

EY's attractiveness survey - Africa 2015 - Making choices
http://www.ey.com/Publication/vwLUAssets/EY-africa-attractiveness-survey-2015-making-choices/%24FILE/EY-africa-attractiveness-survey-2015-making-choices.pdf

Africa attractiveness program - Africa 2016- Navigating Africa's current uncertainties
http://www.ey.com/Publication/vwLUAssets/ey-africa-attractiveness-program-2016/$FILE/ey-africa-attractiveness-program-2016.pdf

Egypt launches Suez Canal expansion
http://www.bbc.com/news/world-middle-east-33800076

Suez Canal Development Project
http://projects.worldbank.org/P004982/suez-canal-development-project?lang=en&tab=overview

Africa one of only two regions achieving FDI project growth – EY
http://www.engineeringnews.co.za/article/africa-one-of-only-two-regions-achieving-fdi-project-growth-ey-2016-07-25/rep_id:4136

Pension funds power Africa's infrastructure
http://www.africancapitalmarketsnews.com/3292/pension_funds_power_africa_infrastructure/

IMF - World Economic Outlook 2017
http://www.imf.org/external/pubs/ft/weo/2017/update/01/pdf/0117.pdf

Companies adapt to local African markets
https://www.ft.com/content/acbe2ed4-a5f2-11e3-b9ed-00144feab7de

As it expands in Africa, Uber adapts to local markets and adopts cash payments
https://techcrunch.com/2016/06/02/as-it-expands-in-africa-uber-adapts-to-local-markets-and-adopts-cash-payments/

Bain & Company - How to succeed in Africa
http://www.bain.com/publications/articles/how-to-succeed-in-africa-hbr.aspx

A conversation about Africa with Nick Blazquez: Lessons for operating success
http://www.bain.com/publications/articles/nick-blazquez-africa-lessons-for-operating-success.aspx

FutureBrand - The Country Brand Index 2016
http://fbi.futurebrand.com/rankings

World Bank Doing Business Ranking 2017 - Cape Verde
http://www.doingbusiness.org/~/media/wbg/doingbusiness/documents/profiles/country/cpv.pdf

Psychology Today - The Art of Happiness
https://www.psychologytoday.com/basics/happiness

The Wall Street Journal - Is Africa Hiding the Next Mark Zuckerberg? https://www.wsj.com/articles/is-africa-hiding-the-next-mark-zuckerberg-the-future-of-tech-talent-1449242360

NEPAD CEO Blog
http://ibrahimmayaki.com/

NEPAD 2016 Annual Report
http://www.nepad.org/resource/nepad-agency-2016-annual-report

The Role of Culture in Doing Business in Africa
https://www.ntusbfcas.com/african-business-insights/content/the-role-of-culture-in-doing-business-in-africa

If you could have one superpower, what would it be?
https://www.gatesnotes.com/2016-Annual-Letter

CIA Factbook - Cape Verde
https://www.cia.gov/library/publications/the-world-factbook/geos/cv.html

CIA Factbook – Mauritius
https://www.cia.gov/library/publications/the-world-factbook/geos/mp.html

World Bank Doing Business Ranking 2017 - Cape Verde
http://www.doingbusiness.org/data/exploreeconomies/cabo-verde

World Bank Doing Business Ranking 2017 – Mauritius
http://www.doingbusiness.org/data/exploreeconomies/mauritius/

World Bank - Country Overview - Cape Verde
http://www.worldbank.org/en/country/caboverde/overview

World Bank - Country Overview - Mauritius
http://www.worldbank.org/en/country/mauritius/overview

African Economies Adopt Record Number of Reforms, Says Latest Doing Business Report
http://www.worldbank.org/en/news/press-release/2016/10/25/african-economies-adopt-record-number-of-reforms-says-latest-doing-business-report

Did you know that there are more Europeans in Africa, than Africans in Europe?
http://www.siliconafrica.com/the-truth-about-africa-immigration-where-do-they-go/

Why more South Africans are leaving the country
https://businesstech.co.za/news/general/92652/why-more-south-africans-are-leaving-the-country/

African migrants: What really drives them to Europe?
http://www.aljazeera.com/programmes/talktojazeera/inthefield/2015/06/african-migrants-drives-europe-150604124356795.html

TOP 10 MOST CORRUPT AFRICAN COUNTRIES
http://www.africacradle.com/africas-top-10-most-corrupt-african-countries/

Top 20 Most Brutal and Ruthless Dictators in Africa
https://www.africanvault.com/dictators-in-africa/

The Universal Declaration of Human Rights (abbreviated)
http://hrlibrary.umn.edu/edumat/hreduseries/hereandnow/Part-5/8_udhr-abbr.htm

United Nations - Universal Declaration of Human Rights
http://www.un.org/en/universal-declaration-human-rights/

What does a rainbow mean in the Bible?
http://www.biblestudy.org/question/what-does-a-rainbow-symbolize-in-bible.html

Obama's Top 50 Accomplishments
http://washingtonmonthly.com/magazine/januaryfebruary-2017/obamas-top-50-accomplishments-revisited/

Africa: Why Africa Has a Brighter Future
http://allafrica.com/stories/201702080394.html

Is Africa's investment dream still on track?
https://thearabianpost.com/tap/2017/01/is-africas-investment-dream-still-on-track.html

Doing Business Regional Profile 2017: Sub-Saharan Africa
https://openknowledge.worldbank.org/handle/10986/25672

Global Impact Investing Network - Impact investing
https://thegiin.org/impact-investing/

Ministry of Investment - GAFI - REASONS TO INVEST IN EGYPT
http://www.gafi.gov.eg/English/whyegypt/Pages/ReasonsToInvestInEgypt.aspx

Egypt Economic Development Conference - Why Invest in Egypt?
https://www.uschamber.com/sites/default/files/why_invest_in_egypt_-_eedc.pdf

Ghana Investment Promotion Centre - Invest in Ghana
http://www.gipcghana.com/invest-in-ghana.html

Ghana country profile - BBC monitoring
http://www.bbc.com/news/world-africa-13433790

FastCompany 2017 Ranking - The Most Innovative Companies - Africa https://www.fastcompany.com/most-innovative-companies/2017/sectors/africa

Ventures Africa - 42 Africa Innovators to watch - 2016 Edition
http://venturesafrica.com/innovators/

Malaik Equity Crowdfunding Platform
https://www.crowdfundinsider.com/2015/12/78211-malaik-debuts-new-impact-focused-equity-crowdfunding-platform-in-africa/

The World's First Impact Focused Equity Crowdfunding Portal
https://www.africa.com/the-worlds-first-impact-focused-equity-crowdfunding-portal-launches-to-fund-pan-african-start-ups/

Africa's large companies are growing faster & making more money than their global peers
https://qz.com/782196/mckinseys-africa-2016-report-highlights-africas-fast-growing-corporate-companies/

Why African Entrepreneurship Is Booming
https://hbr.org/2016/07/why-african-entrepreneurship-is-booming

Tech hubs across Africa: Which will be the legacy-makers?
http://blogs.worldbank.org/ic4d/tech-hubs-across-africa-which-will-be-legacy-makers

Making Africa Work
http://www.economist.com/news/leaders/21696933-continents-future-depends-people-not-commodities-making-africa-work

iHub Kenya
https://ihub.co.ke/about

Fyodor Bio Corp
http://www.fyodorbio.com/company/

This urine test kit for malaria could save thousands of lives in Nigeria and beyond
https://qz.com/537868/the-worlds-first-urine-malaria-test-could-save-thousands-of-lives-in-nigeria-and-beyond/

ONE
https://www.one.org/international/about/

Bill & Melinda Gates Foundation
http://www.gatesfoundation.org/

The Economist - Why does Kenya lead the world in mobile money?
http://www.economist.com/blogs/economist-explains/2013/05/economist-explains-18

The Economist - 1.2Billion Opportunities
http://www.economist.com/news/special-report/21696792-commodity-boom-may-be-over-and-barriers-doing-business-are-everywhere-africas

The Economist - Making Africa Work
http://www.economist.com/news/leaders/21696933-continents-future-depends-people-not-commodities-making-africa-work

Safaricom M-Pesa in Kenya
http://www.safaricom.co.ke/personal/m-pesa

Ushahidi App
https://www.ushahidi.com/about

The Rise of Silicon Savannah and Africa's Tech Movement
https://techcrunch.com/2015/07/23/the-rise-of-silicon-savannah-and-africas-tech-movement/

Global Impact Investing Network
https://thegiin.org/

GIIN - Why Impact Investing?
https://thegiin.org/impact-investing/need-to-know/#s3

CIA World Factbook – Nigeria
https://www.cia.gov/library/publications/the-world-factbook/geos/ni.html

CIA World Factbook - South Africa
https://www.cia.gov/library/publications/the-world-factbook/geos/sf.html

CIA World Factbook – Egypt
https://www.cia.gov/library/publications/the-world-factbook/geos/eg.html

CIA World Factbook – Algeria
https://www.cia.gov/library/publications/the-world-factbook/geos/ag.html

CIA World Factbook – Angola
https://www.cia.gov/library/publications/the-world-factbook/geos/ao.html

CIA World Factbook – Morocco
https://www.cia.gov/library/publications/the-world-factbook/geos/mo.html

CIA World Factbook – Ethiopia
https://www.cia.gov/library/publications/the-world-factbook/geos/et.html

CIA World Factbook – Kenya
https://www.cia.gov/library/publications/the-world-factbook/geos/ke.html

CIA World Factbook – Tanzania
https://www.cia.gov/library/publications/the-world-factbook/geos/tz.html

CIA World Factbook – Tunisia
https://www.cia.gov/library/publications/the-world-factbook/geos/ts.html

Mauritius Foreign Investment Agency - Board of Investment
http://www.investmauritius.com/

Botswana Investment & Trade Centre
http://www.bitc.co.bw/

The DTI - Department of Trade & Industry - Republic of South Africa
https://www.thedti.gov.za/default.jsp

KENINVEST - Kenya Investment Authority
http://www.investmentkenya.com/

Rwanda Development Board
http://www.rdb.rw/home.html

Egypt General Authority for Investment and Free Zones
http://www.gafi.gov.eg/English/Pages/default.aspx

Seychelles Investment Board
http://www.sib.gov.sc/

Ghana Investment Promotion Centre – GIPC
http://www.gipcghana.com/

Nigeria Investment Promotion Commission
http://www.nipc.gov.ng/

Tanzania Investment Centre
http://www.tic.co.tz/

The 2007-08 Financial Crisis in Review – Investopedia
http://www.investopedia.com/articles/economics/09/financial-crisis-review.asp#ixzz4bt0qZytR

The Business Year - Cement Thy Vows – Dangote Strengthens in Tanzania
https://www.thebusinessyear.com/tanzania-2017/dangote-consolidates-position-tanzania/focus

Dubai Chamber - Global Business Forum Series
http://www.dubaichamber.com/what-we-do/trade-international-expansion/dubai-chamber-global-business-forum-series

Africa Global Business Forum
http://africaglobalbusinessforum.com/

Heineken Reports and Presentations - 2016 Results
http://www.theheinekencompany.com/investors/reports-and-presentations?Skip=0&Take=10

INDEX

G

K

L

Q

U

V

INSPIRE FOUNDATION

With the profits from this book I hope to create and fund a foundation to spread access to knowledge, promote entrepreneurship and leadership, named INSPIRE Foundation, with the goal to help young entrepreneurs in Africa achieve their dream of creating something that will make positive impact in our world.

My vision for INSPIRE foundation is to help brilliant minds across Africa achieve their dreams for a better Africa.

My hope is to see the foundation with its own libraries (printed books, digital books, as well as 3D Technology Documentary experiences) focused on the business sector so young people can have access to knowledge that otherwise they wouldn't dream of.

Because I love quotes my intention is to make a promotion by using INSPIRE Foundation name to ask successful entrepreneurs, artists, politicians and anyone who would like to see Africa Rise to Greatness, to buy Inspire Foundation T-shirts with inspiring quotes, from which for every T-shirt sold we will use the funds to buy books to fill the libraries.

The foundation final mission is to have mentors to guide and inspire young entrepreneurs to develop their business ideas from startup into global companies.

Printed in Great Britain
by Amazon